All
About
Eggs

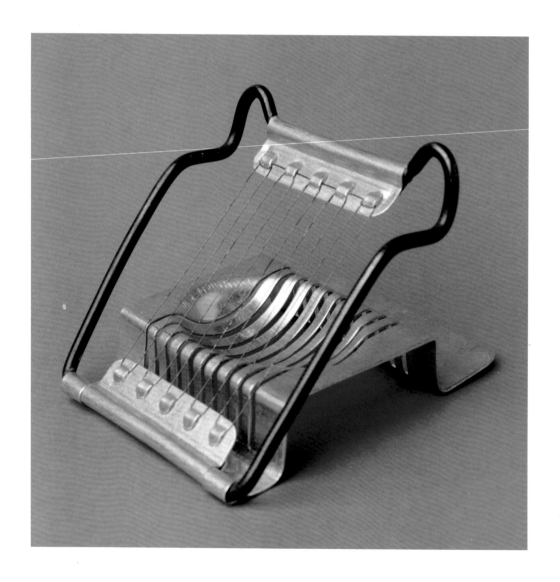

All About Eggs

Everything We Know About the World's Most Important Food

RACHEL KHONG
and the editors of

Clarkson Potter/Publishers
New York

Published in the United States by Clarkson Potter/
Publishers, an imprint of the Crown Publishing
Group, a division of Penguin Random House LLC,
New York.
crownpublishing.com
clarksonpotter.com

CLARKSON POTTER is a trademark and POTTER
with colophon is a registered trademark of Penguin
Random House LLC.

Grateful acknowledgment is made to reprint
the following:
Tortilla Española Clásica from *The Basque Book,*
copyright © 2016 by Alexandra Raij and Eder
Montero, reprinted with permission of Ten Speed
Press.

Saltie's Soft-Scrambled Eggs from *Saltie,* copyright
© 2012 by Caroline Fidanza. Used with permission
of Chronicle Books LLC, San Francisco. Visit
chroniclebooks.com.

Egg Salad from *Vegetable Literacy,* copyright ©
2013 by Deborah Madison, adapted and reprinted
with permission of the author and Ten Speed Press.

Îles Flottantes from *Baking: From My Home to Yours,*
copyright © 2006 by Dorie Greenspan, adapted
and reprinted with permission of the author and
Rux Martin/Houghton Mifflin.

Library of Congress Cataloging-in-Publication Data
Names: Khong, Rachel, 1985– author.
Title: Lucky peach all about eggs: everything
we know about the world's most important food
/ Rachel Khong and the editors of Lucky Peach;
photographs by Tamara Shopsin and Jason Fulford.
Other titles: All about eggs | Lucky Peach.
Description: First edition. | New York: Clarkson
Potter/Publishers, 2017 | Includes bibliographical
references and index. Identifiers: LCCN
2016048977 (print) | LCCN 2016050003 (ebook) |
ISBN 9780804187756 (hardcover: alk. paper) | ISBN
9780804187763 (ebook) | Subjects: LCSH: Cooking
(Eggs) | Eggs as food. | LCGFT: Cookbooks.
Classification: LCC TX745 .K53 2017 (print) | LCC
TX745 (ebook) | DDC 641.6/75—dc23
LC record available at https://lccn.loc.gov/2016048977.

ISBN 978-0-8041-8775-6
Ebook ISBN 978-0-8041-8776-3

Printed in China   **33614080156036**

Design by Tamara Shopsin and
Jason Fulford
Stinkbomben image on page 13 copyright ©
zaphiroff.de

10 9 8 7 6 5 4 3 2 1

First Edition

CONTENTS

1.

IT'S AN EGG WORLD AFTER ALL

For as long as eggs have popped from bird butts, they've been relished the world round—eaten, drunk, steamed, whisked, fried, baked, poached, cracked into dorm-room bowls of Top Ramen, coddled in Michelin-starred restaurants. People eat eggs everywhere. But how did this happen? *Why* did this happen? When did eggs conquer the world?

This first chapter is all about unlikely voyages: the journey that an egg takes from inside a chicken to the outside, and its geographic journey from Southeast Asia, where our domesticated chicken's ancestor originated, onto plates and into bowls all over the world. (And that's just one bird egg's story—the tip of the egg iceberg! We also eat quail eggs, pheasant eggs, duck eggs, and ostrich eggs; in Iceland, people grapple down steep cliffs to harvest the beautiful blue eggs belonging to seabirds called guillemots. In Chile, birds called tinamous lay eggs that seem like ornaments: iridescent and beautiful—page 14.)

Across the globe, despite innumerable cultural differences, we have all come to love eggs for pretty much the same reason: They are delicious. Eggs are what we humans have in common. The English wrap eggs in sausage and call those Scotch eggs (page 28)—but people in India do it, too, and call it *nargisi kofta*. The egg tarts you might order with your dim sum made their way from Portugal to Hong Kong to Macau, and changed like a game of telephone: All the iterations turned out uniquely wonderful. Eggs get hard-boiled and steeped with tea in Taiwan and China (page 228), and in Iran they do it, too, but with onion skins (page 229). Eggs get poached into spicy tomato sauces in the Middle East as *shakshuka* (page 34), which looks a lot like Italian eggs in purgatory, which looks a lot like Mexican Huevos en Rabo de Mestiza (page 35).

This is a book about eggs. But more than that, it's a book about mankind—it's a book about us all. Eggs are often the first things that home cooks learn to cook, yet they're among the hardest ingredients to master. Every great chef boasts a signature egg dish; no diner would ever dream of not offering an omelet. Eggs are a cornerstone of eating, cooking, and, yes, being human. They're the world's most important food.

The JOURNEY of an EGG

Nina Bai

The egg is a single cell, the largest and least mobile of the reproductive cells. Avian eggs must contain all the provisions for a growing chick, barring some exchange of gases and water vapor. They're gargantuan compared to mammalian egg cells, which take up nutrients from the mother via a placenta and can therefore pack light. Where a human egg cell is 0.1 millimeter in diameter, a chicken egg is about 50.

The Yolk

Hens are born with two ovaries, but as in most bird species, only the left one becomes fully developed. This may be an adaptation to cut down on weight for flight. After a hen reaches maturity between four and six months, it lays prolifically. Chickens are known as indeterminate layers, meaning they aim to achieve a certain clutch size (set of eggs) before they stop laying. But if the eggs are taken from the nests by predators—or human collectors—they will keep laying nearly every day. A hen can lay at the rate of about one egg per twenty-five hours. A domesticated chicken kept in conditions that mimic summer daylight hours can produce nearly three hundred eggs a year. A hen invests considerable

effort in her eggs, depositing a quarter of her daily energy and about 2 percent of her body weight into each egg. In human terms, that would be a 150-pound woman creating a 3-pound egg—every day. If a hen lays 275 eggs in a year, she will have converted about six times her body weight into eggs.

The hen's ovary resembles an uneven cluster of grapes, bulging with many egg cells at varying stages of maturity. An egg cell grows over one thousand times in volume during the ten weeks it takes to mature, with most of the action taking place in the tenth week. During this time, the egg cell rapidly accumulates the fats and proteins that form the yolk. These fats and proteins are synthesized by the liver and delivered through the bloodstream. The color of the yolk can vary from pale yellow to deep orange-red and depends on the pigments, called xanthophylls, in the hen's feed. White maize, wheat, millet, and sorghum yield pale yellow yolks, grass and yellow maize produce dark yellow yolks, and supplements of marigold petals or red peppers can create even deeper shades.

On the outside, an egg-laden hen can be heard giving prelaying calls and seen inspecting her nest. Her nervous system

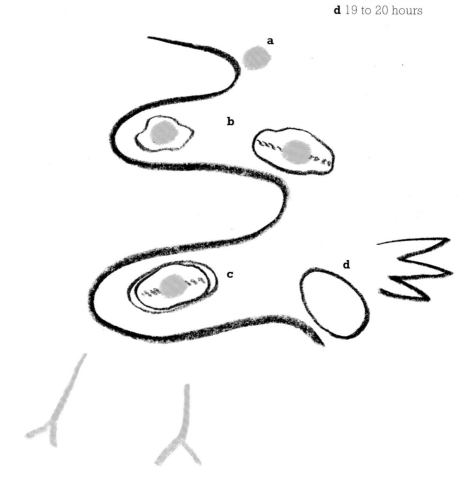

25 hours

a 15 minutes
b 2 to 3 hours
c 1 hour
d 19 to 20 hours

senses the length of daylight, temperature, and food availability and sends the appropriate signals to the pituitary gland.

The White

A burst of luteinizing hormone from the pituitary gland triggers ovulation six to eight hours later. As a completed yolk erupts from the ovary, fleshy writhing fingers projecting from the funnel-shaped opening of the oviduct catch and engulf the yolk. From here, the yolk proceeds on a twenty-five-hour passage through the two-foot-long oviduct and acquires the white, membranes, and shell. (Sometimes two egg cells are released at the same time and become a double-yolked egg. This occurs in roughly one in one thousand ovulations and is more likely to happen in younger hens.)

The first fifteen minutes are spent in the oviduct's funnel-shaped opening, known as the infundibulum **(a)**, where the egg cell has the opportunity to meet its male counterpart. Sperm can be stored in the hen several weeks after mating. This is the juncture where the egg is fertilized. But sperm or no sperm, the yolk travels on to the magnum, the longest section of the oviduct.

For the next two to three hours, peristaltic muscle contractions move the egg along at 2.3 millimeters per minute. Protein-secreting cells of the oviduct coat the yolk with four layers of albumin **(b)** of alternating densities. The first layer is deposited while ridges in the oviduct rotate the egg. This forms a twisted hammock of dense albumin called the chalaza, which acts like elastic cords that suspend and anchor the yolk to each end of the shell. The chalaza protects the embryo from premature contact with the shell. Three more layers of albumin are deposited, forming about half the volume of the egg white in a finished egg.

The Shell

An eggshell protects the embryo from its surroundings while allowing gas exchange. In the next hour, moving at the rate of 1.4 millimeters per minute through a narrow section of the oviduct called the isthmus, the egg is enclosed in two thin-but-tough antimicrobial shell membranes **(c)**. The final nineteen to twenty hours are spent in the two-inch-long uterus or shell gland. First, water and salts are pumped through the membranes to fill the albumen up to full volume. Next, calcium carbonate and protein are secreted by the uterine lining to form the shell. Magnesium and phosphate, in very small amounts, are also critical to the integrity of the shell. (An increase in these levels caused by exposure to pesticides such as DDT and DDE led to an epidemic of eggshell thinning that imperiled species from eagles to penguins in the mid-1900s.)

The shell contains some ten thousand microscopic pores, mostly concentrated at the blunt end of the egg. As the last rite in the shell gland, the egg is coated in a thin cuticle **(d)** that seals the pores to prevent water loss and block bacteria. As the chick grows, however, it requires more access to oxygen. Conveniently, the shell doubles as the source of calcium for the growing embryo, and as the calcium is converted into skeleton, the shell becomes more porous and allows more air exchange.

The cuticle also has a cosmetic effect, coloring the shell with molecules related to hemoglobin, such as porphyrin and biliverdin. Shells come in varying shades of white, brown, blue, green, and speckled patterns depending on the hen's breed.

Hello, World

At the end of the twenty-five-hour journey, muscular contractions of the shell gland push the egg out of the oviduct through the cloaca.

The cloaca is where the reproductive and excretory tracts of the chicken converge, but during laying the cloaca inverts (imagine a sock turned inside out) so that the egg avoids contact with excrement. Although the egg has traveled through the oviduct small end first, it is turned 180 degrees just before laying and comes out blunt end first.

As the egg cools outside the hen, its contents contract, causing the inner shell membrane to pull slightly away from the outer shell membrane, forming an air space at the blunt end. Just before hatching, a chick uses its beak to pierce into this air pocket and take its first breaths.

If the egg was fertilized in the infundibulum, it already contains some twenty thousand cells at the time it is laid. Crack open a typical store-bought egg, however, and you can locate the single nucleus of the unfertilized egg cell in the small white spot on the top of the yolk.

The EGG COLLECTOR

Adam Gollner

My landlord Claude was a kindly, batty old Frenchman—a beardless Santa Claus type, always smiling apologetically. His angel-soft white hair had an uncombable immunity to gravity, making it look like he wore a crown of broken dove wings. Two specific enthusiasms occupied him totally: opera and eggs.

Claude lived alone, a *mélomane* surrounded by his arias. The other collection was displayed in his foyer: over a hundred specimens of bird eggs inside a glass cabinet. I'd sneak peeks at them while paying the rent. They just sat there, their pastel surfaces radiating mystery and reflecting their owner's gentle freakiness.

Not long after I moved into the building—I lived on the second floor, above his ground-floor apartment—Claude invited me to a Sunday afternoon get-together. Twenty or so people showed up, mainly fellow Verdi buffs, but also a few actual opera singers. As Claude greeted different partygoers, he seemed to be kind of hopping around, like a limping rooster. It turned out he had a terrible infection on his left foot. He kept hoping it would go away, he said, and now there was a possibility that he would have to have it amputated. His hobbies had grown so all-consuming that he'd neglected to pay attention to his basic health. When he bird-walked over and asked whether I was enjoying the party, I took the opportunity to inquire about the eggs. "You are interested in eggs?" he asked, his smiling face almost pained with nervous solicitude.

At the time, I wasn't, really. What I was actually interested in was the fact that he was interested in eggs. We turned to the cabinet, where different colored eggs of various sizes had been grouped into neat, oval-contoured formations. "It's just a little assortment," he said, running a hand through his nest of hair. "I'm not too picky—as long as it's an egg, I like it." Most of the eggs were real bird eggs, but some weren't. Expertly carved wooden eggs and smooth-shouldered porcelain eggs and faux-Fabergé-style crystal eggs sat next to matte ostrich eggs and marbled crow eggs and small Tiffany-blue robin eggs.

He told me how the actual bird eggs he'd purchased came with their insides removed through little pinholes at the base. These eggshells had identification tags next to them, although several others didn't have any labels. "I sometimes find eggs on walks around the neighborhood or in the countryside," he explained with a quiet giggle. He picked up a speckled, oblong one—a wild sparrow egg—and handed it to me. "I keep them whole, as is, the way they are in the nest."

I felt its cool, light heft. There was something cosmic about the egg Claude had placed in my hands. Its exterior appeared to be spangled with tiny dots like distant stars in the night sky. Beneath that self-enclosed firmament were primordial waters and translucent proteins and a golden yolk, all crystallizing toward sparrowhood. I wasn't just holding an egg; I was holding an unreadable map of the universe. Or that's how Claude saw it—or how I saw him seeing it.

"Sometimes I hear a loud pop in the night," he continued, in a stage whisper. "I've even gotten out of bed because I'm sure there's an intruder in the house. But it always turns out it is just one of these eggs exploding."

He shrugged in a *what can you do?* way. "If the bird doesn't hatch, at a certain point, the gases and bacteria and what-not build up inside of them and the egg bursts. But not always. I don't know why not."

He may not have known, but I soon understood, firsthand, why it is that decorative eggshells are traditionally divested of their contents. Several times over the next year that I lived there, a putrid, sulfurous-fart smell would emanate from Claude's apartment into the stairwell leading up to my apartment. It always took me a day or two to figure it out. The stench would linger there for close to a week, gradually fading away as the gasified embryo made its way back to the elements.

As revolting as those burst eggs smelled— and as relieved as I was to finally move out— I never looked at eggs the same way again.

*

The first times I saw quail, duck, and goose eggs for sale, I bought them, excited to find out how they differed from hen's eggs. When a new butcher shop in my neighborhood started selling farm-fresh eggs, I noticed that they sometimes had varieties with a blue-green hue. They were from a breed called Araucana chickens, originally from Chile. They may not have tasted any different, but the beauty of their shells seemed to brighten any morning that started with them.

Chilean Bush Tinamou

While looking up Araucanas, I came across a study of another South American bird that lays even more beautiful eggs. Tinamous are an order of partridge-like birds whose iridescent, shimmering eggs have been described by egg-spert Mark E. Hauber (author of *The Book of Eggs*) as being "so unique and unusual that it was hard to take my eyes off them." In photographs, their glossy and reflective shells look as though they've been dunked in fresh paint. These come in a range of colors, from bright green to pale violet to fairy-tale gold. Unfortunately, they don't seem to be available commercially anywhere in the world—except for one farm in the Bío Bío region of Chile, around a five-hour drive to the south of Santiago. When I reached out to the tinamou farmers via their

Facebook page, they responded by inviting me over for breakfast.

*

The tinamou farm I visited is located on the outskirts of Los Ángeles, Chile—not far from the towns of Santa Fe and Santa Bárbara. The owner is Alberto Matthei, fifty-seven, a tall, slender, kind-eyed, lifelong farmer in a thin plaid shirt and dusty jeans. His wife, Carmen Guzmán, is a pretty, glamorous woman who wears billowing wide-legged pants and a cross necklace.

Their farm turned out to be a modest operation, just a few long rows of chicken-wire coops, each large cage containing around fifteen or so tinamous. They have around six thousand birds. They're intentionally keeping it small-scale and semi-free range. "We never want the tinamous to face what chickens do on those big farms," Matthei told me, when we met on a sunny February afternoon.

The tinamous were small and beige, not too different from quails. The birds would spastically rocket off in all directions whenever anyone came near their cages. Guzmán suggested I stand back a few steps in order to not freak them out. But their eggs were as gloriously unique as any I will ever see: a blinged-out purple chocolaty color, kind of like glossy Easter eggs, their surfaces almost mirrorlike. They were more resplendent than any of the eggs in Claude's collection.

"Nobody really knows why their eggs are so decorative," Guzmán explained. It may have something to do with the fact that the male tinamous both incubate the eggs and raise them without any assistance from the female birds. There's been speculation that the eggs may be a means of attracting male incubators. Matthei had only one species of tinamou (*Nothoprocta perdicaria*), but he was hoping to acquire more, including the green-egged elegant crested tinamou (*Eudromia elegans*). There are forty-seven different species of tinamou, and Matthei wants to crossbreed some of them, to see what sort of eggs will arise.

"The tinamou is a very efficient bird," he said. "They don't eat much and each female lays eighty to ninety eggs a year. It's a good business. And we consider the meat, which is very lean, to be just as important as the eggs."

Dinner that evening began with tinamou pâté and ended with tinamou egg meringue pie. The main attraction was fire-roasted tinamous, which reminded me of wild quail but with a tougher, more wiry texture. I felt that their eggs were of greater interest than their meat. Fortunately, I'd be learning more about those extraordinary eggs at breakfast.

We drank liters of pipeño, a light-bodied, refreshing red wine that Chileans like to drink cool. At one point, we all gazed up at the Milky Way glimmering in the dark summer sky above. To me, it looked just like Claude's sparrow egg at his party all those years ago.

*

The following morning, I met Matthei and Guzmán at their home for breakfast. There was a large bowl full of tinamou eggs looking chocolaty and reflective in the early morning light. I picked one up; it almost seemed like it was made of plastic. "They aren't hard to crack," Guzmán assured me.

When I broke one into a bowl, I noticed that the egg white had a slightly pink, coral hue. "That pink color indicates that it is high in iron," Matthei explained. "These eggs are also rich in a protein called ovotransferrin—twenty percent more than chicken eggs. In fact, it has more of everything good than other eggs. It's healthier, more beautiful, and lighter, yet even more delicious."

We tried the eggs in a variety of ways; all of them were good. The boiled eggs retained their delicate pink color, while scrambled tinamou eggs tasted pretty much identical to regular scrambled eggs, perhaps a tad creamier. The yolk in a fried egg was denser than a normal egg yolk, as though thickened with its own natural custard. It had a bit of a duck egg vibe, but less assertive—better.

"If you like eggs, you will like tinamou," summarized Matthei.

I like eggs, so I liked tinamou eggs. A lot. If I could bend destiny, a tinamou egg is the egg I'd have as my everyday morning egg. While we finished our coffees, I thought again of my landlord Claude, and what my life was like back then. So many things had changed, and there was still so much more to come.

The EGGS
We EAT

Fairy

This is a yolkless chicken egg, often laid by a young hen. Usually it has a rough shell. (Also called witch egg, wind egg, and fart egg.) It really spooked people in the olden days. In the 1600s they called these tiny eggs "cock's eggs," and believed that they would hatch glittering-eyed monsters called basilisks (especially if you incubated your egg under a toad).

Quail

About 1 inch long and roughly a fifth the size of a large chicken egg, the quail egg is the smallest commercially available egg. They take just three minutes to hard-boil, and two minutes to soft-boil. Gram for gram, quail eggs are more densely nutritious than chicken eggs, with more B vitamins, iron, and zinc. They're used medicinally in China, and are deep-fried and sold as a street-food snack called *kwek kwek* in the Philippines (page 168).

Chicken

Chicken eggs, the focus of this book, come in an array of sizes depending on many fac-

tors, including the hen's breed and how old she is. Here's how eggs are classified commercially: peewee (1.25 ounces), small (1.5 ounces), medium (1.75 ounces), large (2 ounces), extra large (2.25 ounces), and jumbo (2.5 ounces).

Pheasant

Pheasant eggs are smaller than average chicken eggs and bigger than quail eggs. The shells are a pretty blue on the inside. The ancient Greeks and Romans used to eat them. A pheasant egg contains more yolk than a chicken egg (nearly twice as much), and tends to be yellower.

Duck

Duck eggs have rich, thick yolks with three times the cholesterol of chicken eggs. Their whites also contain more protein than chicken eggs—which means that they can get fluffier than chicken eggs in meringues (page 176) and cakes. People with chicken egg allergies can sometimes eat duck eggs without problems. They're especially popular in Asia, where they get salted (page 244) and preserved (page 238).

Turkey

About one and a half times the size of chicken eggs, turkey eggs contain four times the amount of cholesterol. Centuries ago, these freckled eggs used to be more commonly eaten: Native Americans gathered eggs from wild turkeys; Europeans brought turkeys over to their continent in the sixteenth century, and a seventeenth-century English cookbook writer called the eggs "exceeding wholesome to eate." Delmonico's served them in omelets in the nineteenth century. They've waned in popularity, probably because of their cost in comparison to chicken eggs: Turkeys lay about one hundred eggs a year—a lot fewer than an average chicken's three hundred—and usually sell for $2 to $3 each.

Goose

Goose eggs clock in larger than duck eggs, almost triple the size of jumbo chicken eggs. Like duck eggs they have big, deeply orange yolks, and are prized for their richness. Golden or otherwise, goose eggs aren't super available—probably because geese lay only about forty eggs per year, mostly in the spring.

Emu

Emus, native to Australia, are the second-largest living bird—second only to the ostrich—and their emerald green eggs weigh two pounds a pop. Each one is about the equivalent of a dozen jumbo chicken eggs. But they're milder than chicken eggs and have a white-to-yolk ratio of one to one.

Ostrich

Ostriches are the largest birds on earth, which means they lay the largest eggs. An ostrich egg is equivalent to two dozen jumbo chicken eggs. The shells are five to ten times thicker than a chicken egg's, so they don't break when they're being incubated (at night by their 300-pound fathers, and during the day by their mothers). To open an ostrich egg, a hacksaw or power drill can help.

Guillemot

Guillemots, seabirds found in the Arctic Circle and the North Pacific and Atlantic oceans, lay conical turquoise eggs. The birds spend their lives mostly at sea, only coming to shore to lay their eggs in the spring, when Icelanders will rappel down cliffs to harvest them (they taste "nothing of the sea," according to one guillemot egg harvester, but have a different texture from chicken eggs). These eggs get laid directly on the bare rock ledges, in large colonies without nests, so each female's egg has distinct markings. Their pointy shape means that, if disturbed, the eggs won't roll off the cliffs, but will roll in a circle instead.

Tinamou

Tinamous, found in Mexico, South America, and Central America, lay eggs that are brilliantly colored, glossy, and iridescent. We aren't sure why they're so beautiful, but some say it's to draw the attention of male tinamous, and signal them to incubate the eggs (see page 14).

Gull

Historically eaten in England (and, now, restaurants), the eggs of the black-headed gull have mottled shells and orange, creamy yolks. The eggs have a very short season—about three to four weeks in the spring—and are hand-harvested from nests in salt marshes and wetlands. Egg harvesting is highly regulated, and eggers are permitted to take only one egg from each gull's nest.

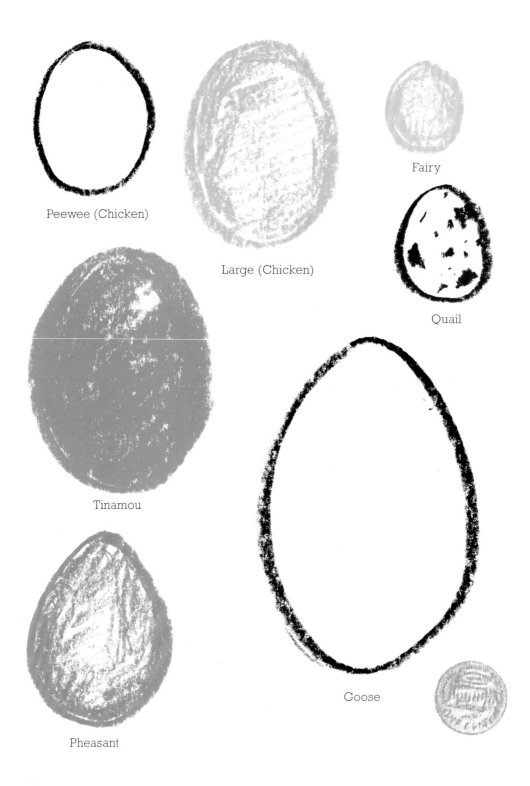

Peewee (Chicken)

Large (Chicken)

Fairy

Quail

Tinamou

Goose

Pheasant

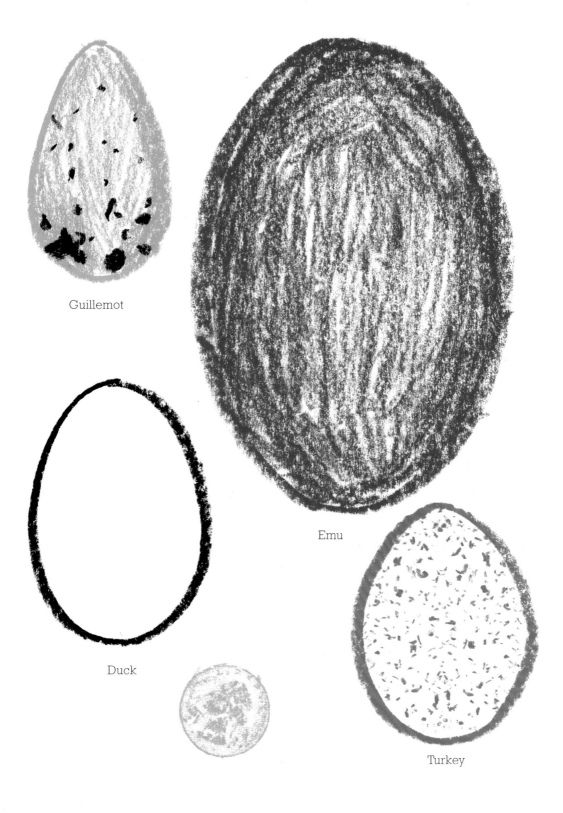

Guillemot

Emu

Duck

Turkey

Tart to Tart: An EGG TART Evolution

Anna Ling Kaye

My introduction to egg tarts happened in childhood, at family dim sum meals in Hong Kong. After we'd knocked back an array of chicken claws, beef balls, and turnip cakes, I'd get sent to find the dessert lady. Clutching our rectangular dim sum chart, I'd navigate the women pushing heavy carts laden with steaming delicacies till I found the cart with glass shelves for fried foods and plated desserts. There, I'd point at the sun-hearted egg tarts (*dan taht*), the whole reason for dim sum, as far as I was concerned. The dessert lady would stamp my chart, and I'd parade back to our table victorious. No matter how much we overate at dim sum, there was always extra room for egg tarts, best washed down with earthy and bitter *bo lei* tea (watered down for us kids).

I have no illusions that I'm alone in my egg tart affinity. (Chris Patten, the last British governor of Hong Kong, was apparently so fond of the pastry he earned the Cantonese nickname "Fatty Patten.") The most symmetrical of desserts, the Cantonese egg tart is concentric circles of golden shortcrust or puff pastry cradling smooth, bright yellow custard. The secret of the traditional egg tart is lard, which allows the crust to crumble in

the mouth and complements the eggy center without overwhelming it. A good Cantonese egg tart has a flat custard that is firm with a gentle give, and its crust brings salty-sweet balance. It is as elemental to a modern Hong Kong childhood as apple pie is to an American one.

So it was a surprise to learn that the pastry is a relatively new export to the Cantonese table. It appeared in Guangzhou bakeries sometime in the first part of the twentieth century, and made its way to Hong Kong tea shops by the 1940s, when it quickly gained menu-must status.

But if the egg tart wasn't a Hong Kong original, where was it from? Some sources pointed to the English custard tart, which has a similar crust. Then I got wind that in nearby Macau they served a more caramelized version of the egg tart, called the Macanese egg tart, or in Cantonese, the *poh taht*.

*

Macau is known today as Asia's casino capital, and to wander there is to navigate flashing neon promising cash and glory, with the accompanying girls in heels and skimpy

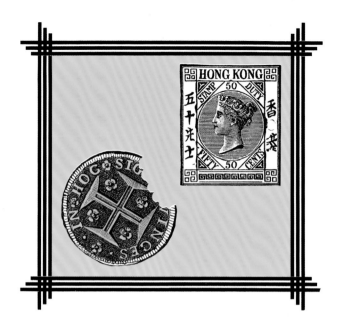

dresses happy to help you spend your hypothetical earnings. But if you know where to go, you will find yourself seeking a different but arguably far more rewarding treasure: the Macanese egg tart.

My go-to spot lies in the shadow of the golden towers of the legendary Hotel Lisboa. Follow the psychedelically patterned black-and-white cobblestone sidewalk of Avenida de Dom João (the street names and cobblestones are vestiges of recent days as a Portuguese colony), and veer a hard right into a quiet alley. Tucked between a local streetside eatery and a motorcycle parking area, you'll find a queue of patiently waiting confection fans trailing out the door and halfway around the block. This is how you will identify the Macanese egg tart mecca of Margaret Wong Stow's Café e Nata.

Café e Nata serves egg tarts fresh out of the oven until they run out, usually by around six p.m., at which point the shutters promptly come down, and any late birds will simply have to try again the next morning.

The Macanese egg tart is a delightfully ugly beast. It's never symmetrical, always tilting to one side or the other, with black blotches on the crumpled, leathery face of its top, and a layered crust of flaky pastry that falls away to the touch like ancient mummy skin. These are all promising signs: The blotches are caramelized sugar, the leathery face is as crisp as the thinnest of crème brûlée shells, and the crust is airily light with a slight salty kick to it. The savory pastry cradles the heart of this lopsided tart—a rich, smoky custard with far more complexity than its paler, more symmetrical Cantonese cousin.

"Everything has to be handmade," owner Margaret Wong Stow tells me, as we walk through the small back room where the egg tarts are made. Two women are on pastry duty, cutting long tubes of puff pastry into coins, which they press into the tart tins by thumb. This small-batch treatment, according to Margaret, makes the pastry layered and flakier. The kitchen staff at Café e Nata can be counted off on one hand, but they turn out 165 trays of 45 tarts, or 7,425 tarts daily. "Even if people try to copy us, they can't," Margaret says confidently.

Another game changer is Café e Nata's use

of margarine in the pastry dough, not the lard popular in Cantonese egg tarts. The margarine is likely what gives Margaret's crust its salty finish. The puff pastry is prepared at an off-site factory, where it is chilled for twelve to twenty-four hours before being sent to the in-town bakery. Once the pastry is molded, the trays are shunted over to the custard chef, who prepares and pours the custard filling: made from scratch with egg yolks, cream, milk, and white sugar. Margaret's daughter, Audrey, offers an important tip for the custard preparation: "You have to dissolve the sugar in the egg yolk in the beginning. And then we add the milk and the cream. Many people use a blowtorch to caramelize the top. We don't need to." Café e Nata's favored custard pouring tool is a repurposed glass coffeemaker pot, which has the perfect handle and spout for mass baking. The tarts are then transferred to a ceiling-high industrial oven kept at a piping-hot 250°C (482°F) all day long, where they are baked for thirty minutes (the high heat creates the hallmark caramelized custard top).

The Macanese egg tart is so iconic it's a major tourist attraction. But Margaret and

Andrew Stow, her husband at the time, baked their first tray of egg tarts in 1990. It's not that there were no egg tarts available in Macau at the time; they just weren't widely available commercially. Macau was still a Portuguese colony then, so Margaret, who is Chinese, and Andrew, who is British, decided there was a niche to be explored in serving the sweets to homesick Portuguese, using a recipe Margaret says was passed to them by the governor's personal chef. Originally a pharmacist, Andrew tinkered with the recipe, switching custard powder for custard made from scratch.

"We took the first tray out from the oven," Margaret told me, "and the local Chinese people said, *No, I don't want it. It's burned, it will give you cancer.*" They didn't sell a single tart, and Andrew was ready to throw the whole batch out. Instead, the couple decided to give away their egg tarts for free.

"They had the first bite. Then they had a second one," Margaret says. "Then they asked me for a third one. And I said, *Money, yeah?*" Their original bakery, Lord Stow's, still stands in its original location in the idyllic backwaters of a local neighborhood called Coloane. Margaret opened her own café in 1992 when the couple divorced. Either you're a Margaret's customer or a Lord Stow's customer, and never the twain shall meet. Unless you are Audrey Stow, that is, in which case you stand to ultimately inherit both. Although the bakeries use the same recipe, their suppliers are different, and this, to discerning customers, makes all the difference. When Margaret sold her proprietary recipe to Kentucky Fried Chicken, the Macanese egg tart craze spread to Hong Kong, Taiwan, Singapore, and the Philippines. Lord Stow's has opened franchises across East Asia.

*

The Cantonese egg tart took off in the 1940s, and the Macanese egg tart with its puff pastry crust only really caught on in the 1990s. They were the innovations. For the original egg tart, I followed the direction pointed by the Macanese egg tart's Cantonese name: poh taht, or the Portuguese egg tart.

In 1496, at the bidding of Portugal's King Manuel I, a large monastery was commissioned to be built on the banks of the Tagus River, now known as the neighborhood of Belém on the outskirts of Lisbon. At the turn of the century, this portion of the Tagus was where the great Portuguese explorers such as Vasco da Gama would launch their world-defining voyages. A century later, the monastery was completed, a fantastical structure with spindly turrets studding its length. When the many, many nuns moved into this architectural jewel, there was a sudden spike in the need for egg whites to starch their clothes and wimples, and as a result, an unanticipated surplus of egg yolks. Thus was born a wide array of decadent egg yolk experimentation, the most famous of which is the *pastéis de nata,* which is easily the Yoda of egg tarts. It has the smallest, gnarliest, lumpiest appearance of the trio, is hundreds of years more ancient, and its flavor profile is immense. Smaller on the palm of the hand than its Macanese or Cantonese kin, the pastéis de nata coddles a creamy, smoked custard, set by high heat, in paper-thin pastry. The result is triumphant balance: The custard is creamy but not eggy, the crust is flaky but not dry, the sweet center delights without cloying. The smallness of the pastéis de nata makes it easy to consume in multiples.

When the Jerónimos Monastery closed in the 1820s because of changing taste in politics and religion, the pastéis bakers struggled to make a living from their egg tarts, which also came to be called *pastéis de Belém.* In 1837, even these destitute bakers were

forced to sell their recipe to a savvy businessman, who began baking the egg tarts in the monastery's neighboring sugar refinery. He's kept the recipe in his family ever since, serving tarts out of the Fabrica dos Pastéis de Belém. Here, egg tarts get elevated from a street-side snack to ritual. Waistcoated waiters take your order at small café tables in a beautiful blue-and-white tiled room. The traditional drink pairing for a pastéis de Belém is espresso, served in china cups. The egg tarts arrive fresh out of the oven, their centers still wobbling and steaming. It's recommended you eat the pastéis in two bites, with a dash of cinnamon (and powdered sugar, for the sweet-toothed).

*

To me, each of the three egg tarts is delicious in its own way. But for a confection with a uniquely global story, my favorite is the smoky-sweet Macanese egg tart, its Portuguese ancestry reimagined and popularized by the experimentations and entrepreneurship of a Chinese woman and a British man.

Yank Sing's Egg Tart   *Hong Kong*

Our Hong Kong–style egg tarts have been on our menu since Alice Chan opened Yank Sing in San Francisco in 1958. We've adapted it over the years, as customer tastes have evolved to favor a lighter, flakier pastry and a more delicate, silky filling. The ingredients have also changed over time: We've replaced shortening with butter. We're looking for a light, melt-in-the-mouth texture, so we try not to overcook the tarts and use only pasteurized eggs for the filling.

—Nathan Waller

Makes 12 tarts

Puff Pastry
1½ sticks (6 oz) cold butter, cut into
    1-inch cubes
1½ cups all-purpose flour, plus more for
    the work surface
1 egg
2 tbsp water

Egg Custard
1 cup water
½ cup sugar
4 eggs
¼ cup evaporated milk
½ tsp vanilla extract
+ salt

1. Make the puff pastry: Mix the butter and ¾ cup of the flour together to form an "oil dough." Knead the dough into a ball, wrap in plastic, and refrigerate for 20 minutes.

2. Meanwhile, mix the egg and water into the remaining ¾ cup flour to form a "water dough." Knead the dough into a ball, wrap in plastic, and refrigerate for 20 minutes.

3. Flour a work surface and remove the water dough from the refrigerator. Roll the dough out into a large square, about 11 × 11 inches.

4. Take the oil dough out of the refrigerator and spread it out on top of the water dough, leaving a large enough border of the water dough to be able to fold over the oil dough entirely. Fold the sides of the water dough over the oil dough.

5. Roll the entire dough out to a large square, again aiming for about 11 × 11 inches, and mark it into thirds. Fold each outer third over the center third and roll the folded rectangle out into a large square again. Repeat two more times.

6. After the third fold, roll out the dough again and this time mark it into fourths. Fold each outer quarter into the center and then roll the rectangle out. Wrap the dough in plastic and place in the refrigerator for at least 20 minutes.

7. On a lightly floured work surface, roll out to a ¼-inch thickness. Cut out disk shapes with a round cutter.

8. Lightly grease the inside of 12 fluted tart molds and press the pastry disks into the molds. Transfer to the refrigerator while you make the filling.

9. Make the custard: Combine the water and sugar in a saucepan and heat over medium heat until the sugar dissolves, 3 to 5 minutes. Remove the pan from the heat and cool.

10. When the sugar syrup has cooled, whisk the eggs into the sugar syrup. Stir in the evaporated milk, vanilla, and a pinch of salt. Strain the mixture through a fine-mesh strainer into a container with a pouring lip.

11. Heat the oven to 350°F.

12. Fill each of the pastry-lined tart molds three-quarters of the way up with egg custard.

13. Position the tarts evenly on a baking sheet and place in the oven. Bake until the crust is golden brown and the filling raises to a slight dome, about 45 minutes. Remove from the oven and leave to cool for 5 to 10 minutes, then carefully tap the molds to remove the tarts.

White-Winged Dove

South America: Put an Egg IN It!

Naomi Tomky

Latin Americans not only "put an egg on it," they also put their eggs in things. When stuffed inside meat, dough, or vegetables, hard-boiled eggs serve a multitude of purposes: helping to stretch expensive ingredients, and adding texture and luxurious flavor. (Plus, they look cool.)

Empanadas

Filling-stuffed dough has infinite variations across the continent, from the dough (wheat, corn, yuca, or plantain) to the filling, but in many countries—particularly those of the Cono Sur—hard-boiled eggs play a key role.

In Argentina, where empanadas are daily bread, the prototypical version is stuffed with ground beef, onions, olives, and hard-boiled egg, the addition of which seems like plain common sense: Eggs are way cheaper than beef and transform the filling into something more complex. In Chile, that egg-and-beef mixture gets combined with raisins and is called *pino;* in Bolivia, it's part of the soup dumpling–esque *salteñas.* Farther north, Nicaraguan *pastelitos* come with a pork or chicken filling, are highly seasoned with a tomatoey sauce, spices, olives, capers, and chopped eggs, then fried and rolled in sugar.

Guatemalan empanadas are made with pork, almonds, sweet spices, and chopped eggs.

Pastel de Choclo

The Chilean *pastel de choclo* is a sort of luxurious corn pudding. A favorite home-cooked casserole in Chile, it combines the colonial-influenced meat filling as a bottom layer and the indigenous corn, caramelized in the oven on top, segregated by slices of hard-boiled egg. In other parts of Latin America, similar meaty casseroles are made with beaten eggs and local starches, like yuca or plantain in the Dominican Republic and Puerto Rico, where they're called *pastelones.*

Torta Pascualina

Because roughly 60 percent of Argentineans are of Italian ancestry, Argentina has happily inherited the traditions of these immigrants (try walking five blocks in Buenos Aires without running into a slice of pizza). One of the more directly adapted dishes is Easter pie—*torta pascualina.* Beneath a puff pastry crust, a dense filling of greens and ricotta cheese houses whole eggs, making a rich vegetarian dish perfect for Lent, as well as quite the visual spectacle when sliced. From inches

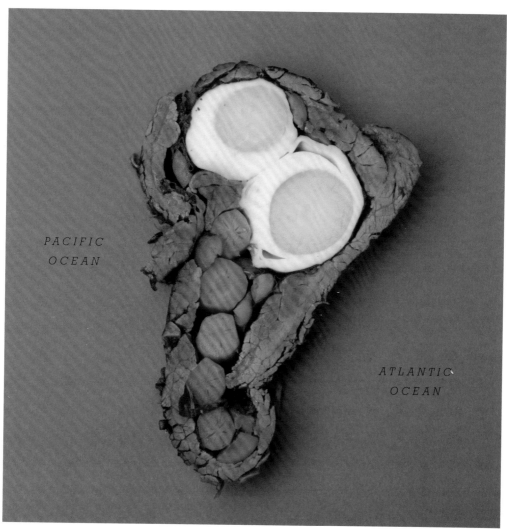

*PACIFIC
OCEAN*

*ATLANTIC
OCEAN*

Matambre

of solid green peek sunny yellow yolks, bordered by white.

Matambre

Matambre is Argentinean steak stuffed with vegetables and eggs, and means, in Spanish, "hunger killer." Served warm as an entree or cold as an appetizer, it's a butterflied flank steak lined with vegetables and hard-boiled eggs. Rolled and pinned, it's cooked either by braising in red wine or on the grill, and then sliced so that each cross-section is a beautiful pinwheel slice of meat, vegetable, and squished-up hard-boiled egg.

Scotch Eggs   *England*

A Scotch egg is a boiled egg coated with meat and bread crumbs—a spherical and portable snack with a yolk at its core. But why? To what end? Whose idea was it?

The story everyone tends to run with is that the Scotch egg comes from the fancy London department store Fortnum & Mason. They like to take full responsibility for the Scotch egg. They claim that in 1738 London's wealthy travelers demanded it for their long and arduous carriage rides. Around that time, so the story goes, Fortnum & Mason had a special kitchen that produced pies, cakes, and breads for travelers. The Scotch egg would have come out of that kitchen. (Other items designed by the kitchen included a meat lozenge, which is like a big fruit pastille, but meat—a protein hit for travelers, sportsmen, and MPs on all-night parliamentary sittings.)

"We had been supplying travelers' baskets for some time," says Dr. Andrea Tanner, the store's archivist. "The Scotch egg was most likely a natural progression, based on the perceived demands of the travelers. It is a compact snack that required no cutlery, and could be transported easily—even in a pocket, wrapped in a handkerchief."

Back then, the egg would have come from a pullet—a young hen, which isn't really in the business of laying proper eggs yet—and would have been much smaller than eggs are now. The covering would have been made from forcemeat (lean meat, ground up and bound with fat) rather than the sausage we use these days. It would've been heavily seasoned with pepper and mace.

But no chef creates meat-covered egg balls in isolation. Anonymous must have taken inspiration from somewhere. A search of Victorian cookbooks reveals numerous receipts for egg balls—hard-boiled eggs, put through a sieve, mixed with parsley, flour, cayenne pepper, and raw egg, rolled into balls and re-boiled—and forcemeat balls: veal, pounded through a sieve, mixed with butter, bread crumbs, parsley, shallots, and egg, rolled into balls and boiled. In *The English Art of Cookery, According to the Present Practice* (1788), Richard Briggs writes, "In almost every made dish you may put in what you think proper, to enlarge it and make it good; such as sweetbreads, ox palates boiled tender . . . force-meat balls, egg balls." The Scotch egg was the Cronut of the eighteenth century: a hybrid ball.

These days, Scotch eggs are pub snacks. And in that context, they are perfect. I'm not sure I'd ever eat one like a hand fruit on the bus, or on a horse-and-cart ride to my house in the country (I'd get crumbs on my bustle!). But cut in half, fresh from the fryer, egg yolk gently relenting, they are beautiful.

Michael Harrison, head chef of the Cornwall Project, which brings produce up to London from Cornwall and turns it into perfect pub food, talked us through his basic Scotch egg formula, which is infinitely adaptable.

—Laura Goodman

Makes 10 Scotch eggs

2 lb breakfast sausage, casings removed
    if links
+ salt
10 eggs, at room temperature, plus
    2 eggs, beaten
+ extra-virgin olive oil
⅓ cup whole milk
1 cup panko bread crumbs
1 cup rolled oats
2 cups all-purpose flour
+ neutral oil, for deep-frying
+ sea salt

1. Divide the sausage meat into 10 balls (about 3.25 oz each). Chill them.

2. Bring a large pan of water to a boil. Add salt until it starts to taste unpleasantly salty. Have a timer ready to count down 5 minutes 35 seconds. Half-fill a same-size container with ice, water, and salt. When the water is boiling, take the 10 eggs and dip them into the boiling water with a slotted spoon—dip once, twice, and then gently lower them in and start the timer. The water must keep boiling vigorously. At the end, drop them into the ice bath and let them sit for 10 minutes. Peel them carefully, as they're soft inside. Dry the eggs and chill them.

3. Rub your hands with a thin film of extra-virgin olive oil. Press a ball of meat flat onto your hand, so that it's about ⅓ inch thick.

4. Place the egg in the middle and wrap the egg with the meat. Pinch the edges together and smooth the ball so that there are no gaps or bumps. (If the covering isn't even, the Scotch egg will split during cooking.) If you're struggling with the wrapping of the egg, try covering your work surface with oiled plastic wrap and pressing the balls flat on that, rather than on your hand.

5. Beat together the remaining 2 eggs and the milk in a shallow bowl. In a second shallow bowl, combine the panko and oats. Dredge the balls in the flour. Roll them in the milk-egg mixture, then in the panko-oat combo. (I use panko for texture and stability, mixed with oats for presentation and crunch.)

6. Heat the oven (preferably convection) to 350°F.

7. Heat the oil in a deep fryer to 350°F.

8. Deep-fry the eggs in batches for 1 minute, then bake them in the oven until the sausage is cooked through (firm to the touch and 160°F), about 10 minutes.

9. Serve them straight away (or the eggs will keep cooking). Season the yolk with a good sea salt (preferably Cornish!). I finish mine with cracked green pepper and sliced celery leaf. Lots of condiments work. I use brown sauce flavored with wildflower honey and Cornish ale. If you'd rather serve them cold, take them out of the oven after 8 minutes and the yolk will still be runny.

India does it, too! Northern India is home to the nargisi kofta, *a deep-fried meatball with a hard-boiled egg inside, served with curry.*

Aioli   *France*

Hunger is the best sauce, yes, but aioli is second best—homey and luxurious, the perfect eggy emulsion. In the villages throughout the Provençal region of Var, shops serve it with their salt cod on Fridays. In Solliès-Toucas, aioli and salt cod get served with boiled potatoes, carrots, and snails. Throughout Provence, summer festivals serve *aïoli monstre* on their final day: Village populations turn out to watch fireworks, fill their plates with cod, potatoes, carrots, green beans, artichokes, chickpeas, beets, hard-boiled eggs, snails, and squid stew, and top it all with a generous cap of aioli. In that spirit, put this aioli wherever you want an alluringly garlicky condiment: on vegetables raw or boiled, on fish, in sandwiches instead of mayo. Traditionally it's made start to finish by hand—in a mortar and pestle—but I am impatient, so I do just the mashing-garlic part in the mortar and pestle, and the rest in the food processor.

Makes 1 cup

2 garlic cloves
+ salt
1 egg yolk, at room temperature
a few drops water
¼ cup canola oil
½ cup extra-virgin olive oil
1 tbsp fresh lemon juice

1. Pound the garlic cloves with a big pinch of salt in a mortar and pestle until they're a paste. Set aside.

2. Slide the egg yolk into a blender or mini food processor and blend. Add a few drops of water from your fingers and ¼ teaspoon salt. Add a few drops of canola oil, and run the processor. Glug more canola oil in with the food processor running, then the olive oil. You'll see the emulsion start to take when the food processor starts to get louder, and the oil will turn from clear to opaque. Add more drops of water if the mixture becomes too thick or looks like it may break.

3. Once the aioli is emulsified and thickened, stop the machine. Taste. Add more salt to taste. When it's salty to your liking, add the garlic paste and the lemon juice. If the aioli breaks or doesn't emulsify, start over with a new egg yolk and use the broken mixture in place of the oil.

Great Blue Heron

Egg Curry   *India*

This is a recipe my mom would make when there was little else on hand and she had yet to go to the store. It's a great recipe for a hangover or when you're feeling lazy or both. Some people quarter the eggs so the yolks fall apart and make the sauce thicker, but I find that too muddled. Others throw in some boiled and peeled baby potatoes too. We used to make this dish when we had unexpected guests to feed and it never disappointed. I love the fiery tomato sauce and like to sop it up with whole pieces of toast.

—*Padma Lakshmi*

Makes 4 servings

2 to 3 tbsp butter
1 tsp cumin seeds
3 whole cloves
1 pod black cardamom
1 cup diced red onion
1 tbsp chopped fresh ginger
2 garlic cloves, minced
2 or 3 fresh bay leaves
2 to 3 serrano chilies, seeded and sliced
½ cup diced green bell pepper
1 tsp garam masala
½ tsp amchoor (optional)
4 cups chopped tomatoes
¼ cup water
+ salt
1 cup yogurt
+ crushed black pepper
8 hard-boiled eggs (page 90), peeled
2 tbsp fresh lime juice
2 slices sourdough toast, cubed into
    croutons
1 cup cilantro, roughly chopped
+ rice or rotis, for serving

1. Melt the butter in a deep skillet over medium heat until just slightly browned, about 2 minutes. Add the cumin, cloves, and black cardamom and stir until fragrant, 1 to 2 minutes.

2. Add the onion, ginger, garlic, bay leaves, chilies, and bell pepper. Stir and sauté until the onions are glassy, about 5 minutes.

3. Add the garam masala and amchoor (if using) and stir until the spices begin to darken slightly, about 3 minutes.

4. Add the tomatoes, water, and salt to taste. Stir, cover, and cook for 5 to 7 minutes more.

5. In a small bowl, whip the yogurt with a fork until runs a bit thin. Season with salt and black pepper.

6. Stir the tomato gravy, adding a bit more water if needed. Add the whole boiled eggs to the skillet, gently nestling them into the tomato gravy, and pouring some over the eggs to cover them. Cover and cook for 5 to 7 more minutes.

7. Remove from the heat and stir in the lime juice. Transfer the egg curry to a serving dish. Drizzle the yogurt evenly all over and then garnish on top with the croutons and cilantro.

8. Serve with rice or rotis.

Egg Hoppers   *Sri Lanka*

In Sri Lanka, curry is a given at just about every meal—what changes is the starch with which you eat it. At breakfast it's often the incredible bowl-shaped, egg-cuddling rice-flour crepe called a hopper, or *appa*, which means "rice cake" in Tamil. Hoppers are also eaten in southern India, but on this neighboring island they reach their culinary destiny—served as a common breakfast and occasional dinner.

Anchored by the twin pillar ingredients of Sri Lankan cuisine, rice (in flour form) and coconut (in milk form), hoppers combine a fun shape with a sourdoughesque zing. They come either sweet or savory, and can be eaten with any type of curry or condiment. But the best of them have an egg dropped in the center and fused to the bottom of the pancake (ideally with the yolk still runny).

At the open-air food stalls of Sri Lanka, cooks—often shirtless and sarong clad—expertly swirl the lightly fermented batter of rice flour and coconut milk in pans made specifically for hoppers. They look like tiny woks. Swirling the batter along the sides of the hot pan forms crisp, lacy edges. An egg gets cracked directly into the center, cooking with the pancake. After a few minutes, the edges of the pancake brown and curl away from the pan and the whole bowl-shaped breakfast slides out with ease, ready to be dolloped with *lunu miris*—the local sambal (spicy condiment)—and dipped in whatever curry gravy is lying around.

Because *appachatti* (hopper pans) aren't easy to track down outside the subcontinent (nor is toddy, the local palm wine used to ferment the pancakes), it takes some improvisation to make these at home. Subbing in a small wok or a pan with gently sloping sides, it's possible to make a pretty decent copycat.

—Naomi Tomky

Makes 6 hoppers

½ tsp active dry yeast
½ cup plus 2 tbsp warm water
1 cup rice flour
¼ tsp salt
¼ tsp sugar
1¼ cups coconut milk
⅛ tsp baking soda
1 tbsp neutral oil
6 eggs
+ curry, sambal, or hot sauce, for
   serving

1. Dissolve the yeast in the warm water and let it sit for a few minutes, until active.

2. Mix together the rice flour, salt, and sugar in a large bowl. Add the yeast mixture and stir the batter until smooth.

3. Cover the batter and leave in a warm spot for 2 to 3 hours (many recipes call for "room temperature," but be advised that room temperature in Sri Lanka is often over 90°F).

4. Stir in the coconut milk, re-cover, and return to the warm spot for an additional hour. After the hour has elapsed, add the baking soda.

5. Heat a hopper pan, small wok, or omelet pan over medium-high heat. If you are using an omelet pan, roll the pan around over the burner, making sure that all the pan's sides and bottom are quite hot. Very lightly oil the pan. This is best done with an oil mister or pastry brush, as the oil needs to cover both the bottom and sides, and too much oil will make the hoppers greasy.

6. Ladle about ¼ cup of the batter into the bottom of the pan, then immediately begin to roll the pan, swirling it around so that the batter climbs up the sides of the pan. Keep doing this until there is no batter left swirling and it is in a thin layer

all over the inside of the pan (including the sides). Crack an egg into the center. Cover the pan immediately and leave to cook for 3 to 4 minutes.

7. When you lift the lid to check on it, the top edges should be browned and crisp, starting to pull away from the edges, and the white of the egg should be cooked through. If so, use a spatula to gently separate the pancake from the pan. If it's sticking, it may need a little bit more time over the heat.

8. Slide the pancake onto a plate and repeat with the remaining batter and eggs.

9. Serve right away, with curry or sambal. If you don't have or don't want to make curry, a spoonful of any good hot sauce is a more than worthy accompaniment.

Common Loon

Shakshuka

Middle East & Africa

Algeria, Israel, Morocco, Saudi Arabia, Libya, Yemen . . . People in lots of places eat *shakshuka,* eggs poached in peppery tomato sauce. (In Italy there's *uova in purgatorio,* or eggs in purgatory; Mexico does it, too! See opposite.) It's popular for obvious reasons—it's delicious. But one theory goes that once upon a time in the Ottoman Empire, there was a meze called *saksuka*—an eggless meat-and-vegetable stew. In Maghreb, the Jewish population turned saksuka into shakshuka: a meatless dish, with eggs. Here's a not-at-all-traditional one I like to make, adapted from cookbook author David Lebovitz's inspired recipe.

Makes 4 servings

3 tbsp olive oil
1 yellow onion, chopped
1 green bell pepper, chopped
1 serrano chili, chopped
1½ tsp salt
4 garlic cloves, minced
½ tsp freshly ground black pepper
1 tsp caraway seeds, crushed
1 tsp paprika
1 tsp ground cumin
⅛ tsp cayenne pepper
1 can (28 oz) whole tomatoes
2 tbsp tomato paste
2 tsp honey
1 tsp red wine vinegar
½ cup water
1 cup chopped kale or chard
¼ cup feta cheese or whole-milk yogurt
4 eggs (preferably cracked into
    ramekins)
1 tbsp chopped parsley
+ bread or toast, for serving

1. Heat the olive oil in a large skillet over medium heat. Add the onion, bell pepper, serrano, and ½ teaspoon of the salt. Cook until soft, about 8 minutes. Add the garlic, black pepper, caraway, paprika, cumin, and cayenne. Cook, stirring so nothing sticks, until fragrant, another 2 to 3 minutes.

2. Break up the whole tomatoes and add them, along with all their juices, to the pan. Stir in the tomato paste, honey, vinegar, water, and remaining 1 teaspoon salt. Reduce the heat to medium-low and simmer until the sauce has thickened, 12 to 15 minutes. Stir in the kale or chard and remove from the heat. If you're using feta (and not yogurt), mix it in at this point.

3. Make 4 indentations in the sauce with the back of a big spoon and slide each egg into its own well. Use a fork to intermingle the whites with the sauce a little. Turn the heat back on, to low, so the sauce is at a gentle simmer, and cook until the whites turn opaque around the sides and middle, 7 to 8 minutes. Cover the pan and cook until the whites are fully opaque but the yolks are still runny, about 3 more minutes.

4. Remove from the heat and sprinkle the parsley all over. Serve with bread or toast, and the yogurt if you opted out of the feta.

Huevos en Rabo de Mestiza

Mexico does it, too!

"This is the perfect thing in the summer when tomatoes and chilies are at their peak," says Karen Taylor, the chef and owner of El Molino Central in Sonoma, California, of *huevos en rabo de mestiza*. "But it needs a new name."

The translations for *rabo de mestiza* are as colorful as the dish itself: from "tattered clothing of a mixed-race girl" to "a whore's ass." (*Mestiza* was a term ascribed to the daughter of a Mexican and a Spaniard in the colonial era.)

Thought to have originated in the Central Mexico state of San Luis Potosí, a peasant dish of eggs poached in spicy tomato sauce à la *shakshuka* and Italian eggs in purgatory, huevos en rabo de mestiza is now a popular brunch dish throughout Mexico. Some variations call for hard-boiled eggs instead of poaching the eggs directly in the sauce, but traditional chefs do not always approve. This is Karen Taylor's recipe.

—*Aralyn Beaumont*

Makes 4 servings

3 tomatoes
2 serrano chilies
1 tbsp salt
4 poblano chilies
¼ cup olive oil
1 small white onion, sliced into thin
    half-moons
2 epazote sprigs
1½ cups chicken stock
8 eggs
8 thin slices queso fresco

1. Fill a medium saucepan with water and bring to a boil over medium heat. Add the tomatoes and serrano chilies and boil for 5 minutes.

2. Remove the tomatoes and chilies from the water and place on a plate lined with paper towels. When they're cool enough to handle, place them in a blender or food processor and add the salt. Blend until smooth.

3. Char the poblanos over a gas flame or under the broiler, then put them in a plastic bag. Once cool enough to handle, peel the poblanos and slice them into thin strips.

4. Heat the olive oil in a large saucepan over medium heat. Add the poblanos and onion and sauté until softened, 10 to 12 minutes. Add the puréed tomato-serrano mixture and the epazote, and cook for 10 to 15 minutes. Add the chicken stock and cook 5 minutes more.

5. Working with one at a time, crack an egg into a small bowl and slide it into the tomato-chili sauce. Try not to crowd them.

6. Cover the pan and cook the eggs until they're halfway done, about 5 minutes.

7. Add the slices of queso fresco, cover, and cook until the eggs are set and the cheese is melted, 5 to 7 minutes. Serve right away.

Huevos Divorciados *Mexico*

In Mexico, we regularly eat eggs for breakfast, preparing them in many different ways with various sauces—spicy red and green tomato sauces being the most common. *Huevos divorciados* is two fried eggs, each topped with one of the sauces. You get a dish that is half red and half green, which inspired the name "divorciados," because we usually eat fried eggs with just one sauce in Mexico. The dish is generally accompanied with refried beans, though some people will ask for chilaquiles on the side. Chilaquiles turn green, red, or black, depending on the sauce used. This is the recipe of my mom, Titita Ramírez Degollado—it's very popular at our restaurants.

—*Raúl Ramírez Degollado*

Makes 1 plato

2 **Fried Eggs** (page 103)
¼ cup **Salsa Roja** (recipe follows)
¼ cup **Salsa Verde** (recipe follows)
+ refried beans and/or chilaquiles, for serving

1. Place the fried eggs next to each other on a plate. Top one egg with the salsa roja and the other with the salsa verde.

2. Serve with refried beans and/or chilaquiles.

Brown Pelican

Salsa Roja

Makes 4 cups

4 garlic cloves
½ medium onion, chopped
1 tbsp vegetable oil
2 jalapeño chilies, chopped
2 lb plum tomatoes or 1 can (28 oz)
    whole tomatoes
1 small bunch epazote, finely chopped,
    or ½ cup chopped cilantro
1 tsp salt

1. Place the garlic and onion in a blender or food processor and blend until smooth.

2. Heat the oil in a medium pot over medium-low heat. Add the blended garlic and onion, reduce the heat, and simmer for 15 minutes, stirring occasionally.

3. Working in batches if necessary, add the jalapeños and tomatoes to the blender and blend until smooth. Add the mixture to the simmering pot along with the epazote, mix to combine, and let simmer for 45 minutes, stirring occasionally. Stir in the salt and let cool.

Salsa Verde

Makes 4 cups

3 tbsp vegetable oil
½ medium onion, finely chopped
2 lb green tomatoes or tomatillos,
    husked
2 jalapeño chilies
½ cup roughly chopped cilantro
+ salt

1. Make a *sofrito de cebolla*: Heat 2 tablespoons of the oil in a medium skillet over medium-low heat. Add the onion and sauté until soft and translucent, about 15 minutes. Remove from the heat and set aside.

2. Place the tomatoes and jalapeños in a medium pot and fill with water to cover. Set the pot over high heat, bring the water to a rapid boil, then drain the tomatoes and jalapeños and leave to cool.

3. Once cooled, stem the jalapeños. Working in batches if necessary, place the tomatoes, jalapeños, and sofrito de cebolla in a blender or food processor and blend until smooth.

4. Add the remaining 1 tablespoon oil to the drained pot and heat over medium-high heat. Pour all but a few tablespoons of the tomato mixture into the pot and bring to a light boil.

5. Meanwhile, add the cilantro to the blender. Blend with the remaining sauce into a smooth paste.

6. Before the salsa starts to boil rapidly, add the cilantro paste and mix to combine. Once the salsa is at a full boil, add 1 teaspoon salt and cook for 2 minutes. Remove from the heat, season with more salt if necessary, and chill the salsa before serving.

Spaghetti alla Carbonara

Italy

This is pasta that's been made with egg and sauced in egg, so it was more or less mandatory in this egg book. Carbone, Italy, has nothing to do with carbonara—this is a Roman dish. It's possible that carbonara *did* come from a restaurant called La Carbonara in Rome, but we can't be 100 percent sure. What we *do* know is that carbonara (a spaghetti dish that's finished with a mixture of beaten eggs, pecorino, and bacon or guanciale or pancetta) didn't become internationally popular until after World War II. Historians speculate that the original pasta carbonara was a modernized version made by food-strapped cooks with leftover American war rations (in which bacon and powdered egg yolks would have been bountiful). The original was a dish endemic to central and southern Italy, and consisted, simply, of pasta dressed with melted lard and beaten eggs and cheese. Carbonara is simple to put together—provided you temper the eggs, warming them up with the pasta water a little at a time so they don't curdle—and best eaten within a few minutes of cooking.

Makes 4 servings

4 oz guanciale, finely diced
+ salt
12 oz spaghetti
2 eggs
2 egg yolks
1 cup finely grated pecorino cheese
1 tsp freshly ground black pepper

1. Place the guanciale in a large cold skillet and set over medium heat. Cook, stirring often, until the guanciale is crisp and rendered, about 12 minutes. Remove the meat to a bowl and reserve the drippings.

2. Bring a large pot of water to a boil, salt it well, then add the spaghetti. Cook until al dente, 8 to 10 minutes.

3. Meanwhile, whisk the whole eggs and the yolks, pecorino, pepper, and 3 tablespoons of the guanciale drippings together in a large heatproof bowl. Gradually temper the mixture with ⅓ cup pasta water. Reserve in a warm spot.

4. When the spaghetti is al dente, lift it with tongs from the pot directly into the bowl with the egg mixture, and toss it vigorously in the sauce until the sauce thickens and clings to the noodles, about 30 seconds, adding splashes of pasta water if necessary. Add the guanciale and toss again.

5. Divide among four warm bowls and serve immediately.

Uitsmijter   *Netherlands*

Uitsmijter, pronounced outs-my-ter, means "out-thrower" in Dutch. As in the person who kicks you out of the bar when you've had a few too many Heinekens—the bouncer. How this egg-and-bread dish came to be named is unknown, but it probably has something to do with the fact that uitsmijter is Holland's national late-night food. After a long night of drinking, you might order an uitsmijter at the bar or at a nearby *eetcafé* (literally "eating café") to soak up all that booze. Cheap, hot, and easy to make, uitsmijter is also what you serve your friends after a house party. My cousin Martijn subsisted solely on uitsmijters during his first year of college, when he lived in a frat house overlooking one of Leiden's famous canals.

The thing about uitsmijter is that it allows Dutch ingredients—creamy butter, fantastic cheese, and really fresh bread—to shine. Although the fresh produce of this gray, soggy nation isn't anything to write home about, iconic Holstein cows turn rain-soaked grass into delicious butter and cheese. The very best cheese for uitsmijter is the creamy-yet-sliceable *jonge* (young, aged about four weeks) *boerenkaas* (farmers' cheese), an EU-protected designation that ensures the cheese was produced with raw milk that came from the same farm where it was aged. But if you can't find boerenkaas, it's fine to use gouda or any other semi-firm cheese available.

Although high-quality cheese and bread will enhance your uitsmijter experience, they're not necessary at all: Uitsmijter is the great leveler. Simple enough to make while hung over (or still drunk) and composed of things most folks have in the fridge, it's satisfying every time.

—Sascha Bos

Makes 1 serving

1 tbsp butter
2 eggs
2 oz semi-firm cheese, such as gouda, sliced
2 slices ham
2 slices white or whole-wheat sandwich bread, lightly toasted
+ salt and freshly ground black pepper

1. Melt the butter in a medium skillet over medium-high heat. Gently crack the eggs into the foaming melted butter and fry until the white is almost set and the yolk is still quite runny—just a bit less cooked than you like your sunny-side-up eggs—about 2 minutes. It's okay if the whites merge together to form one super-egg. Reduce the heat.

2. Arrange the cheese slices over the whites of the eggs, tearing to fit around the yolk. Cover the skillet, and allow the cheese to melt. When fully melted, remove from the heat.

3. Place a slice of ham on each piece of toast and top with a cheesy egg. Season with salt and pepper. Eat immediately.

2.

EGGS TODAY

Humans have been eating eggs since before recorded history—for a very, very, VERY long time. And as with any epic love story, any multimillennium relationship, there have been ups and there have been downs; there have been good times, and there have been horrifically bad. There have been times when, terrified of cholesterol, we thought it was a good idea to make omelets using just egg whites. And there have been egg creations so masterful, so breathtaking, we couldn't improve upon them if we tried. Our relationship to eggs has ranged from fraught to blissful to fraught again. Eggs have been medicine, and they have been poison; they've been vilified and celebrated and anointed.

The thing is, it's not eggs, it's *us*. As the more dramatic party in my long-term relationship, I know the swinging of moods all too well: Eggs have always just been, straightforwardly, eggs.

At least, that's true for the most part. In the process of our crazy ups and downs, humans have changed eggs, too. Somewhere down the line, eggs became Big Business, and we transformed chickens into egg-laying machines, in the process depriving them of everything chickens like in life (the outdoors, for example). Now, too, there's a proliferation of nonfactory egg options in the egg case—organic, free-range, omega-3. Backyard chicken flocks abound. You can get your eggs both fresh and factory. In other words, humans made things complicated, as we do.

Herein we explore the State of the Egg. Here we also have three recipes for egg sandwiches that are not an Egg McMuffin, the most widely consumed egg sandwich in the world today.

The Test of TIME

Aaron Thier

There is no prohibition against eggs in the Hebrew Bible. Yahweh limits himself to an injunction against taking eggs from the nest when the mother bird is watching, and that's just good manners. But what God won't proscribe, human beings will—and we're not apt to be consistent in our proscriptions either. An egg dish that would have fortified you in the seventeenth century might have killed you in the twentieth. One century's nutriment is another century's heart-disease risk factor.

1600s

In the seventeenth century (and until the nineteenth century), medicine is dominated by the humoral theories of Hippocrates and Galen. Disease is believed to be the result of imbalances, not infectious agents. Since everything you ingest affects that balance, the distinction between food and drugs does not exist. The consistency and temperature of various foodstuffs—their similarity to the body's humors—is an indication of how good they are for you, and since the consistency of eggs is transformed by cooking, the method of preparation is the most important consideration when determining whether an egg dish is nutritious or not.

According to an early English translation of the didactic fourteenth-century Latin poem *Regimen Sanitatis Salernitanum,* or "The Salernitan Rule of Health," poached eggs are best. They're easy to digest, nourishing, and most important they "engender blood," which is why "they be exceeding good for such as be recovered from sicknesse, for aged folke, and for weake persons, and specially the yolke." Poached eggs are better than "Egges roasted, hard or rere." (Rere meant partly boiled eggs, or in the subject of physics "rarefied" or "diffused.") Rere roasted eggs have their virtues, since they are also easy to digest, but they're nowhere near as nourishing as poached eggs. Hard-boiled eggs should be avoided: They are difficult to digest, "descending slowly to the stomacke, and slowly they enter therein."

The theory of the humors produces another association—one that persists to today: eggs as aphrodisiac. In *The Secret Miracles of Nature,* published in 1658, Levinus Lemnius explains that eggs, like certain other "meats of good juice," have a tendency to "stir up venery, and breed seed for generation."

Etmullerus Abridg'd: or, a Compleat System of the Theory and Practice of Physic, published in 1699, lists a number of uses for the different parts of an egg. The yolks are good for tooth sensitivity; the cooked whites are good for "numness of the teeth." Paronychia (an infection of the nail bed or cuticle) can be cured by placing the finger inside a newly laid egg. Bladder stones can be cured by placing the penis into a mixture of egg whites, human milk, and camphor.

1700s

Eighteenth-century writers also sing the praises of raw eggs. In his *Pharmacopoeia Universalis,* published in 1747, Robert James is refreshingly clear and direct on the rationale: "The white of a new laid Egg raw, pretty much resembles the Serum of the Blood, and is the Nutriment, from which all the solid Parts of the Chicken is form'd; hence 'tis perhaps, the very best Nutriment, where a Weakness of the digestive Organs prevails."

A 1793 article in *The Scots Magazine* echoes the view that the whites, when boiled hard, are difficult to digest.

1800s

In *Five Thousand Receipts in All the Useful and Domestic Arts,* published in 1829, Colin Mackenzie is restrained in his assessment, acknowledging that "the eggs of birds are a simple and wholesome aliment." He specifies that turkey eggs are best. Boiled or fried

eggs—no specificity as to hardness—are difficult to digest, a difficulty only increased by the addition of butter.

Belief in the aphrodisiac properties of eggs remains unchallenged: In 1834, *The London Medical and Surgical Journal* lists eggs as one of the foods that have "a specific action on the sexual organs," and Robert Druitt writes that eggs are a cure for impotence. *The Enchiridion Medicum: Or, Manual of the Practice of Medicine* says the same thing in 1836, although here the benefit appears to derive from their wholesomeness and not from any "specific action" on the genitals.

Thomas Andrew, author of *A Cyclopedia of Domestic Medicine and Surgery* (1842), is a raw egg man. They are especially good in the morning, he says, and are recommended as a remedy for jaundice and for problems with the liver and gallbladder. And yet he emphasizes individual variability as well: "Many persons, not otherwise remarkable for a vigorous digestion, can eat a great many eggs, not only with impunity, but with advantage," while other people may feel "oppressed" if they eat more than one at a time.

In 1845, Julius Vogel makes a scientific claim that will have momentous consequences for egg-eaters and egg-producers in the twentieth century: In his medical text, *The Pathological Anatomy of the Human Body,* Vogel observes that cholesterol (more abundant in eggs than in most animal products) is an important constituent of arterial plaques.

The idea that raw or soft eggs were good for invalids had been based on humoralist doctrine—they were like blood in their nature—but humoralism gives way to the germ theory of disease.

1900s

Although earlier writers have observed that the egg yolk is mostly oil, *Winfield Scott Hall's Nutrition and Dietetics,* published in 1910, warns us—presciently, it now seems—against making too much of this fact: "While eggs contain a considerable amount of fat, approximating ten per cent, this does not make a sufficient amount of fat, even in the half dozen eggs [!] that might be taken in one day's rations, so that we would be justified in looking upon the egg as an appreciable source of fat."

It is not until the 1950s that a biologist and physiologist named Ancel Keys popularizes the idea that dietary lipids are a risk factor in heart disease, rates of which had skyrocketed among American men in the previous two decades. In 1952, he publishes an article called "Human Atherosclerosis and the Diet." People have known for a hundred years that cholesterol is a component of atherosclerotic lesions, but though Keys does say that serum cholesterol levels are elevated in people suffering from heart disease, he emphatically denies that *dietary* cholesterol is harmful.

Then, in 1955, Dwight D. Eisenhower suffers a heart attack, which in many ways is the climax or culmination of the heart disease epidemic. Within six months, the American Heart Association, led by first lady Mamie Eisenhower, broadcasts a fund-raiser warning Americans about dietary lipids, and by 1961 the organization's official guidelines assume a familiar form, urging Americans to reduce total fat, saturated fat, and cholesterol. (This despite a 1957 report to the AHA that agrees with Keys and speculates that cholesterol has been singled out as "the villain underlying arterial catastrophe" simply because a new technique has made it easier to measure than other lipids. The authors say this test has "dragged a blue-green herring across the trail of investigation by concentrating too much attention on cholesterol.")

Bad news for eggs, in any case. In 1977, the Senate Select Committee on Nutrition and Human Needs publishes a report entitled *Dietary Goals for the United States.* The recommendations are stark: "Decrease consumption of butterfat, eggs and other high cholesterol sources." Egg and meat producers are quick to protest, additional hearings are convened, and a second edition is issued later that year. In one of the many prefaces to this second edition, three of the committee members acknowledge the great uncertainty about cholesterol and contend that "because of these divergent viewpoints, it is clear that science has not progressed to the point where we can recommend to the general public that cholesterol intake be limited to a specified amount." And yet the report recommends that cholesterol intake be limited to a specified amount: 300 milligrams per day, only slightly more than that contained in a single egg.

The 300-milligram recommendation will not go away, although there was and is little evidence to support it. In 1989, nine health organizations, meeting at the instigation of the American Heart Association, reaffirm all the earlier warnings about fat and cholesterol and retain the 300-milligram limit. And

IMPOTENCE

CURED

RADICALLY

& AT ALL AGES

through the use of

VIRILINE

PRICE:

10 Francs per box

ORDER ADDRESS:

18 Chaussée

FREE POSTAGE

after payment

even though the AHA emphasizes the danger of saturated fats in 1996—saturated fats have the largest impact on low-density lipoprotein (LDL) cholesterol levels—they do not revise their recommendations for cholesterol.

2000s

The tide may be turning. Studies published in 1999 and 2006 suggest that eggs do not increase the risk of heart disease in healthy men and women, although they may increase the risk for diabetes patients. A statement on the Harvard School of Public Health website suggests that "eggs also contain nutrients that may help lower the risk for heart disease."

Harold McGee's *On Food and Cooking* issues no warning whatsoever. McGee says that cooked egg "is one of the most nutritious foods we have . . . unmatched as a balanced source of the amino acids necessary for animal life." He dismisses the cholesterol debate: "Blood cholesterol is raised far more powerfully by saturated fats in the diet than by cholesterol itself, and most of the fat in egg yolk is unsaturated. It also appears that other fatty substances in the yolk, the phospholipids, interfere with our absorption of yolk cholesterol. So there no longer seems to be any reason to bother counting our weekly yolks."

Today, the belief that eggs will cure impotence is still held, judging by the huge abundance of recipes on the Internet: eggs with ginger and honey, eggs with chopped carrots, quail eggs, and so on.

In 2015, the 300-milligram recommendation for daily cholesterol intake is finally removed from the US Dietary Guidelines, though with the caution that "this change does not suggest that dietary cholesterol is no longer important to consider when building healthy eating patterns."

As for Ancel Keys, he died in 2004 at the age of one hundred, so whatever he was doing, he was doing something right.

How to Tell If Your Egg Is FRESH

There's a time and place for old eggs, and that is chapter 8 (page 237). When it comes to NON-preserved-egg cookery, however, you'll want to seek out a fresh egg. Here are four ways to tell if your egg is fresh.

Method 1

Break it open and look at the white. If it's cloudy, it's fresh! If it's clear, it's still okay to eat. If it looks a little pinkish, it's bad (unless it's a tinamou egg!).

Look at the yolk. If it sits up and looks perky, it's fresh! (If it flattens out, it's not that fresh.)

Look for the chalazae, the two ropey, goopy strands on either side of the yolk that keep it centered. When they're visible, the egg is fresh. When they're hard to find, the egg is not as fresh.

Method 2

Drop it into a glass bowl full of water. As an egg gets older, the water inside it evaporates. That water is replaced by air—or, in the case of a rotting egg, smelly gases.

If it sinks and lies horizontally at the bottom of the bowl, it's very fresh—1 to 3 days old.

If it sinks but bobs or stands diagonally, it's quite fresh—about 1 week old.

If it sinks but stands vertically, it's pretty fresh—about 2 weeks old. (This is a good age for hard-boiling.)

If it floats, it's a month old or older. It's not only not fresh, it's bad. Don't eat this egg!

Method 3

Shake the egg near your ear. If you don't feel or hear any movement, the egg is fresh. If you feel or hear the egg moving around inside, it's bad!

Method 4

Hold it up to the light. Fresh eggs are transparent in the center; old eggs are transparent at the ends.

Less fresh (flat)

More fresh (perky)

The Egg Carton GLOSSARY

Michael Light

Egg cartons today have a lot to explain, and for good reason: Among conventional egg producers, unsavory practices are commonplace. There's "forced molting": starving chickens so they'll molt at the same time, go out of production for a couple weeks, and return with rejuvenated reproductive tracts—making them better layers of better-quality eggs. There's painful, stressful "beak trimming," which prevents cannibalism and violence when hens are kept in close quarters. So there's no question that seeking out better eggs is well worth it. But when it comes to terminology, what do "Cage-Free," "Natural," "Organic," "Omega-3," and on and on, really mean?

Below are Government Certifications:

Cage-Free: According to the USDA, a cage-free chicken "[can] freely roam a building, room, or enclosed area with unlimited access to food and fresh water during their production cycle, but does not have access to the outdoors." Though this is an upgrade from the conventional battery cage (roughly 8½ × 11 inches), cage-free facilities, while allowing their hens more space, have much higher mortality rates (often the result of hen-on-hen violence) and lower air quality than facilities that use cages.

Free Range: Unlike cage-free hens, free-range hens must have access to outdoor space. It doesn't have to be much—sometimes it's a cat door to a screened-in porch.

No Added Hormones: This simply means that the egg-laying hen did not receive hormones. Which is a funny thing to mention, because administering hormones and steroids to poultry is prohibited across the board by the FDA. *All* eggs sold in the United States are hormone free.

No Added Antibiotics: This term is regulated by the USDA and FDA, and means an egg-laying hen received no sub-therapeutic antibiotics. But only a very small percentage ever receive added antibiotics to treat sickness, and their eggs are "diverted from human consumption" anyway.

Vegetarian Fed/Feed: "Vegetarian Fed/Feed" means an egg-laying hen was fed a diet devoid of any animal products during its production. Which is actually kind of sad!

Hens aren't naturally vegetarian, but omnivorous (they love worms and bugs). That said, conventional hens who *aren't* vegetarian fed are not likely being fed those worms and bugs they love so much, but a diet rich in animal by-products, from feather meal to chicken litter. So really, when you're buying vegetarian-fed eggs it's a lesser-of-two-evils situation.

Local: A term regulated by the USDA, "local" eggs must have come from a source flock located less than four hundred miles from their processing facility or within the state where the eggs originated and were processed.

Organic: Eggs marked with the USDA's National Organic Program label were laid by uncaged hens that are technically free to roam and have access to the outdoors, in addition to being fed an organic diet produced without conventional pesticides or fertilizers. Which all sounds great and is for the most part great—organic is a pretty decent option. But the problems with organically produced eggs are the same as those for free range: the absence of cages in a barn

or poultry house doesn't usually translate to a wealth of actual free-roaming space per hen, and what qualifies as access to the outdoors can be as insignificant as a cat door to a wired-in patch of cement.

Omega-3 Enriched: Eggs with higher levels of omega-3 fatty acids come from hens that were fed diets high in fatty acids: anything from flax to chia seeds to fish oil to algae, added to a bird's regular wheat- and/or corn- and/or canola-based foodstuff. Omega-3-enriched egg cartons are required by the USDA to state the amount each egg contains, and the eggs can have five times the concentration of omega-3s than conventionally raised or free-range eggs.

Pasteurized: Pasteurization occurs when an egg is heated in an effort to destroy pathogens. Egg products are *required* to be pasteurized. It's regulated by the FDA.

In addition to all of the hubbub mentioned above, eggs can be certified by third parties, further complicating this task of ingredient buying. Below are Third-Party Certifications in Decreasing Order of Goodness:

Animal Welfare Approved: This gold standard requires that each hen in a flock of no more than 500 birds has 1.8 square feet of indoor floor space and continuous access to at least 4 square feet of outdoor foraging space covered by vegetation; be able to nest, perch, and dust-bathe; be fed a diet containing no meat or animal by-products; and not be subject to forced molting or beak cutting.

Certified Humane: Humane Farm Animal Care breaks their certifications down into three distinct tiers. The HFAC disallows farms across the board from force-molting their birds, but allows beak cutting. Regular "cage-free" hens must be uncaged and able to nest, perch, and dust-bathe, but may be kept indoors at all times. "Free-range" hens must have at least 2 square feet of outdoor space (which should be covered by living vegetation where possible) and access to that space for at least 6 hours a day. "Pasture-raised" hens must be placed on a pasture for at least 6 hours each day, where each has at least 108 square feet of space.

American Humane Certified: Similar to the Certified Humane label, the American Humane Association divvies their eggs into categories. Hens in "Enriched-colony cages" each must have at least 0.8 square foot in their "furnished cage" and be provided with nests and perches. "Cage-free" hens must be uncaged and provided perches and nesting boxes in addition to their 1.25 square feet of roaming space, but can be kept indoors at all times. "Free-range" hens must have 28 square feet of outdoor space on a pasture with substantial vegetation coverage. "Pastured" hens must have 108 square feet of outdoor space including portions of range fenced off for regrowth of vegetation, in climatic conditions suitable for hens to access that exterior for the majority of the year.

Food Alliance Certified: Disallows hens from being fed meat or animal by-products; allows beak cutting; requires they be provided 1.23 square feet each of uncaged indoor floor space and be able to perch, nest, and dust-bathe; necessitates access to natural daylight or a living-vegetated outdoor area for at least 8 hours a day.

United Egg Producers Certified: No forced molting allowed; beak cutting allowed. "Caged" hens must have at least 0.46 square foot of cage space. "Cage-free" hens must have 1 to 1.5 square feet of roaming space.

Inside Yolk

Harold McGee

A deeply colored yolk is beautiful to behold and reflect on, but it doesn't really tell you anything about how the hen was raised, or how flavorful or nutritious the egg is. Sorry. It's true that uncaged farm hens and backyard hens accumulate yellow-orange pigments from green plants and maybe from bugs that battery hens don't. But feeds for battery hens routinely include ingredients for coloring their yolks that are rich in the same—or similar—pigments related to vitamin A (mainly lutein and zeaxanthin, both important for keeping our eyes healthy). Among those ingredients are yellow maize, meals made from marigold petals, alfalfa, grass, or algae, paprika extract, and (in Europe, not the United States) synthetic pigments.

Egg producers in different regions formulate their feeds to match consumer preferences, which are measured on scales like the Roche Yolk Color Fan (there are similar color scales for salmon flesh). According to a recent European review, Ireland and Sweden prefer light yellow yolks of Roche 8–9, France and England a deeper 11–12, and northern Europe and Spain an orange 13–14.

A number of other factors also affect yolk color, including the hen's breed, age, and other feed components. So the only way to know where a beautiful yolk got its color is to know the hen's owner and ask what it eats.

The best way to highlight yolk color is to avoid cooking the egg fully. Just as happens in the white, the heated proteins form microscopic aggregates that scatter light rays and eventually turn the liquid into a cloudy solid. The more moist you leave the yolk, the clearer and deeper its color will remain.

Chickens of PORTLANDIA

Liz Crain

On the other end of the spectrum, the practice of raising backyard flocks is alive and well! Meet some of the big-personalitied chickens who call (or called, RIP) Portland, Oregon, home.

Roberta is a small, all-black Burmese Silky with a crazy mop-top afro who was won in a raffle fund-raiser for KPSU and named after Robert Smith of The Cure. She is very small and so are her eggs, which have light green shells. Though they're tiny, they're mighty. A friend of Roberta's owner once rolled one of Roberta's eggs off the kitchen counter, and it didn't crack.

Mayonnaise & Dirty Mayonnaise were two high-strung, manic White Leghorns who laid loads of eggs but were always convinced their owners were going to kill them. The irony is that their owners took care of them, fed them, cleaned up their stinky poop, and bedded them every night . . . until coyotes ate them. The Mayos' owners vowed to never get white chickens again because of their high visibility to predators.

Tinkerbell was a Wyandotte who refused to lay her eggs in the coop and instead made every day a sort of Easter egg hunt. For a while, she laid her eggs in the alley behind her owners' house on the other side of the fence. One night, not realizing she was in the alley, they closed up the coop. At three a.m., Tink's owner heard a racket in the alley and ran out in his underwear. A possum was eating Tink's eggs and Tink was lurking at the end of the alley—a black silhouette. Still wearing only underwear, he chased Tink around the neighborhood for half an hour until he lost her. He never saw her again.

Brave Tetra was one of several video-game-princess-named chicks: Zelda, Peach, Yorda, and Tetra. All of these fuzzy baby chicks were brought home by their owners one February, kept warm and well fed. In the spring, when they were plucky teenaged pullets, the owners introduced them to their new coop in the backyard. They flapped and danced under the quince tree, and caught the attention of the Cooper's hawk living in the park next door. The owners heard a kerfuffle, and got to the window in time to see Tetra fighting off the hawk. A week later, the hawk returned, but this time Brave Tetra lost the battle.

Wilhelmina was a tiny Bantam hen in a flock of six. One day, while her owners were away, a neighbor's tomcat got through a tennis ball–size hole in the fence and killed five fellow members of her flock. Wilhelmina was nowhere to be found. A week later, one of her owners came home and heard a hen calling from the side yard. It was Wilhelmina. When he approached her, she took off. Once he finally caught her, a neighbor across the street hollered out, "Is she yours?" The neighbor told him that she'd roosted in their tree for the past week. Don't ever call that chicken a chicken.

Dolly Parton was a hardy Buckeye Heritage Breed. When she was a chick, her owner kept Dolly in her pocket for about two hours every day. As a hen, Dolly would squat down and wiggle her tail feathers when her owner came in the coop, which was a signal for the owner to scratch Dolly's downy booty. Her owner would do just that, and then scoop her up, and Dolly would nuzzle her head into her owner's neck. Dolly was the sweetest until—there's no easy way to put this—she was eaten by a raccoon. As it turns out, "I will always love you" was written by Dolly for Dolly.

What Shall We Name the Chicken?

Ardis . . . . "Fervent or eager" (*Latin*).

Barbara . . . . "The stranger". DIM. Bab, Babs, Babette.

Eldrida . . . . "Sage counselor" (*Anglo-Saxon*).

Frodine, Frodina . . "Wise, or learned, friend" (*Teutonic*).

Laïs . . . . A Greek name of obscure meaning. A favorite with the poets.

Lalita . . . . Perhaps "artless, straightforward".

Portia . . . . It comes from the title of an ancient Roman clan, the Porcii, called "pig men", probably because their ancestors were swineherds.

Ramona . . . . "Wise protectress" (*Teutonic*).

Sela . . . . "A rock" (*Hebrew*).

Solita . . . . "The wonted, or accustomed" (*Latin*).

Thera . . . . "The unmastered, or wild" (*Greek*).

Trista . . . . "The sorrowful" (*Latin*).

Una . . . . "The one".

Wanda . . . . "The wanderer" (*Teutonic*).

Zandra . . . . "Helper of mankind" (*Greek*).

Eggs Kejriwal

Even in a city as full of anachronisms as Mumbai, the old clubs scattered around town feel decidedly old-fashioned. The most famous of the clubs—foremost among them the Bombay Gymkhana and the Willingdon Sports Club—were built by the British as rarefied realms where they could rub shoulders with the city's anglicized elite, colonial and native alike. They had terrace restaurants full of wicker furniture and wood-paneled bars stocked with whisky and gin sold at heavily subsidized rates. (They still do; if you have a friend with a membership, the clubs are the best places in town for a cheap drink.)

At the Willingdon Club, the restaurant on the whitewashed verandah still looks out on one of the only open spaces in town, and waiters are still summoned using little brass bells left on the tables. The Willingdon is also responsible for the invention of Mumbai's most famous example of club grub: eggs Kejriwal.

Here's what we know about eggs Kejriwal: They were invented several decades ago by a rich businessman named Devi Prasad Kejriwal, who hailed from the conservative Marwari community. Kejriwal had a penchant for eggs, which were, unfortunately for him, strictly proscribed by his staunchly vegetarian family. On his daily visits to the Willingdon, he would throw caution to the wind and order an egg dish of his own invention: toast topped with a slice of Amul cheese (a processed white cheese that melts like rubber and tastes like nostalgia), a pair of fried eggs, and a healthy garnish of chopped chilies. In time, the Willingdon made the dish an official part of the menu, whence it spread to club kitchens all over the city.

You can still order your eggs Kejriwal at the Willingdon, but in truth, the original isn't all that great. It usually turns up lukewarm, with dry toast, overcooked eggs, and inexplicably unmelted cheese. In the last year, a wave of nostalgia has brought eggs Kejriwal to fashionable restaurants and cafés across Mumbai, first (and best) among them being the version turned out by Thomas Zacharias at the Bombay Canteen, the restaurant opened by Floyd Cardoz—his first in his native Bombay—back in February 2015. Zacharias's version is only slightly fancier than the original, replacing white bread with homemade brioche, and the chopped chilies with his South Indian grandmother's coconut oil–flavored green chili chutney.

—*Michael Snyder*

Makes 4 servings

2 to 3 tbsp butter, at room temperature
4 slices brioche (preferably round)
4 eggs
1 cup grated Amul cheese (see Note)

1 tsp chopped green chili (skinny, green, spicy—found in Indian groceries)
Green Chili Chutney (recipe follows)
1 tbsp chopped cilantro

1. Heat the oven or toaster oven to 425°F.

2. Apply butter to the bread slices and toast them golden brown. (Leave the oven on.)

3. For a pretty restaurant presentation, fry the eggs in ring molds: Heat a non-stick skillet over medium heat. Set the molds in the pan and allow them to heat as well. Drop a knob of butter into each ring mold, then crack an egg inside. Cook undisturbed until the white is half set but still loose and a bit translucent on the top. Use an offset spatula to loosen the egg from the inside of the mold, if needed, then remove from the skillet. (If you're not worried about presentation, fry the eggs normally and serve on a square piece of brioche.)

4. Put the fried eggs on the toasted bread, cover each with ¼ cup grated cheese, and sprinkle ¼ teaspoon of the chopped green chilies on top.

5. Transfer to a baking sheet and bake until the cheese is melted but the yolk is still runny, about 3 minutes.

6. Serve with green chili chutney and a sprinkle of cilantro.

Note: Amul cheese is the classic processed cheese that Indian kids grow up eating, similar—at least culturally— to Kraft Singles. It's mildly salty and extremely gooey when melted. In its absence, any grated cheddar or jack cheese would be a fine substitute.

Green Chili Chutney

Makes ⅔ cup

¼ cup seeded and diced green chilies
2 tbsp diced shallots
½ tsp sugar
+ salt
+ fresh lime juice (Indian nimbu, available at Indian groceries, are ideal here, but key limes or normal limes will work fine, too)
1 tbsp coconut oil
5 tbsp vegetable oil

1. Bring all the ingredients to room temperature. (This makes sure they'll emulsify properly.)

2. Place the chilies, shallots, sugar, salt to taste, and 1 teaspoon lime juice in a food processor and blitz to a smooth, pale green purée.

3. Add the coconut oil and continue blending until it reaches the desired consistency.

4. Add the vegetable oil a couple teaspoons at a time to emulsify. When it's nearly finished, adjust for taste, adding lime and salt as needed. The final product should be smooth and thin, almost like pea soup, and have a good balance of sweetness, salt, and acidity, but with the flavors of chili and coconut dominating.

5. Refrigerate for at least 1 hour to thicken before serving.

Egg and Beef Sandwich

In Hong Kong tea restaurants (*cha chaan teng*), this was traditionally known as the *mai ngau ju*, meaning the "haven't vomited yet" sandwich. You can imagine the state of the clientele to whom it's usually served.

The ladies who cook it up at Sun Han Yuen, a twenty-four-hour cha chaan teng just around the corner from the night market in Sham Shui Po, simply call their version *dahn ngou jee*, which pretty much means an egg and beef sandwich (though it serves the same purpose as the classic, if you so require). There are many other versions around Hong Kong. Some use canned corned beef. Others use a fried egg. Sun Han Yuen's is the best version: fresh chopped, savory beef topped with a perfectly crisp, yet fluffy scrambled egg between slices of hot, buttered white toast.

Owner Mr. Chow knows it's good. His dad started making it in 1968, when the restaurant was just a *dai pai dong*, a street stall down the street. He refuses to divulge the housemade *shacha* recipe, the Hokkien seasoning of finely ground shrimp paste, shallots, green pepper, ginger, and garlic, behind the ridiculously flavorful beef, but this version comes close.

—*Tienlon Ho*

Makes 4 sandwiches

1 lb beef brisket
3 tbsp shacha (Bull Head brand
    barbecue sauce works)
1 tbsp soy sauce
1 tbsp Shaoxing wine
+ peanut oil
8 slices white sandwich bread
+ salted butter
4 eggs
+ salt

1. Roughly chop the beef, working whatever sinew and fat there is evenly into the meat, stopping when it is still something coarser than hamburger. This takes time. Use a large cleaver or two. Mix in the shacha, soy sauce, and wine.

2. Coat a very hot skillet with peanut oil. Add the beef and cook, tossing, until cooked through and browned, about 5 minutes. Remove from the pan and set aside. Cook in portions if your pan is too small.

3. For each sandwich, lightly toast 2 slices of white bread. Trim off the crusts and spread butter over the toast.

4. Beat 1 egg per sandwich, and season with a pinch of salt. Pour 1 portion into the very hot oiled pan, allowing the egg to spread to about twice the size of a slice of sandwich bread. Cook over high heat until it has browned, crispy edges, about 1½ minutes.

5. Make the sandwich, placing a generous a layer of beef followed by the crispy egg folded in half. Cut into 2 triangles, and serve.

Egg Banjo

Since circa World War II, an egg banjo has been troop treat food. It's a fried egg, slotted between two pieces of (often stale) white bread, cut thick and brushed liberally with melted butter or margarine, all wrapped up in greaseproof paper. Sometimes, there's a mug of gunfire (black tea with a splash of rum) to go with it. Egg banjo is armed forces food, which means variations aren't acceptable: Add bacon, or sausage, or exchange the bread for something grainy, and it becomes too luxurious to be a banjo—it's a sandwich.

A banjo is a banjo because, so they say, when the yolk runs down a person's clobber (clothing), the person's instinct is to lift their sandwich-holding hand out of harm's way and "strum" the egg from their top using their other hand, accidentally impersonating a banjo player.

There couldn't be a simpler way to eat an egg, and yet ex–military personnel talk about egg banjos like they're dream food. On one forum, ex-members of the Royal Air Force discuss how they'd get them at the beginning or the end of an exercise, either to get them off to a good start or to send them cheerfully home. "The best food I remember was an egg banjo," writes one. "Always used to cheer up the dark mornings when the Banjo's arrived," agrees another.

The egg banjo is essentially a butty, a sanger, a sarnie. It's a sandwich, but in the specific way of British people at the weekend, made using thick cuts of squishy white farmhouse loaf—a doorstep sandwich. With a proper cuppa, it's a very fine way to eat an egg.

—Laura Goodman

Makes 1 sandwich

2 tbsp margarine or butter
2 thick slices white bread
1 **Fried Egg** (page 103), over easy

1. Spread 1 tablespoon margarine or butter over each slice of bread.

2. Sandwich the egg between.

3. Eat. If yolk dribbles onto your clobber, strum it away!

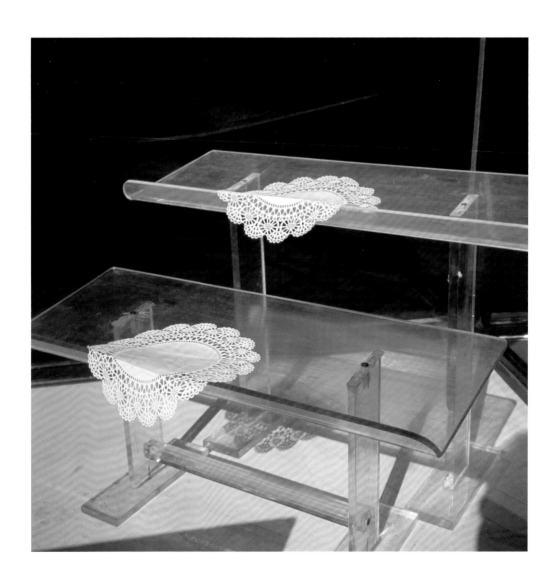

3.
OMELETS

Omelets were first described by Randle Cotgrave in his 1611 *Dictionary of the French and English Tongues*: "Haumelette, an Omelet, or Pancake of egges." But the word "omelet" now calls an endless range of egg pancakery to mind: There's the restrained, without-color, classic French omelet, cooked with nothing but butter, then folded primly, or the just-as-classic diner omelet, packed with fixings either intermingled with or tucked into the eggs, oozing with cheese (page 79). Elsewhere, it might mean *tamagoyaki* (page 62 and page 64), the Japanese layered omelet cooked with sweet dashi, or the herb-dense, Middle Eastern *kookoo sabzi* (page 69). Then there are those stuffed, fat omelets that grandma might make: *tortilla española* (page 76), hefty with potatoes and browned on all sides, and frittatas (page 80), holding anything from rice to meats to greens, arguably the best vehicle for leftovers. Then there's everything in between.

Whether exacting or forgiving, stuffed or slender, what all omelets have in common is pretty straightforward: beaten eggs, cooked over heat. This is an exploration of that golden delicacy—the rare item that unites the global culinary capitals of Paris and Denver. This is a celebration of all the forms an omelet can take.

Daniel Boulud's
Omelette Farcie

Daniel Boulud's perfect omelet is a classic *omelette farcie* (stuffed omelet), but the farcie is more eggs. Picture a perfect yellow French omelet, rolled three-quarters of the way, with a line of soft-scrambled egg spooned into the center. "This is an affair with a partner," Boulud says of the wet, hot scrambled eggs stuffed into the taut omelet. "When they meet . . ." he trails off.

He was fifteen when he first made this omelet as an apprentice in Lyon. All the young chefs had to demonstrate the technique before judges to advance their careers.

The perfect omelet can't be rushed: It needs thirty minutes, at least. The time- and labor-intensiveness is why Boulud doesn't make omelets ten times a night, or serve it at his restaurants, or regularly make it for himself at home. When he does, he says he likes it with warm buttered pain de mie, crème fraîche, and smoked salmon. Or caviar.

—*Genevieve Ko*

Makes 1 omelet (2 to 4 servings)

8 eggs
+ salt and freshly ground white pepper
3 tbsp cold unsalted butter, cut into
    ½-inch cubes
3 tbsp super finely sliced chives, plus
    more for garnish
+ clarified butter

1. Beat 5 eggs with a fork to blend, season with salt and white pepper, and beat again to mix. Don't beat any foam into the eggs. Set aside.

2. Bring 2 inches of water to a steady simmer in a saucepan that will hold a large metal bowl snugly.

3. Whisk the remaining 3 eggs in the metal bowl to break, then whisk in a pinch of salt and a twist of pepper. Set the bowl over the simmering water and whisk constantly, adjusting the heat to keep the water just simmering and to prevent the eggs from curdling too

fast. The eggs will foam on top, then the foam will subside and the eggs will start to thicken and become opaque and creamy. This process will take 20 to 30 minutes. You will whisk them steadily and constantly the entire time.

4. Once the scrambled eggs coalesce and form tiny curds—they'll resemble a loose porridge—remove the bowl from the saucepan and immediately add 2 tablespoons of the cold butter to slow the cooking. Whisk in the butter until melted, then fold in the chives. Set aside.

5. Heat a 12-inch black steel or non-stick omelet pan over medium heat until hot. Add enough clarified butter to the omelet pan to coat the bottom and the sides, then add the remaining 1 tablespoon cold butter. As soon as it melts, add the reserved beaten eggs. Swirl to coat the bottom and ½ inch up the sides of the pan. Let stand until the edges are just set, then immediately pull in the edges with a fork and beat the eggs by moving the fork in a circular motion while vigorously swirling the pan in the opposite direction. When the eggs are barely set but still runny, slam the pan flat against the stove grate.

6. Use an open palm to forcefully rap the pan's handle near where it meets the pan. The egg should slide and roll a bit. Repeat the tapping until the egg has rolled three-quarters of the way. Spoon a line of the scrambled eggs onto the open flap, leaving 1 inch on all sides. Tap the

pan again for the final roll, then flip the omelet onto a dish, seam side down.

7. Drape a clean kitchen towel over the omelet and gently encourage it into a torpedo shape. With a sharp knife, cut a slit down the center, leaving 2 inches uncut on both ends. Use the tip of the knife to carefully open the slit an inch wide, and spoon the remaining scrambled eggs in and on top of the slit. Garnish with chives and serve immediately.

Pigeon Guillemot

Michael Anthony's Tamagoyaki

Michael Anthony is the chef of New York City's acclaimed Gramercy Tavern. His style is seasonal and vegetable-centric, his flavors clean and intense. But he actually started cooking on the other side of the globe. He studied Japanese in college, hopped a plane to Tokyo the day after he graduated, and ended up in Saitama, a semirural satellite suburb north of the city. Officially, he was there to teach English. And he did, trading language classes for cooking lessons with a group of middle-aged women. "I was interested in learning how people ate at home, from a cultural perspective as well as a culinary one," he tells me. "Every Friday morning, I'd go to my friend's house and she and her friends would teach me the basics of home cooking. *Tamagoyaki* was the first dish they taught me." At its best, tamagoyaki (aka *dashimaki tamago*) is a rolled log made from numerous golden-brown layers of savory-sweet egg cooked in a traditional heavy copper square pan called a *makiyakinabe*.

The ingredients are simple—eggs, soy, dashi, sugar. Anthony worked to get the balance just right. He likes to add extra yolks for richness and uses white soy sauce because it's saltier, more savory, and makes for a paler omelet. Equipment-wise, Anthony admits a lightweight nonstick skillet would be easier to maneuver than his makiyakinabe. Nowadays, Japanese markets sell lighter square nonstick pans for the weak of arm. To aid with the egg-rolling, Anthony flips the finished omelet onto a sushi mat and gently presses it into a rectangular cylinder.

—*Genevieve Ko*

Makes 1 omelet (2 to 4 servings)

5 eggs
3 egg yolks
2 tbsp sugar
1 tsp salt
Dashi (recipe follows)
2 tbsp white soy sauce, plus more for
    serving
2 tbsp fresh mitsuba leaves or flat-leaf
    parsley leaves, finely chopped
+ grapeseed oil
+ daikon radish, peeled
+ baby green radish (optional), peeled
+ baby white turnip (optional), peeled
    and trimmed
+ microgreens (optional)

Great Horned Owl

1. Mix the whole eggs, yolks, sugar, and salt in a medium bowl with chopsticks until well blended, but not foamy. Mix in the dashi and soy sauce until incorporated, then stir in the mitsuba.

2. Heat a well-seasoned 8-inch square copper makiyakinabe or 10-inch nonstick or cast iron pan over medium heat. To check if the pan is ready, draw a line of beaten egg in the pan. It should coagulate on contact. When the pan's ready, soak a paper towel with oil and rub a generous coating all over the bottom and sides of the pan. Pour in enough egg to form a thin layer, swirling the pan to evenly coat the bottom.

3. Cook the eggs, tapping down any bubbles with chopsticks, until the bottom is completely set and golden brown and the top is glossy. Pick up one far corner of the egg and pull it in 2 inches and fold it over. Repeat on the other far corner so that there's a 2-inch strip of golden brown egg folded over the remaining omelet. Let it set for a second, then grip the center of the fold with the chopsticks and gently lift and roll it over while pushing the pan away from your body and bring it back more gently in a circular motion. So, you're simultaneously pulling the egg toward you while rotating the pan away from you. Repeat until the omelet is fully rolled and snug against the handle-side of the pan.

4. Gently scooch the roll to the far side of the pan and press it firmly against the side. Soak the oiled paper towel again and lube the pan, letting oil seep under the roll. When the oil's hot, add another thin layer of egg. Lift the roll to let the wet egg run under it. Once this layer is set, repeat the rolling and rotating technique. Keep adding egg and rolling until all the egg is used up. Be warned: the rolling gets harder with each layer as the roll gets heavier.

5. When the roll is complete, carefully turn it out onto a sushi mat. Wrap the mat around the roll and press it gently, squaring off the edges. Transfer the roll to a cutting board and cut it into 1-inch slices. Transfer to a serving dish. Tamago also tastes good cold or at room temperature, though it is best hot.

6. To garnish, grate the daikon on a Japanese grater or fine Microplane. Squeeze out any excess liquid, then press into a little snow hill on the dish and drizzle with soy sauce. If using, cut the radish into paper-thin slices and the turnip into wedges. Arrange on the plate like a zen garden with the microgreens and serve.

Dashi

Makes ½ cup

2-inch square of kombu
⅔ cup water
3 tbsp loosely packed katsuobushi
    (dried bonito flakes)

1. Simmer the kombu and water in a small saucepan for 20 minutes. Remove from the heat.

2. Discard the kombu and add the katsuobushi. Stir well and let stand for 15 minutes. Strain through a strainer into a bowl.

Tamago-no-Shinzo Yaki

Just as there are many ways to cook a Western omelet, there are countless ways to cook a Japanese omelet. *Tamagoyaki* can be sweet or savory; it can contain fish, crab, or shrimp paste, or grated mountain yam, which gives it a fluffy texture. I like to put minced chives in mine. You can be bold and throw in a piece of grilled eel to give it a smoky flavor. When dashi is added, tamagoyaki becomes *dashimaki tamago*. Japanese love to splash dashi in everything, as Italians do olive oil. Dashi is the hidden flavor that gives depth to the eggs.

The common tamagoyaki (like Michael Anthony's, page 62) is made in a squarish tamagoyaki pan. A thin egg batter is poured into the sizzling hot pan and then the thin layer is made into a roll. Then more batter is poured under the first roll to form another layer. Eventually, you create a spiral, which is made by rolling together several layers of thinly cooked eggs. This takes a little practice.

My mother's tamagoyaki defied all tamagoyaki conventions. She didn't bother making the spirally layers. She didn't even own a square pan. She used a round 10-inch cast iron skillet to make a communal tamagoyaki. Hers was basically scrambled eggs packed together like an ugly pillow. She called it *shinzo-yaki* ("pan-fried heart"), and sure enough, it looked like an organ. She'd learned it from Hamako Tatsumi, a popular cooking teacher and neighbor in Kamakura. I remember tagging along to these cooking lessons when I was a girl—it's a dish that's stuck with me all these years. Every time I watched my mother make this tamagoyaki, it looked like a disaster. But she didn't seem worried. She was a brave cook. She would stir the eggs in the simmering dark broth and push the cooked eggs to one side of the pan and keep stirring. The most important step was to scoop up the dashi and pour it on the tamagoyaki repeatedly, until all the dashi was gone. The final step was letting the tamagoyaki brown on both sides. The kitchen smelt irresistibly good, like burnt caramel. The tamagoyaki didn't look so bad in the end, and it tasted amazing: sweet and juicy from all the dashi that seeped inside.

—*Sonoko Sakai*

Makes 1 omelet (2 to 4 servings)

10 eggs
1½ cups dashi
½ cup sake
¼ cup sugar
2 tbsp soy sauce
½ tsp sea salt
2 tbsp sesame oil
1 cup grated daikon radish (optional)

1. Whisk the eggs, dashi, sake, sugar, soy sauce, and salt in a large bowl.

2. Heat the sesame oil in a well-seasoned cast iron or nonstick pan over medium heat. Pour the soupy egg mixture into the heated pan all at once and stir until the eggs split from the broth and start to coagulate. Using a spatula, start to push the cooked eggs to one side of the pan, packing the tamagoyaki so it holds together and scraping the bottom of the pan to make sure it is not sticking. When most of the egg has bound together in a heap at one side of the pan, after about 10 minutes, reduce the heat to low. Work the omelet into the middle of the pan, packing it into a wiggly oval. It will be very tender so treat it gently. Ladle the broth pooling in the skillet over the entire tamagoyaki while moving it around in the pan so it cooks evenly. Repeat until the tamagoyaki absorbs all the broth, about 15 minutes.

3. When there is only syrupy dashi left in the skillet, and the bottom of the omelet is caramel colored, carefully flip the tamagoyaki and caramelize the other side, about 5 minutes.

4. Carefully transfer the tamagoyaki to a cutting board. Let it cool slightly, then cut it into square or rectangular pieces and serve it with grated daikon radish, if desired.

Thick-Billed Murre

World's Fastest Omelet MAKER

interviewed by Lauren Ro

Howard Helmer, also known as the Incredible Egg Man, worked as a spokesman for the American Egg Board for over forty years, traveling the world to educate people on the benefits and joys of cooking with eggs. He also happens to hold three Guinness World Records—all involving omelets. Helmer is the world's fastest omelet maker. He once made 427 two-egg omelets in thirty minutes. He is also the fastest single omelet maker (whole egg to plate in forty-nine seconds), and the fastest omelet flipper (thirty flips in thirty-four seconds).

I come from a Russian immigrant family who came to Chicago in the 1920s, from Belarus. We were a poor family, so whatever was left over from the dinner my grandmother made, she would mix with eggs the next day, and serve it. Eggs, as a result of that, became kind of my soul food. That's my propensity for eggs! I love eggs, and I love to use them in different ways.

I came to New York because I was dazzled by it. My first visit to New York at age twelve convinced me that I wanted to live there. After a stint in the air force, I learned that the American Egg Board was looking for a home economist for their New York office. I went to interview for the job. Even though I'm not a home economist, I do know what public relations is. I talked the person at the Egg Board into sending me to New York so that I could encourage the media to publish egg recipes, instead of focusing only on nutrition. I started with them forty-five years ago, and today I show people how to make omelets in under a minute.

One year, I decided to attempt the Guinness World Record for fastest omelet making. The AEB was opening an omelet restaurant on Main Street in Disneyland, and we wanted to create excitement. This was 1978 and there was Guinness fever. There were TV shows about record breakings, and so I went into training. Now I've got a Guinness World Record credential, which really beats a Harvard PhD!

If you put on a headset, put on some rap music, and make omelets to the cadence, you'll really keep your pace going. At Mont Saint-Michel in France there's a restaurant called La Mère Poulard, which is like omelet central for the world (see page 70). It's where these rosy-cheeked Norman kids have these copper frying pans with long handles

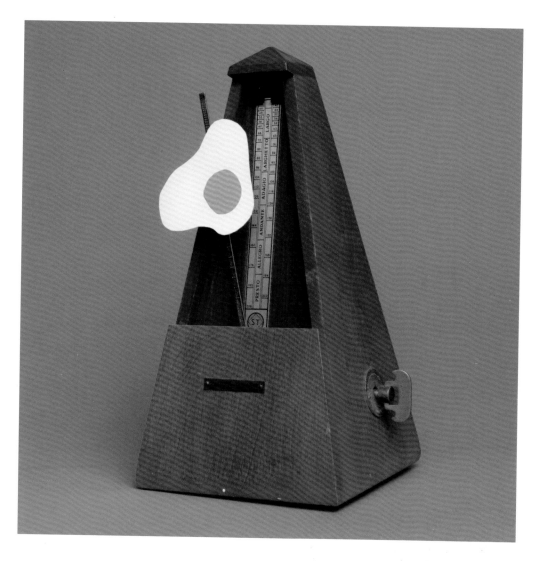

that they put into what is essentially a wood-burning oven, and they beat on the long handle of the frying pan, which creates a ripple effect, so that by the time it gets down to the frying pan the eggs are dancing in the oven. When I went to visit, I identified myself as the world record holder, so they invited me into the kitchen to watch. They attributed the success of their omelets to the beating on the handle and the cadence. I thought, Well, I'm going to make my omelets to a cadence. I started doing it, and before you know it, there was no stopping me.

The omelet technique that I use is different from the classic one. My omelet-making technique is really to make a simple egg pancake: fill it, fold it, and turn it upside down on the plate.

The French way of making omelets can be intimidating. The French don't put any liquid in their eggs, so they'll take generally two or three eggs, whisk them up, put them in a frying pan, and shake the pan while twirling the egg in the frying pan with the back of the fork, lifting the egg off the bottom of the pan as they twirl the fork. It is complicated. And then they grab the handle of the pan, roll the egg to the lip of the pan, turn the pan upside down, out comes an omelet.

My way is the dig-a-hole-and-fill-it method, where instead of twirling a fork in the pan, you put the eggs in the pan and with an inverted spatula draw the cooked egg, which sets up right away in the pan, from the perimeter of the pan to the center of the pan while at the same time tilting the pan so that the raw egg flows onto the space of the pan you just vacated! You can get the omelet ready to fill in twenty seconds, then by the time you add the filling and turn it out onto the plate only a minute has elapsed.

My recipe for an omelet is two eggs and two tablespoons of water. If I substitute a dry white wine for the water, the egg takes on a whole new wonderful flavor and I can fill that with shredded gruyère cheese and bacon, and it's a classic.

The quintessential egg dish is, of course, the omelet. People have told me that if a classically trained chef goes for a job in the kitchen, the first thing he's asked to do is make an omelet—that all of his culinary skills are judged by the way he makes the omelet. That tells you a lot. I like the omelet for its versatility. I make a dessert omelet with fresh fruit that I flambé with flavored brandy, which I think is terrific. People love it! I make an open-faced omelet that I slide onto a heated flour tortilla, that I then roll and serve as a burrito. There's so much you can do with an omelet.

If you came to my house for dinner, I'd serve you the omelet I described before. I put some dry white wine in the egg batter,

I fill the egg with shredded gruyère cheese and bacon, turn it out onto the plate, and serve it with a spoonful of Dijon mustard. You would love it!

I have more respect for the egg than any other food and I think the reason is that I know it so well, inside and out, and if anybody knew eggs as well as I do they too would celebrate them.

Life without eggs would be dull. Life without eggs would leave us with not a whole lot of recipes to cook. I'm so happy to do this, to talk about eggs.

Kookoo Sabzi

Iranians treat herbs not as a seasoning, but as a vegetable: Copious fresh herbs are the foundation of many Persian recipes. This is especially the case in spring, when Nowruz, the Persian new year, pulls everyone out of their homes to go on picnics, where *kookoo sabzi* is always part of the spread. It's a frittata-like dish of fresh greens bound by just enough egg to hold it together. Every family has its own combination of herbs. My family's recipe starts with onions lightly caramelized with turmeric for subtle sweetness, basil for its aroma, and the unusual addition of romaine lettuce, which helps give the kookoo a fluffy texture.

—Tannaz Sassooni

*Makes 4 main-course servings,
or 8 as part of a larger spread*

½ cup neutral oil, such as grapeseed
1 tsp ground turmeric
1 white onion, finely chopped
¾ cup finely chopped flat-leaf parsley
¾ cup finely chopped dill
½ cup finely chopped basil
1 cup finely chopped spinach leaves
6 leaves romaine lettuce, finely chopped
5 scallions, finely chopped
¼ cup fresh fenugreek leaves or
    1 tbsp dried (optional)
½ cup finely chopped garlic chives
    (optional)
3 eggs
¾ tsp salt
¼ tsp freshly ground black pepper
1 tbsp all-purpose flour
+ flatbread and yogurt, for serving

1. Heat ¼ cup of the oil in an 8-inch nonstick skillet over medium-high heat. Add ½ teaspoon of the turmeric and the onion, and sauté, stirring occasionally, until the onions are lightly browned, 12 to 15 minutes. Add all the greens, parsley through scallions (and fenugreek and garlic chives if using), and stir to combine (the pan will be very full). Wilt the vegetable mixture for about 4 minutes. Transfer to a bowl. Wash the pan.

2. Whisk together the eggs, salt, pepper, flour, and remaining ½ teaspoon turmeric in a medium bowl. Add 2 cups of the vegetable mixture and stir to combine completely. If there's still egg puddling at the bottom of the bowl, add more of the vegetable mixture, ¼ cup at a time, until the egg is fully incorporated. (Save any leftover vegetable mixture for something else, like a scramble.)

3. Return the pan to the stove over medium heat and add the remaining ¼ cup oil. Add the egg mixture and quickly spread it into an even layer. Cover and cook, reducing the heat as necessary to maintain a gentle bubble, until the bottom is browned and the top has set, about 10 minutes. With the side of a spatula, divide into quarters. Flip each quarter and continue cooking, covered, 2 to 3 minutes. Halve each quarter to make 8 slices. Serve with warm flatbread and tart yogurt.

Poulard Omelet

The Poulard omelet is a hearth-cooked omelet that's like an egg-in-egg purse: puffy, soufflé-like outsides are folded over runny, buttery, lightly cooked eggs that ooze out onto the plate like a sauce. As with all French omelets, a fork cuts effortlessly through it and each bite is egg-forward in flavor, with a slight toastiness from the open fire.

In 1888, Annette Poulard and her husband opened the Auberge de Saint-Michel Tête d'Or on Mont Saint-Michel, a small monastic island turned prison turned travel destination off the coast of Normandy. Day after day, the restaurant served the same 2.50-franc lunch menu with complimentary cider and butter: an omelet with ham, salt marsh lamb cutlets, potatoes sautéed in butter, roasted chicken, salad, and dessert.

By the time Madame Poulard retired in 1906, her inn and restaurant had become a popular tourist attraction. In 1922, she addressed rumors circulating about her recipe in a letter to French food writer Robert Viel: "I break some good eggs into a bowl, I beat them well, I put a good piece of butter in the pan. I throw the eggs into it and I shake it constantly. I am happy, monsieur, if this recipe pleases you." Apparently, Madame Poulard preferred this style of omelet, popular in communes throughout Normandy, to the Parisian-style omelet in fashion at the time. She passed away in 1931, at eighty years old.

—Aralyn Beaumont

Makes 1 omelet (1 or 2 servings)

3 eggs, at room temperature
¼ tsp salt
1 tbsp butter

1. Heat the oven to 350°F.

2. Crack the eggs into a metal, preferably copper, bowl. With a large whisk, begin beating the eggs, working air into them for a few seconds. Season with the salt and continue whipping until the eggs have creamy, soft peaks, and hang for a quarter second from the whisk before falling back into the bowl in a fluffy ribbon. This will take about 3 minutes of vigorous whisking (don't give up!).

3. Set a seasoned 8- or 9-inch carbon-steel pan over medium-high heat and heat until very hot, about 3 minutes. While you wait, continue beating the eggs so they don't lose volume. Add the butter to the pan, swirl to coat it in fat, and pour in the whipped eggs. Let cook, undisturbed, for 1 minute. Transfer the skillet to the oven and bake for 2 minutes. Remove and return to medium-high heat for about 1 minute, until the bottom of the omelet is browned and the omelet releases from the bottom of the pan.

4. Use an offset spatula to half-slide the omelet onto a large plate. Use the inner edge of the pan to fold the omelet over itself on the plate, allowing the soft, souffléed filling to ooze out of the omelet, creating a crescent border of soft egg around the omelet. Serve immediately.

Hangtown Fry

This Gold Rush–era bacon-and-oyster omelet makes a single, rib-sticking serving: suitable for fortifying you for a demanding day of gold-mining.

Makes 1 serving

1 tbsp butter
2 slices thick-cut bacon, cut into
    1-inch pieces
6 shucked oysters
2 eggs
1 scallion, sliced
+ salt and freshly ground black pepper

1. Heat a small skillet over medium heat, melt the butter in the pan, then add the bacon. Cook until nearly crispy, about 8 minutes. Add the oysters and cook until they plump, about 60 seconds.

2. Beat the eggs with the scallion, salt, and pepper, then pour over the oysters and bacon. Shake the pan until a soft scramble forms, about 60 seconds. Let cook undisturbed for a few seconds to set the bottom. Flip and cook for 1 minute. Invert onto a plate and serve immediately.

Golden Eagle

Taiwanese Oyster Omelet

Taiwan does it, too!

In their raw states, oysters and eggs are textural twins—equally liquid and jelly, the quivering consistency of, well, mucus. Because chewy, bouncy, and slippery textures are fetishized in Taiwan, and the island's coasts are clogged with oysters, the oyster omelet (*o ah jian*) is a humble, cheap roadside snack. Oysters and eggs are barely set together with a few rapid tosses in a wok, and bound by another slippery substance: a cooked sweet potato starch slurry. The resulting omelet is less Hangtown Fry (page 71) than savory mochi. It's all drenched in a sweet-sour, thickened sauce made from ketchup and soy, so that you have to slurp the bites up with chopsticks quickly before they slip away. First popularized in coastal towns with oyster farms nearby, it's now a night-market staple.

Make the sauce ahead, and use it on everything from scallion pancakes to french fries. As it's milder than ketchup, you can drench it liberally on everything, as the Taiwanese do. Celery leaves are a fragrant and classic touch, but can be substituted with shredded bok choy, mustard greens, cabbage, lettuce, or any other greens you have on hand.

—Cathy Erway

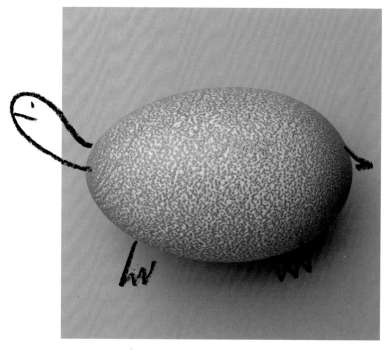

Bennett's Cassowary

Makes 1 omelet (about 2 servings)

4 eggs
+ salt and white pepper
1 tbsp sweet potato starch
½ cup cold water
2 tbsp vegetable oil
8 shucked oysters
1 cup loosely packed celery leaves
+ **Sauce** (recipe follows)
+ rice, for serving

1. Beat the eggs in a bowl with salt and white pepper. In a separate bowl, mix the sweet potato starch and cold water.

2. Heat 1 tablespoon of the oil in a large nonstick or cast iron skillet over high heat. Once the oil is hot and starting to pop a little, add the oysters to the pan. Let cook for 1 minute, stirring occasionally.

3. Stir the starch mixture once more and pour it onto the oysters. Let it bubble for a couple seconds, then pour the beaten egg mixture into the pan on top of the starch. Push the edges in with a spatula to create a somewhat round shape. Once the eggs are almost set, scatter the celery leaves on top. Carefully loosen the bottom of the omelet from the pan using a spatula. If the underside is completely loosened and slightly browned, carefully flip the entire omelet over (using two spatulas if needed). Cook on the opposite side to lightly brown, about 1 more minute. Invert the omelet onto a plate. Top with the sauce and serve immediately, with rice.

Sauce
Makes 1 cup

¼ cup ketchup
¼ cup rice vinegar
1 tbsp sugar
1 tsp soy sauce
1½ tsp cornstarch
½ cup cold water
+ salt

1. Combine the ketchup, rice vinegar, sugar, and soy sauce in a small saucepan and stir to mix thoroughly. Bring to a simmer over medium-high heat, stirring occasionally, until the sugar dissolves, 1 to 2 minutes.

2. In a separate bowl, whisk together the cornstarch and cold water. Stir into the ketchup mixture and continue to simmer until thickened, 2 to 3 minutes. Season with salt. Remove from the heat and allow to cool to room temperature.

China Café's
Egg Foo Young

Egg foo young—also spelled *egg fo yeong, egg foo yong, egg foo yung, egg fu yung*—the small omelet-like disk of egg, bean sprout, onion, and minced meat or seafood, topped with gravy, may have descended from *fu rong*, a custardy egg dish served at Cantonese banquets. But it more closely resembles the omelets and goopy gravy of American diners, probably because it was first meant to appeal to American palates.

When the hopes of striking it rich from the California Gold Rush dwindled, opening restaurants became a viable career path for many Chinese immigrants, most of whom had no professional cooking background. These restaurants weren't places for immigrants to find a taste of home, or for adventurous eaters to try a new style of cooking. They were purely money makers with menus listing typical American dishes alongside Americanized Chinese dishes: the Big Three being chop suey, chow mein, and egg foo young.

Since its heyday throughout the first three-quarters of the twentieth century, egg foo young and its fellow Big Three have fallen off in popularity as regional Chinese cuisines have become more popular. You'll still find it on take-out menus and in old-school Chinese-American restaurants, or in the form of a sandwich in the Midwest (i.e., the St. Paul Sandwich: egg foo young, lettuce, pickles, onion, and mayo between white bread).

China Café has been serving multiple varieties since it opened at Grand Central Market in downtown LA in 1959. Though the restaurant counter has changed ownership three times, the recipe has remained the same. Out of respect for lifelong customers, Rinco and Susie Cheung have held on to China Café's cooks and the original menu since they purchased the business in 2012. Rinco refers to the egg foo young (they call it "egg fo yeoung") as very simple, old-style food, but likes it all the same. Serve it with pork, chicken, or shrimp on top, but never forget the gravy and side of rice.

—Aralyn Beaumont

Makes 6 pieces (2 to 3 servings)

4 eggs
½ cup all-purpose flour
4 oz bean sprouts, finely chopped
    (about ¾ cup)
½ large white onion, finely chopped
+ salt
+ neutral oil
+ rice, for serving
+ **Gravy** (recipe follows)
+ chopped scallions

1. Combine the eggs, flour, bean sprouts, onion, and a pinch of salt in a bowl and mix until the batter is smooth, but do not overmix—it should resemble pancake batter.

2. Heat a skillet over medium heat. Working in batches, add 1 tablespoon neutral oil and when it is hot, pour batter by ¼ cupfuls into the skillet. Cook the patties until light golden and almost cooked through, about 2 minutes per side.

3. Remove the patties from the skillet and repeat with the remaining batter until you have 6 patties. At this point, the patties can be refrigerated for a day.

4. Pour 2 inches of neutral oil into a deep fryer or saucepan. Bring the oil to 350°F.

5. Add a couple of patties at a time, deep-frying until deeply browned, crisp, and puffy in the center, 3 to 4 minutes.

6. Serve with rice and top with gravy and chopped scallions.

Gravy

Makes 1 cup

1 cup chicken broth
2 tbsp cornstarch
1 tbsp vegetable oil
½ tsp salt
½ tsp sugar
⅛ tsp sesame oil
+ pinch of white pepper
1 tbsp mushroom or regular soy sauce

Combine the chicken broth, cornstarch, vegetable oil, salt, sugar, sesame oil, and pepper in a small saucepan and bring to a boil, whisking often. Add the soy sauce and taste, adding more if desired. Cook until the gravy has thickened, about 3 minutes. Set aside, but keep warm.

Chaco Finch

Tortilla Española
Clásica

Learning how to make *tortillas* makes you a better cook. You learn how to apply heat, remove heat, preheat, reduce heat, carry over cooking—you learn a million skills in one recipe. You learn how to poach potatoes in olive oil, which is confit. There are so many concepts in this one dish. Then the most important part is intimacy. Every time you'll make it, you'll work at it a little differently. You'll smell it differently. There's just so much to observe and respond to in one dish. And it's really something you can work on—that you can get better and better and better at. Because you have to be completely engaged. It's not passive. Which I think is true of most egg cooking.

Tortillas can be juicy or dry, and either way is correct. It's just a question of how you like them. Spaniards prefer their tortillas soupy, but you can cook them through if you're concerned about raw eggs. No one can teach you how to perfect a tortilla; you have to learn as you go. But here are a few tips: Use the smallest pan you can, one that will just accommodate the size of the tortilla—I like a 9- to 10-inch pan—and, if you can, work over a gas burner. You want the flame to lick up the sides of the pan, which is essential for forming the sides of the tortilla and preventing broken edges. Commit to flipping the tortilla: Use deliberate, purposeful movements and don't hesitate once you've begun. You can patch up any cracks or holes with a bit of beaten egg, should the need arise. The side of the tortilla that you sear first should be facing up at the end. That's important because it made contact with the pan when the surface was the hottest, so it is the sturdiest.

—Alex Raij

Makes 4 to 6 servings

1½ lb russet (baking) potatoes
    (2 to 3 medium)
1 Spanish onion, thinly sliced
    (about 2 cups)
1 cup canola oil, or as needed
1 cup plus 3 tablespoons extra-virgin
    olive oil, or as needed
+ salt
10 eggs, at room temperature

1. Peel the potatoes, then rinse under cool running water and cut lengthwise into quarters. Cut the quarters crosswise into ⅛-inch-thick slices. You should have 4 cups potato slices.

2. Combine the potatoes and onion in a large deep skillet and add the canola oil and 1 cup of the olive oil to cover, adding more of each if needed to cover. Add enough salt to season the vegetables, not the oil. Place over low heat and cook until the vegetables are tender, 25 to 30 minutes. Remove from the heat and strain the vegetables, reserving the oil. Set the vegetables aside. Carefully strain the oil through a fine-mesh strainer and store in the fridge for future use.

3. Heat 2 tablespoons of the olive oil in a 9- to 10-inch nonstick skillet over high heat. While the oil is heating, beat the eggs with ½ teaspoon salt in a bowl just until blended. If you're not squeamish about raw eggs, taste them and adjust the seasoning. Add the potatoes and onions to the eggs, folding them in with a heat-resistant spatula to combine.

4. When the oil is smoking, make sure to swirl it up on the sides of that pan to prevent the tortilla from sticking. Pour the egg mixture into the pan and toss the mixture aggressively, as if sautéing it or flipping pancakes, about three times, then stop to give it time to form a skin. You want to heat what will be the inside of the tortilla, but you want to make sure that it doesn't coagulate so much that it doesn't form a foundation. Prod the mixture with the spatula around the edges to give it shape and to prevent it from sticking to the bottom of the pan. Begin to shape the sides of the tortilla by using the spatula to pull the mixture gently from the sides of the pan, shaking the pan to make sure the mixture isn't stuck. Reduce the heat to medium-low and cook until the egg begins to set, running the spatula around the edges, about 2 minutes.

5. Invert a large plate on top of the pan. Firmly grasp the pan handle, choking up on it with the help of a kitchen towel, place your free hand palm down over the plate, and flip the pan and plate over together, dropping the tortilla onto the plate.

6. Place the pan back on the burner, wipe it clean of any stuck-on bits, and recoat it with the remaining 1 tablespoon olive oil. Heat the oil over high heat until it begins to smoke and then quickly and deliberately slide the tortilla off the plate into the pan, using a pushing-and-

pulling motion. Pat down the tortilla and begin shaping its sides again. Cook for 1 minute.

7. Repeat the flip and return process and cook for another 2 minutes over very low heat; you shouldn't need more oil at this point. Repeat the flip one more time, cooking for 3 more minutes on low heat. Now repeat the flip one final time to get the presentation side facing the bottom of the pan. Using a clean plate, flip the tortilla out so the pretty side is up.

8. The tortilla will taste best if you let it rest for an hour before serving, but do not refrigerate it. Cut it into wedges to serve. If you do have to chill it, warm it slightly before serving.

Chipsi Mayai

Tanzania does it, too!

Chipsi is chips, *mayai* means eggs. I was living in a town called Arusha, in northern Tanzania, when I first encountered *chipsi mayai.* It's street food—a french fry omelet. The chips are made first, over a wood or charcoal fire. You get these big chunks of fries that have been fried at low temperature and are therefore exceptionally soggy and greasy. Those are fried first, and set aside. When you order a chipsi mayai, the cook heats the fries back up again in oil, and then pours beaten eggs over them and fries it into an omelet. It comes either on newspaper or on a metal or plastic plate, with a tomato sauce that's like a watery Heinz ketchup—sometimes spicy, sometimes not. It'll come in a really flimsy plastic bottle that somebody has spiked the top of with a nail to make a hole for you to squeeze your sauce out of. I was a vegetarian at the time, so I'm sure I ate at least one chipsi mayai a week for three years. Oh my god, it was so terrible eating chipsi mayai all the time.

—*Peter Freed*

Makes 1 omelet (1 or 2 servings)

+ neutral oil, for deep-frying
¾ lb white or Yukon Gold potatoes, peeled and cut lengthwise into ½-inch-wide wedges
2 eggs, beaten
+ salt
+ ketchup
+ hot sauce

1. Make the chips: Pour 2 inches of oil into a pot or deep skillet. Bring the oil to 300°F over medium heat.

2. Add the potatoes and cook until they are tender and golden, about 10 minutes. Lift from the oil and drain on paper towels or plates. Frying the chips can be done up to 1 hour before assembling the omelet.

3. Combine the chips and 2 teaspoons oil in an 8-inch seasoned or nonstick skillet and set over medium heat. Warm up the potatoes, tossing them in the pan, until they sizzle, about 2 minutes. Add the eggs and swirl the pan to coat the bottom evenly with egg. Cook undisturbed for 3 minutes, then loosen the omelet from the pan and invert it onto a plate. Slide the omelet back into the pan and press on it with a spatula, packing it down into an even layer of potato and egg. Press again and cook for 1 minute. Invert and slide back into the pan, cooking for 1 final minute.

4. Transfer the omelet to a plate and season with salt. Serve with ketchup mixed with hot sauce.

Denver Omelet

The Denver omelet, a diner staple in the American West, is most likely a relative or descendant of egg foo young (page 74). This is a thing I learned recently, not a thing I knew as a kid, when I would order Denver omelets at Denny's. (Did it destine me to be an egg-obsessed weirdo, that I didn't think to order pancakes or french toast as a child? Probably.) The eggs-and-bell-pepper pairing is a motif we'll revisit, because it's one of those love-and-marriage, horse-and-carriage kind of combos.

Makes 1 serving

2 tbsp butter
2 tbsp diced onion
2 tbsp diced green bell pepper
¼ cup diced ham
+ salt and freshly ground black pepper
3 eggs, beaten
+ Tabasco
1 oz cheddar cheese, grated
+ buttered toast, for serving

1. Melt the butter in an 8- or 9-inch nonstick skillet over medium heat. Add the onion and bell pepper and cook, stirring, for 1 minute. Add the ham and season generously with salt and black pepper. Sauté until the onions and peppers are limp and not at all browned, about 1 minute.

2. Pour the beaten eggs into the skillet and shake to combine with the vegetables and ham. Let cook, undisturbed, until the omelet is set and browned on the bottom, about 2 minutes. Flip the omelet, then dash the surface with Tabasco to taste, and sprinkle with the cheese. When the omelet is browned on the underside, fold in half and slide onto a plate. Serve hot with buttered toast.

Peasant's Frittata

My first childhood trip to Italy helped me understand where my love for this simple protein came from: It's in my DNA, because Italy loves the egg as much as I do. In Italy, I was happily surprised to find that I didn't have to wait all day and night to enjoy my favorite ingredient: Eggs are not just for breakfast but can be served for lunch as a frittata, for dinner as the perfect fried egg with truffles, or even for dessert as zabaglione.

My favorite of all egg dishes is the frittata. Frittata roughly means "fried" in Italian and it is probably the easiest dish to make. At least that's what I tell my cooks. In reality it takes restraint to not throw in everything but the kitchen sink. You need the ingredients to complement each other, to harmonize. I like to think of my frittatas as a compass on a map. Each one points to a season and a region of Italy. Summer in Sicilia, spring in Toscana—it's so easy for the ingredients to transport you to a specific moment in time. The frittata has to be the most versatile dish because anything can be added and it can be served individually, hot out of the oven or even at room temperature. My version is softer and looser, like velvety scrambled eggs with seasonal ingredients.

Right now I'm inspired by a recent trip to Piemonte, so I'm using porcini, cardoons, and robiola cheese; but you can use any combination of vegetables and cheese you like. When I make this dish I can smell the wet grape leaves and the black dirt of the vineyards, and feel the chilly fog rolling in over the hills of Barolo. We cook our frittatas in our wood-burning oven, but you can make it in a regular oven just as easily.

—*Frank DeCarlo, as told to Joanna Sciarrino*

Makes 4 servings

2 tbsp fresh lemon juice
2 medium cardoons (or 2 artichoke
    hearts, chopped)
2 tbsp olive oil
¼ lb mushrooms, thinly sliced
    (about 1½ cups)
8 eggs
¼ cup heavy cream
2 tbsp roughly chopped flat-leaf parsley
½ cup crumbled robiola or grated
    fontina cheese
+ salt and freshly ground black pepper

1. Prep the cardoons: Fill a large bowl with cold water and add the lemon juice. Strip the leaves from the cardoons, rinse under cold running water, and use a sharp peeler to remove the thick, stringy skin. Cut them into 1-inch pieces and put them in the lemon water while bringing a pot of salted water to a boil. Drain the cardoons from the lemon water and add to the pot. Simmer the cardoons until nearly tender, 20 to 30 minutes. Drain and pat dry.

2. Heat the oven to 350°F.

3. Heat 1 tablespoon of the olive oil in an ovenproof 10-inch skillet over medium heat. Add the cardoons and cook, stirring often, until softened and lightly browned, about 5 minutes. Transfer to a plate. Add the mushrooms to the pan and cook, stirring often, until the mushrooms release their liquid and it evaporates and the mushrooms are lightly browned, about 8 minutes.

4. Meanwhile, whisk the eggs, cream, and parsley in a large bowl. Mix in ¼ cup of the cheese. Season with salt and pepper.

5. Increase the heat under the skillet to medium-high, add the remaining 1 tablespoon oil, return the cardoons to the pan, and pour the egg mixture over the vegetables, shaking the pan to evenly distribute the mixture. Cook the frittata, without stirring, until its edges begin to set, about 3 minutes.

6. Sprinkle the remaining ¼ cup cheese over the eggs and transfer the skillet to the oven. Bake until golden brown and the center is set, about 10 minutes.

Groove-Billed Ani

Chicken with Eggs Tagine

This Moroccan tagine, *d'jaj souiri,* is quite different from the traditional ones in that it looks more like a *tortilla* (Spanish omelet) than like a stew. It has a distinct taste of cinnamon. Like most other tagines it can be prepared well in advance, but wait to add the eggs after reheating the chicken for serving.

—*Anissa Helou*

Makes 4 servings

1 whole chicken (3 lb), cut into 8 pieces
1 medium onion, thinly sliced
2 tbsp extra-virgin olive oil
+ pinch of saffron threads, crushed
1 cinnamon stick (3 inches)
+ salt and freshly ground black pepper
4 cups water
6 eggs
½ tsp ground cinnamon
¼ tsp ground cumin
½ cup finely chopped flat-leaf parsley
+ juice of 1 lemon, or to taste
1 tsp paprika
+ bread, for serving

1. Put the chicken pieces in a sauté pan and add the onion, olive oil, saffron, cinnamon stick, a little salt, ½ teaspoon black pepper, and the water. Bring to a boil over medium-high heat, then cover and cook for 30 minutes. Uncover and continue to simmer until the chicken is done and the sauce has thickened, about 15 minutes.

2. Meanwhile, lightly beat the eggs in a bowl with the ground cinnamon, cumin, salt to taste, and ½ teaspoon black pepper. Cover and set aside.

3. When the chicken is ready, remove the skin if you like. Stir in the parsley and lemon juice and let bubble for a few more minutes. If the sauce is too liquid, reduce it further by boiling uncovered.

4. Pour the eggs all over the chicken and gently shake the pan to mix the eggs and sauce. Cook gently, covered, for 4 to 5 minutes or until the eggs are set to your liking. (I keep them quite soft, like a thick sauce.)

5. Sprinkle with the paprika and serve very hot with good bread.

Khai Jiao

My oldest, best friend, Jessica, whose family lived in Chiang Mai, Thailand, for a few years when she was in high school, makes a Thai omelet called *khai jiao* that I love. It's simple but deceptively complex: Fish sauce caramelizes the omelet's outsides. It's sometimes filled with ground pork, sometimes served with ketchup, always served with jasmine rice, and "on every menu in Thailand," Jess says. This recipe makes a funnel cake–esque khai jiao with crispy outsides and pillowy insides.

Makes 4 servings

+ neutral oil, for frying
3 chicken eggs or 2 duck eggs
1 tsp fresh lime juice
1 tsp fish sauce
+ pinch of sugar
1 tsp chopped garlic chives
+ jasmine rice, for serving

1. Pour 1 inch of oil into a wok and heat to 350°F.

2. While the oil is heating, beat the eggs in a bowl with the lime juice, fish sauce, sugar, and chives, until smooth.

3. Drizzle the eggs into the hot oil and leave to fry until the whole bottom of the now-omelet is set and crispy, about 3 minutes, then flip. Continue cooking until golden brown, another minute or two. Remove, let drain, and serve with jasmine rice.

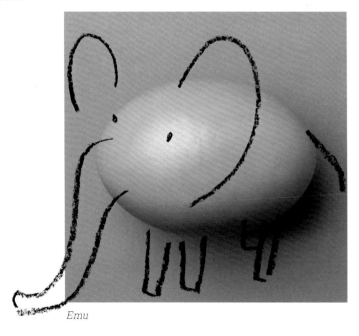

Emu

Courgette Omelets

These omelets, called *'ejjet kussa,* are a perfect example of the ingeniousness of Lebanese cooks, who never waste any food. My mother always made them when she prepared stuffed courgettes (zucchini) so that she didn't waste the pulp, but I often make them with whole courgettes because I really like them this way and it is simpler to prepare courgettes from scratch than to spend hours coring and stuffing them! You can vary this dish by using aubergine (eggplant) pulp, or simply make parsley omelets (*cejjet baqdunes*) by leaving out both courgette pulp and garlic. Follow the instructions below for either variation, the only difference being that you need to sauté the aubergine pulp in a little vegetable oil to soften it before adding it to the eggs.

—*Anissa Helou*

Makes 12 little omelets (4 servings)

+ pulp from 1 lb pale green zucchini (about 2 cups pulp), very finely chopped, or 1 medium pale green zucchini, coarsely grated (about 2 cups)
+ salt
3 eggs
¾ cup thinly sliced scallions
¾ cup finely chopped flat-leaf parsley (about ½ bunch)
2 garlic cloves, crushed into a paste (about 2 tsp)
1 tbsp all-purpose flour
¼ tsp ground cinnamon
¼ tsp ground allspice or Lebanese seven-spice mixture (black pepper, allspice, cinnamon, nutmeg, coriander, cloves, ginger)
⅛ tsp finely ground black pepper
2 tbsp water
+ extra-virgin olive oil, for shallow-frying
+ yogurt, for serving (optional)

1. Sprinkle the zucchini with 1 teaspoon salt and rub it firmly with your hands until soft and mushy. Squeeze between the palms of your hands to extract the excess liquid (there should be at least ⅓ cup). You should have about ⅔ cup squeezed zucchini.

2. Break the eggs into a bowl and beat well. Add the scallions, parsley, and garlic paste. Mix well, then add the zucchini, flour, spices, and water. Season with salt and mix well.

3. Pour ⅛ inch olive oil into a large skillet and set over medium heat. When the oil is hot, drop in 2 tablespoons of the egg mixture and spread it into a medium-thin round, about 3 inches in diameter. You should be able to make 3 or 4 small omelets per batch. Fry until golden on both sides, 5 to 6 minutes total, then remove with a slotted spatula and leave to drain on several layers of paper towels. Repeat with the remaining batter, adding oil as necessary to maintain ⅛ inch for frying. Serve the omelets warm, with yogurt, if you like.

Masala Omelet

The best place to sample a masala omelet is on an Indian Railways station platform. As a child, I would travel the rails from Mumbai, where our flight would land, to Pune, where my parents emigrated from and where my extended family lived. At one of the journey's many stops, one of my family members would leap from the carriage and order a freshly made masala omelet, served with a *pav,* or a soft bread roll, and ketchup, to go.

This well-seasoned, strongly flavored, spicy omelet—thin and lightly browned, almost pancake-like—is always accompanied by sweet, soft bread or toast and a cloying condiment.

—Pooja Makhijani

Makes 4 servings

2 eggs
+ salt and freshly ground black pepper
1 tbsp chopped cilantro leaves
1 green chili pepper, finely chopped
¼ cup finely chopped onion
¼ cup finely chopped tomato
¼ cup finely chopped green bell pepper
1 tbsp vegetable oil

1. Whisk the eggs in a bowl with salt and pepper to taste until frothy.

2. Add the cilantro, chili, onion, tomato, and bell pepper.

3. Heat the oil in a heavy-bottomed, nonstick skillet over medium heat until shimmering but not smoking. Pour the egg mixture in, spread it into an even layer, and let fry, undisturbed, until the bottom is set and golden brown, about 3 minutes. Flip over gently and fry until the second side is golden brown, another 1 to 2 minutes. The omelet should be lightly browned, and thin enough to be folded into quarters. Serve immediately.

4.

BREAKFAST

The French epicure and cheese-lover Jean Anthelme Brillat-Savarin once wrote, "A dessert without cheese is like a beautiful woman with only one eye." Well, breakfast without eggs is a woman with no eyes at all. What would you pop on top of your corned beef hash? What would you put into a little cup, carefully cut the top off of, and dip your toast soldiers into? What would you fry into the punched-out hole in your bread? How would you turn regular toast into french toast? Imagining breakfast without eggs is like imagining the sky without the sun—too dreary to even consider.

This book, among other things, should make abundantly clear that eggs need NOT be confined to breakfast. But lest we neglect to acknowledge that eggs first thing in the morning—or for a leisurely weekend brunch—are, without question, one of life's greatest pleasures, here's a chapter on the eggs we eat for this most important meal of the day: boiled, poached, scrambled, and fried. They're the subject of strong preference: *How do you like your eggs?* The question comes preloaded. They are the thing you can order, any style. They stimulate, fortify, and sustain us. EGGS!

Why Do We Eat Eggs for BREAKFAST?

Sascha Bos

It's difficult to answer this question without also asking, *Why do we eat breakfast?* The Ancient Romans ate breakfast, which they called *ientaculum,* and included eggs, if available. When the Romans were pushed out of Europe, breakfast left with them, and throughout the Middle Ages Europeans ate two large meals (in contrast to the Roman three). The Normans had dinner around nine a.m., making a wake-up meal superfluous. Physicians and religious leaders of the time suggested that it would be gluttonous to eat before dinner, and so breakfast was a meal reserved for children, the elderly, and manual laborers, who needed energy first thing in the morning.

In the West, it is not until 1620 that an English medical writer, Tobias Venner, actually suggests eating eggs for breakfast: poached, with salt, pepper, and vinegar, and served with bread and butter. In one of the oldest known cookbooks, *The Closet of Sir Kenelm Digby Knight Opened* (1669), Sir Digby, chancellor to Queen Henrietta Maria, suggests eating "two New-laid-eggs for breakfast" (he also recommends them poached). This brings us to another theory: Since chickens lay eggs in the morning, it made sense for farmers to grab them for breakfast.

(This isn't, strictly speaking, true: Chickens lay eggs on a twenty-five-hour cycle, depositing their eggs later in the day until they hit that magical three p.m. mark when they start all over again.)

The English began taking their dinners later and later (as late as four or five p.m. by the end of the eighteenth century), pushing supper even later and creating the need for a third meal: breakfast. It's in the 1800s that breakfast really takes off. The Industrial Revolution ushers in the need for workers, who in turn need heavy breakfasts, and the Second Industrial Revolution and rise of the nouveau riche sees the creation of the Full English: an egg-laden meal that can be dressed up (three-course breakfast spreads) or down (beans, toast, and an egg).

Throughout its history, breakfast has been the domain of the worker. Those who could afford to eat more lavishly, later in the day, often did. Workers needed protein and fat—slow-metabolizing energy sources—to get them through the day, and eggs provided a cheaper alternative to meat. The need for a filling breakfast meant that eggs would serve as breakfast's primary protein—uniting workers of the world.

Boiled Eggs

Ah, the boiled egg—austere, yet luxurious. Simple, yet complex (and perfect!). Easily adorned, yet impossible to improve upon. Whether soft-boiled or hard-boiled or somewhere in between, a boiled egg refers more to an outcome than to a cooking method, as an egg cooked in its shell to a firm white with a runny or hard yolk is often not cooked in boiling water, rather boiled water that reaches some equilibrium with a cool egg.

Soft-Boiled Egg(s)
Makes 1 to 12 eggs

1 to 12 eggs

1. Bring a large saucepan of water to a boil and gently add the egg(s). Stir the water and egg around the pot for 60 seconds. This will center the yolk inside the egg white, yielding a more evenly cooked egg. Stop stirring and simmer the egg, reducing the heat as necessary to maintain a light bubble, for 3½ minutes longer.

2. Remove the egg and plunge it into an ice bath. When the egg is cool enough to handle, peel it carefully. Alternatively, set the hot egg in an eggcup and use an egg topper to remove the pointed end of the egg. Serve with a small spoon and toast soldiers.

Hard-Boiled Egg(s)
Makes 1 to 12 eggs

1 to 12 eggs

1. Put the egg(s) in a saucepan of cold water and bring to a full boil. Once you see big bubbles, remove the pan from the heat and let stand 8 minutes for a fudgy yolk, 10 minutes if you'd like the yolks firmer. Plunge the egg(s) into an ice bath and let cool.

2. Crack the egg(s) against a flat surface. Peel the egg(s) and rinse under running water to remove any bits of shell. Eat right away, or refrigerate until ready to serve.

Half-Boiled Eggs

These are a Malaysian breakfast fixture: custardy "half-boiled" eggs with soy sauce and pepper. They're lazier than a hard-boiled egg, less fussy than soft-boiled (you just crack them into a bowl). Suck these down with something sweet, like condensed milk–sweetened tea. Another worthy companion is *kaya,* coconut jam, on white toast—the fluffiest you can find—with the crusts cut off.

Makes 1 serving

1 tsp salt
2 eggs
+ soy sauce
+ white pepper

1. Bring a saucepan of water to a boil. Once boiling, turn off the heat and stir the salt into the water.

2. Lower the eggs into the pot using a spider or slotted spoon. Cover and let sit for 5 minutes. Take them out of the water.

3. Crack the eggs (which will be hot!) into a small bowl, scraping out any whites, which should be just set, that cling to the shell.

4. Season with soy sauce and white pepper to taste. I like a lot of both. You can pop the yolk and mix it all around (I like a little white and yolk in each spoonful), or do what my great-grandpa liked to do: eat the whites first, then suck the yolks down whole.

Mockingbird

The HARDBOILED Detective

Harold McGee

Peeling can be an unpredictable and frustrating job. Sometimes the shell comes away cleanly, but sometimes it clings to the white, gouging or tearing divots in it. In a given carton there'll usually be both easy eggs and recalcitrant eggs, and you can't tell which is going to be which.

Over the years I've tested many different methods for making eggs easier to peel. The latest is the oral method, much demonstrated on the Web: You partly peel a hard-boiled egg at both ends, then place your mouth on the narrow end and blow the egg through the other.

Blowing eggs is certainly quick and showy, but not especially hygienic. And recalcitrant eggs still pop your ears before they pop their shells. No more reliable is prepoking the shell, boiling with baking soda, or shocking in ice water.

After blowing failed to be the answer, I decided that it was time to solve the peeling problem for real. How tough could it be?

Well, the egg turns out to be a very sophisticated package—mysterious and not so easy to manipulate. I did finally come up with a reliable peeling method, but it takes some pretty inelegant, brute-force chemistry, and it's kind of messy. But entertainingly so.

I started by revisiting the scientific literature on egg peeling to see what solid information we have these days. It still comes down to one not-so-new fact: Eggs become easier to peel as they age. Freshly laid eggs slowly lose moisture and carbon dioxide through their porous shells, and the loss of carbon dioxide causes their whites to become more alkaline. The pH of a freshly laid egg's white starts out at a slightly alkaline 7.5. Food scientists have found that when the pH rises above 9, the egg becomes easy to peel.

Apparently, the change in pH makes the egg-white proteins adhere less strongly to the thin, tough membrane attached to the inner surface of the shell, but we still don't know how or why. It might involve a well-documented stabilization of the major egg-white protein, or the recently discovered "peri-albumen layer," a microscopically thin envelope around the egg white that disappears in a few days as a fertilized egg develops.

In any case, the fresher a farm-fresh egg, the more likely it is to peel ugly.

The pH of a fresh egg white rises from 7.5 to a peelable 9 after a few days at room temperature, but it takes much longer in the refrigerator. Cold temperatures helpfully slow general deterioration, but they also slow the egg's loss of carbon dioxide and the rise in pH and peelability. According to a couple of recent studies, a refrigerated egg may take 2 or more weeks for its albumen pH to reach 9. So even when they're not especially fresh, the eggs we buy may not have become alkaline enough to peel cleanly.

The challenge is to raise the pH of eggs reliably and quickly, faster than leaving them in the back of the fridge for weeks. My first thought was to hold them at room temperature or in a warm oven to speed their aging. This does work, but it still takes several days for enough carbon dioxide to pass through the membranes and shell. Then I tried immersing eggs in a very alkaline solution at pH 12, to raise the inner pH artificially. That also worked, and also took days.

I realized that the shell itself is the main

obstacle to changing the chemical environment within. How could I make the inner egg more accessible to an alkaline bath? By starting with alkali's opposite: acid. I found that I could etch away much of the shell by immersing it in acid for about an hour. This acid treatment also conveniently makes the shell weaker and easier to break during peeling. Once the shell's been thinned out by acid, a few hours in an alkaline solution is enough to raise the pH of the egg white just beneath the shell.

The entire process takes about 4 hours—maybe 30 minutes of real attention—and a couple of odd ingredients. One is citric acid, the main acid in citrus fruits. Pure citric acid is used in Middle Eastern cooking, and is much stronger than vinegar. It's available online and is often sold in ethnic markets or in the kosher section of supermarkets as "sour salt." Buy plenty; you'll need almost half a pound for a dozen eggs.

The second ingredient is baked baking soda. By spreading baking soda out on a baking sheet and heating it in a 350°F oven for a couple of hours, you transform sodium bicarbonate into sodium carbonate. Baking soda itself is a weak alkali that can't create a pH above 9, but a carbonate solution can get up to pH 12.

To treat a dozen eggs, dissolve about a cup (200 grams) of citric acid in a quart of water in a bowl that's large enough to keep all the eggs immersed. Add the eggs. They'll quickly fizz over with tiny bubbles of carbon dioxide created from the acid's reaction with the shell's calcium carbonate. Then the eggs will rise to the surface and start doing barrel rolls as the bubbles grow and detach from the shells.

As the shells continue to dissolve and some of their protein is released, the bubbling creates a foamy scum. To speed up and even out the shell etching, gently rub the scum off each egg back into the liquid every 15 or 20 minutes. (If your hands have any recent nicks, wear gloves or expect some stinging.)

After about 45 minutes, start checking the eggs. When they've developed little clear spots where the acid has etched away nearly all of the shell, remove and rinse them. Don't let the spots grow into large clear patches. All the eggs should be well etched in 45 to 90 minutes.

At this point, immerse the etched eggs in a solution of baked baking soda—4 teaspoons (10 grams) dissolved per quart of water. Let them sit for at least 2 hours—or as long as 6 hours—gently stirring every 15 or 20 minutes. After the soak, rinse them off and either proceed to the cooking or refrigerate them for later use.

I've handled several dozen eggs this way, all as fresh as I could find at stores and farmers' markets, and only a couple of eggs tore when I peeled them. The acid-alkali method works pretty well. The weakened shells often peel off in long, papery spirals.

Whether you etch the shells or not, once you cook eggs it's best to immerse them in cold or iced water and let them cool down before trying to peel them. This firms the white and further helps it resist tears and gouges. Gently tap or squeeze the shell all around to fracture it into many small pieces. The egg's narrow end is especially vulnerable, so press the shell down on the very tip with one finger while peeling up to it.

If you're adventurous, let the eggs sit in the soda solution overnight or longer before cooking them. When the pH of the outer white approaches 12, it develops an opalescent translucency and stronger flavor. You're on the way to the Chinese century egg and real edginess (page 238).

More Than One Way to Poach an Egg

Tienlon Ho

There's an episode of *Julia and Jacques Cooking at Home,* where the two poach eggs in Julia's sunny kitchen in Cambridge, Massachusetts. Julia Child is beginning to bend under her eighty-eight years but ever spry. Jacques Pépin, barely sixty-five, vibrates with enthusiasm.

"I'm going to use a mechanical device, and Jack is going to use his own hands and ingenuity," Julia declares, without a tinge of apology.

Julia pokes a pinhole in the large end of her eggs, then boils them in the shell for ten seconds. Then she brings out her gizmos, four oversize perforated spoons with perpendicular handles. She doesn't need these to get the eggs right, of course. She has by that time hosted a dozen cooking shows and printed forty editions of her first cookbook. Julia is trying to tell us to do whatever you need to make this work for you.

Jacques cracks his eggs and slides the contents into the simmering water with the efficiency that only people who have cracked a million eggs can have. A few seconds in, he waves a slotted spoon over a jumble of egg to get it to roll over, and it instantly reorders itself into a tidy pillow.

When Julia cooks, she is teaching confidence. When Jacques cooks, he is teaching sleight of hand. Both are key to mastering any technique.

In the end, Julia's eggs are soft and expansive, while Jacques's are plump with a round protrusion of yolk on top, and they admire each other's handiwork.

"Oh that came out beautifully and it looks very eggy," Julia says. After all, it doesn't matter how you get to the finish line. As Julia was known to say, "If you're alone in the kitchen, who is going to see?"

Jacques's Poached Eggs

When making poached eggs, the fresher the eggs the better. The older the eggs, the more the whites will tend to spread in the water. A dash of vinegar (white vinegar preferably) is added to the water to help firm the egg white. Salt is omitted because it has the reverse effect and tends to thin down the white. Eggs can be poached several hours, even a day, ahead (as most restaurants do), eliminating any last-minute panic when you want to serve several people at once.

—Jacques Pépin

Makes 6 poached eggs

¼ cup distilled white vinegar
6 eggs

1. Place 2½ to 3 quarts of water and the vinegar in a large saucepan. Bring to a boil, then reduce to a slow simmer: You want small bubbles just at the sides of the saucepan. Break one egg at a time on the side of the saucepan. Holding it as close as you can to the water (to avoid splashing), open it with both thumbs and let it slide into the water. If you are afraid of burning your fingers, break the eggs into a saucer or bowl and slide them into the water. (Cracking directly into the saucepan can also lead to weird egg shapes; sometimes there's a sticky tail of white that lingers on the shell.)

2. Go as fast as you can putting the eggs into the water so that the difference in cooking time is not too great between the first and the last egg. Keep the water at a bare simmer, or let it "shiver" as it is said in France.

3. As soon as all the eggs are in the water, drag the bottom of a large slotted spoon across the surface of the water to move the eggs about a bit and keep them from sticking to the bottom of the pan. Once some of the whites have hardened, the eggs will not stick anymore.

4. Large eggs take 3 to 4 minutes of cooking. If you like them more runny or more set, the timing should be changed accordingly. Check the eggs by lifting them, one at a time, with a slotted spoon and pressing them slightly with your fingers. The white should be set, but the yolks soft to the touch.

5. As soon as an egg is cooked, transfer it to a bowl of ice water. This stops the cooking and washes the vinegar off.

6. When the eggs are cold, lift each one from the water and trim off the hanging pieces with a knife or a pair of scissors. Place in a bowl of fresh cold water.

7. Drain well if you use them cold, or keep refrigerated in cold water. They will keep for at least a couple of days. To use hot, place in a strainer, lower into boiling water for about 1 minute, drain, and serve immediately.

Julia's Poached Eggs

In *Julia and Jacques Cooking at Home,* Julia says: "In my method, you crack the egg into an egg poacher—a perforated-metal oval egg-shaped container—set in shimmering water. The egg takes on the oval poached-egg shape." Those oval egg poachers turn out to be tricky to find these days, but as it turns out, the real trick is in the pinprick and parboiling, which sets the whites and helps keep the egg in shape.

Makes 4 poached eggs

4 eggs

1. If you're using egg poachers, set them in a large saucepan with at least 3-inch sides, and measure in enough water to cover them by ½ inch. Remove the poachers and bring the water to a boil. If not using poachers, fill the water to 2 inches high, and bring it to a boil.

2. With a pin, prick the large end of each egg—going through the shell and into the body of the egg to make a small hole (no egg should come out)—then place in a strainer and lower into the boiling water.

3. Submerge the eggs for exactly 10 seconds and lift out with a slotted spoon.

4. Now reduce the heat to a gentle simmer, just so there are the tiniest bubbles at the bottom of the pan. Set the poachers in the saucepan, if using.

5. Once the water is at a simmer, rapidly crack an egg into each of the poachers, holding it as close to the water as possible. If you aren't using poachers, crack your eggs directly into the water (again,

as close to the water as possible), the first one at the pan's twelve o'clock.

6. Rapidly continue with the rest of the eggs, going clockwise.

7. Poach for 4 minutes per egg. When the time is up, slip the eggs out of the poachers onto a plate or, if you are not planning to use them right away, into a bowl of ice water.

Flamingo

The POACHED Egg Murder

Rachel Levin

Across from a Jack in the Box, in downtown San Francisco, Pinecrest Diner serves just about everything, as any respectable, forty-eight-year-old, twenty-four-hour diner should. Salisbury Steak. Shrimp Louie. Pastrami on Rye. Two Eggs Any Style.

Except for one.

We regret that we cannot prepare poached eggs, states the oversize plastic menu—as it has since 1969, when a local Greek man named Bill Foundas opened shop on the bustling corner of Geary and Mason. After five decades, at ninety-nine years old, Foundas still comes in daily to watch over his family's restaurant from his perch at the counter, sipping black coffee in his three-piece suit.

But, somehow, he wasn't there that summer day in 1997: the day a waitress was killed by the cook who'd agreed to poach the eggs for a pretty customer.

Hashem Zayed, a fifty-nine-year-old Jordanian immigrant, father to children back in the Middle East, and husband supposedly several times over, had been flipping pancakes and burgers at Pinecrest since 1975. From behind the counter, he'd chat up customers and joke with regulars and, because of house rules—and the limitations of Pinecrest's tiny

kitchen—refuse special requests that would only further slam their only short-order cook.

Unless the request came from an attractive woman, as it did on July 23, 1997. The woman wandered in, grabbed a stool at the counter, and simply asked the cook for eggs the way she liked them, as egg eaters do.

But the server, Helen Menicou, a forty-seven-year-old mother of two, originally from Cyprus, who, like Hashem, had also worked at Pinecrest for two decades, was a stickler. If the menu said no poached eggs, then no one—no matter how pretty—got 'em poached. And that was that.

Until the next morning, which, for Helen, began like every morning: early, in a black skirt, at the diner, with coffee and Hashem. The two were apparently longtime frenemies—he, a card gambler who'd recently lost a bundle and lived in a Tenderloin SRO and often made Helen lunch; she, the suburban wife of a retiree, known and loved by everyone and who, just days before, had loaned Hashem a few hundred bucks to send home to his family.

But at seven a.m., on July 24, Hashem was still holding a grudge. And a gun.

He hadn't slept all night and was still upset

about the eggs, he'd told Helen. And then he shot her in the arm. Surrounded by screaming customers, he shot her again, in the back. Then, as she lay on the floor behind the counter where they had worked together, side by side, for twenty years—he shot her one more time, in the neck.

Mayhem ensued as Hashem just stood by the door, waiting for the police. Helen was whisked off to San Francisco General and, within the hour, pronounced dead. Hashem was convicted of first-degree murder and sentenced to twenty-five years; he died in prison from a brain tumor a few years later.

Today, little is spoken about the tragedy at Pinecrest. Obnoxious customers used to come in and flippantly order their eggs poached, but that eventually died down. Occasionally, someone sidles up to the counter asking about the veracity of the rumored murder. "Polite men have no memory," a line cook once responded. But the murder predated him, anyway. No one who currently works at Pinecrest was present—save for owner Bill Foundas and his family. Somehow, none of them happened to be there that ill-fated day, said daughter-in-law and manager Sylvia Foundas. Bill had been in the hospital . . . His son-in-law had run out of gas . . . Sylvia was at home pregnant. . . .

It was a mystery. What made Hashem snap? everyone asked. Why would he kill a waitress? Why would he kill *Helen*? What ever happened to the pretty woman who preferred her eggs poached?

We may never know. Pinecrest's past is the past, buried beneath pallets of fresh eggs and slabs of perfectly crisped hash browns. The diner churns on, as diners do. All day, every day, scrambling, folding, frying six thousand plus eggs a week, a time warp in the rapidly changing city around it. The only gunshots come from the ever-grittier street corner outside. Its cushioned booths and

faux-leather stools are filled with decades' worth of crumbs, and conventioneers and late-night partiers and tourists from around the world pour in for grilled pork chops and whipped-cream-topped pancakes and a taste of a true American greasy spoon—but never, ever for poached eggs, per the fine print.

Eggs Benedict

Eggs Benedict originated circa 1894, when the chef at Delmonico's in New York committed to paper the recipe for Eggs à la Benedick, named after a favorite patron, LeGrand Benedict, which instructs readers to "Cut some muffins in halves crosswise, toast them without allowing to brown, then place a round of cooked ham an eighth of an inch thick and of the same diameter as the muffins on each half. Heat in a moderate oven and put a poached egg on each toast. Cover the whole with Hollandaise sauce." Another slightly less believable story goes that during that same year a man named Lemuel Benedict, a well-to-do Wall Street stockbroker, walked into the restaurant at the Waldorf one morning with a spectacular hangover and demanded to be served poached eggs, toast, bacon, and a hooker of hollandaise sauce. Whatever the truth, whether Lemuel or LeGrand, this is fancied-up eggs, toast, and bacon—an ideally absorbent weekend brunch. Also, once you try these English muffins—inspired by Model Bakery's, in Napa, California, you'll never go back to store-bought.

Makes 4 servings

4 **English Muffins** (recipe follows)
8 slices Canadian bacon or ham
8 **Poached Eggs** (pages 96 and 97)
+ **Hollandaise Sauce** (recipe follows)
+ chopped chives (optional)
+ shaved truffles (optional)

1. Split the English muffins with a fork and toast until lightly browned. Arrange each on a plate, nooks and crannies up.

2. Meanwhile, warm the Canadian bacon in a skillet over low heat until steamy but not yet browned, about 1 minute.

3. Place one slice of bacon on each muffin half. Top each piece of bacon with a poached egg and cover with hollandaise. If desired, sprinkle with chives (and truffles, if you're fancy).

English Muffins
Makes 12 muffins

BIGA
½ cup bread flour
¼ cup water
¾ tsp active dry yeast

DOUGH
1⅓ cups water
¾ tsp active dry yeast
1½ tbsp olive oil
1½ tsp fine sea salt
3½ cups all-purpose flour, plus more for dusting
¼ cup stone-ground cornmeal
6 tbsp butter, melted

1. Make the biga: The day before making the muffins, stir together the bread flour, water, and yeast in a bowl. Cover and refrigerate for 12 to 24 hours.

2. Make the dough: Combine the biga, water, yeast, olive oil, and salt in a bowl or the bowl of a stand mixer and stir with a whisk or the paddle attachment until creamy. Add 3 cups of the flour and stir to form a sticky dough. Cover the bowl with plastic wrap and let stand for 20 minutes.

3. Add the remaining ½ cup flour and stir to form a soft dough. Knead with the dough hook or by hand until the dough is smooth and elastic but still a bit moist and tacky, about 10 minutes.

4. Shape the dough into a ball and transfer to an oiled bowl. Cover and let rise until doubled in volume, about 2 hours at room temperature or 12 hours in the refrigerator. Bring to room temperature before proceeding.

5. Scatter the cornmeal on a rimmed baking sheet. Scrape the dough onto a lightly floured work surface and pat to 1 inch thick. Using a 4-inch biscuit cutter, punch out 12 rounds of dough and place them on the cornmeal-dusted baking sheet. Flip the dough rounds over so both sides are coated with cornmeal. Cover loosely with plastic wrap and let rise in a warm spot until the muffin dough is puffy, about 1 hour.

6. Pour 1 tablespoon of the melted butter into a large skillet set over medium-low heat. Add 2 to 3 muffin doughs and cook until they are golden on the bottom and domed on top, about 6 minutes. Flip and continue cooking, reducing the heat as necessary so the muffins cook through without scorching, 5 to 6 minutes longer.

7. Place the cooked muffins on a wire rack to cool, wipe out the skillet, and repeat with the remaining butter and

muffins. Let the muffins cool completely before splitting and toasting.

Hollandaise Sauce
Makes 2 cups

1 small shallot, chopped
1 tsp black peppercorns, cracked
¼ cup white wine vinegar
¼ cup water
3 egg yolks
2 tsp fresh lemon juice, plus more to taste
½ tsp salt
2 sticks (8 oz) butter, melted
+ cayenne pepper

1. Make the gastrique: Combine the shallot, peppercorns, and vinegar in a small saucepan. Bring to a boil over medium-high heat and cook to sec, the moment the pan is nearly dry; immediately stir in the water and remove from the heat. Strain the gastrique into a bowl (discard the solids).

2. Bring 1 inch of water to a simmer in a saucepan. Whisk the gastrique, egg yolks, lemon juice, and salt in a large, heatproof bowl. Set the bowl over the saucepan of simmering water and whisk until the mixture is frothy and slightly thickened, about 5 minutes. Add a few drops of the melted butter, whisking vigorously to incorporate, then begin adding the butter in a thin, steady stream. Whisk the mixture constantly until you have a creamy, slightly fluffy, emulsified sauce. Season with a pinch of cayenne and thin with a drop of water or lemon juice as needed. Keep warm until ready to serve.

Çilbir

Çilbir—poached eggs on a bed of garlicky yogurt, drizzled with spiked butter—is a Turkish egg dish. This is Filiz Hosukoglu's recipe. She is a culinary researcher from Gaziantep, Turkey, who has worked with chefs like Paula Wolfert, Claudia Roden, Anissa Helou, and Rick Stein on cookbooks and TV shows. She talks about resting the eggs on top of the yogurt (rather than hiding them beneath) to show them off, and I get her entirely—everything sits on this whipped white backdrop; the yolks are the stars. Çilbir's uniqueness rests on the sourness of the yogurt and the softness of the whole thing— there is nothing to crunch. If you love to sop up an egg yolk with some bread at the best of times, this bowl of creamy, yolky wonder is for you.

—*Laura Goodman*

Makes 2 servings

1 garlic clove
1¾ cups whole-milk yogurt
4 tbsp butter
1 tsp Aleppo chili flakes
½ tsp paprika
4 **Poached Eggs** (pages 96 and 97)
+ salt and freshly ground black pepper
+ mint leaves (optional)
+ pide or pita bread, for serving

1. Crush and pound the garlic to a paste in a mortar and pestle; mix it in with the yogurt. They must be properly mixed. These two ingredients are good company—leave them alone.

2. Meanwhile, combine the butter, chili flakes, and paprika in a small saucepan. Set over medium-high heat to melt and froth a little, about 2 minutes.

3. To assemble, spread the garlic yogurt on a plate and place the poached eggs on top, so you can see the beauty of the eggs.

4. Drizzle with the chili butter, and season generously with salt and pepper. If you like, tear some mint leaves over the top for some extra color and texture. Serve with bread.

Fried Egg

Fried egg, I'm in love! There are probably thirteen ways of looking at a fried egg but here are four ways to cook one. A sunny-side up egg has a purely white albumen that is fully set, including where it meets the yolk and the yolk is not opaque or coagulated but warm to the palate. An over easy egg has a purely white albumen that is flipped and fully set. The yolk is warm and the outside of it is coagulated. When cut, the yolk will run past the edge of the white. An over hard egg has a fully set, pure white albumen, flipped and cooked so the yolk will not run, though it retains a creamy and not chalky consistency. An over medium egg lands in between.

Makes 1 egg

+ oil, butter, lard, or other edible fat
1 egg
+ salt

1. Warm a teaspoon of fat in a small nonstick skillet over medium-low heat. Crack the egg into the pan and run a heat-resistant spatula through the egg white where the cohesive albumin meets the runnier albumin. This will create a uniform white.

2. Cook the egg undisturbed until the white is set. Doneness can be tested by dragging a spoon across the white near where it meets the yolk; the white should collect in the spoon in a soft curd, like a scrambled egg. It should not be rubbery. Depending on the size of your pan and burner, it will take 60 to 90 seconds to reach this stage. This is a sunny-side up egg.

3. For an over easy egg, flip the egg and cook for 15 seconds, sealing the yolk in coagulated protein. For over medium, cook for another 15 to 30 seconds, until the yolk feels like a cheek when poked. The yolk will have thickened but not be firm throughout. For over hard, continue cooking for another 30 seconds, until the yolk feels like where your thumb meets your palm. It should be firm but creamy. Slide onto a plate, season with salt, and serve.

Huevos Motuleños

This is a very straightforward breakfast dish from Motul on the Yucatán Peninsula. The contrasts really appeal to me: the sweetness of the plantains with the saltiness of the ham and the spiciness of the sauce. Some people put sour cream on it, but I don't think it needs any because of the queso fresco. Huevos Motuleños already has all the perfect elements, if you can get a bite of everything together in your mouth at one time. It's a classic breakfast dish.

—*Karen Taylor*

Makes 2 servings

+ vegetable oil
4 corn tortillas
2 tbsp butter
1 ripe plantain, cut into ¼-inch-thick coins
4 eggs
4 thin ham slices
+ **Habanero Salsa** (recipe follows)
½ cup green peas
½ cup crumbled queso fresco
+ black beans, for serving (optional)

1. Fill a large pan with 1 inch of oil. Heat the oil over medium heat until a tortilla crumb sizzles gently when it hits the oil. Add a tortilla and fry until halfway crisp. Remove and let drain on a cooling rack. Repeat with the remaining tortillas.

2. Heat 1 tablespoon of oil and 1 tablespoon of the butter in a pan over medium heat. Add the plantain and sauté until golden, about 6 minutes. Reserve for plating.

3. In the same pan, heat another 1 tablespoon oil and the remaining 1 tablespoon butter over medium heat. Add the eggs and fry until you have soft yolks.

4. Assemble the motuleños: Place 2 tortillas on each plate, and layer each tortilla with 1 slice of ham and 1 fried egg. Top each egg with habanero salsa, 4 or 5 slices of plantain, the peas, and queso fresco. Serve with black beans, if you like.

Habanero Salsa
Makes ½ cup

1 large tomato
1 habanero chili
+ salt
1 tbsp vegetable oil
¼ cup diced white onion
+ water or chicken broth, if needed

1. Fill a small pot with water and bring to a boil. Blanch the tomato until its skin has shriveled and it is heated through, about 2 minutes. Drain and reserve on a paper towel until cool enough to handle. Remove the skin and core.

2. Roast the habanero under a broiler or in a dry skillet until soft and charred all over, about 3 minutes. Remove the habanero stem and discard.

3. In a blender or food processor, blend the tomato and habanero until smooth. Salt to taste.

4. Heat the oil in a large saucepan over medium heat, then add the onion and sauté until it's soft, about 5 minutes.

5. Add the tomato-habanero mixture and cook for a few minutes, until slightly thickened and fragrant. Thin with water or chicken stock if needed to make a cohesive salsa.

Albatross

Corned Beef Hash

This is not an egg recipe. But corned beef hash is one of the most classic, most perfect eggcompaniments, and this is why it's included here. There is no better medium for soaking up egg ooze: Paired with an egg or two or three, poached or fried, it is one of the world's great breakfasts.

Makes 4 servings

1 lb cooked corned beef
4 tbsp butter
1 onion, finely chopped
1 green bell pepper, finely chopped
1 lb russet (baking) potatoes, peeled
    and finely diced
+ salt and freshly ground black pepper

1. Chop the corned beef: If you have a meat grinder, grind the beef through the coarse plate. If chopping by hand, cut into rough ¼-inch pieces.

2. Melt 2 tablespoons of the butter in a 12-inch skillet over medium heat. Add the onion and bell pepper and cook until the vegetables are softened, about 5 minutes. Add the potatoes and season generously with salt and black pepper. Toss to combine everything, then cover, reduce the heat to medium-low, and cook until the potatoes are tender, about 10 minutes.

3. Uncover and fold the corned beef into the vegetables. Increase the heat to medium-high and add the remaining 2 tablespoons butter around the edges of the pan. Let melt and cook undisturbed until the hash is crispy, about 6 minutes. Flip over in two or three large pieces and cook until browned, 3 to 4 minutes longer. Divide among plates and serve with eggs.

Saltie's Soft-Scrambled Eggs

Before opening my restaurant, Saltie, I had a real phobia about cooking eggs—really, anything in regard to brunch in general. When you work in restaurants, it's always, *Ugh we have to do brunch now.* The restaurant had to change personalities to do all of this short-order cooking—and for some reason, I was not good at short-order cooking. So I developed a real phobia.

When we opened Saltie, we didn't have enough space to cook other kinds of protein in here—so it turned into a mostly vegetarian menu. The egg entered the picture in full force. There was a lot of being with the eggs: thinking about them, dreading them.

But Rebecca Collerton, one of my co-owners, had this technique for eggs that was the best of both over easy and scrambled, where you scramble the whites in the pan, leaving the yolks whole, and then you break them at the last minute, folding them into the whites. For so long, I had this idea of what a scrambled egg was, and it wasn't exciting. This was an exciting way to cook. The technique changed me. It was so easy, and it had such a better texture than the small-curd scramble method. It was . . . rugged. It was easy. It was a joy.

It's funny that for this little simple food, there are so many cooking techniques: so many styles, times, and temperatures. This took all the stress out of cooking eggs. It became the signature way for us to do it—there is no other way. I still, to this day, love it. It's the one thing where I say, "I love cooking these eggs." It still makes me really happy.

—*Caroline Fidanza, as told to Brette Warshaw*

Makes 1 serving

1 tsp unsalted butter
2 eggs
+ salt
+ finely chopped herbs, for garnish
   (optional)

1. Melt the butter in a nonstick skillet over medium heat. Break the eggs into the pan when it is warm but not yet hot. Sprinkle the eggs lightly with salt.

2. Let the pan heat up, and don't move the eggs until the egg whites begin to set. Using a heat-resistant spatula, move the whites around the pan to help them cook through, while keeping the yolk unbroken, for about 30 seconds. When the whites fluff up and are almost completely set, remove from the heat and fold the yolks into the whites. The residual heat should cook the whites through and leave the yolks soft. This is kind of like scrambling an over easy egg.

3. To emphasize: Be careful not to overcook the eggs. Err on the side of runny rather than dry. Sprinkle with herbs, if desired.

Buvette's Steamed Scrambled Eggs

I don't think I had ever seen this technique of cooking eggs before, but I had this piece of equipment—the espresso machine—and wondered what else I could do with it. I steamed milk, hot chocolate, wine, even soup, so why not eggs? They're light and fluffy and are a fixture on our breakfast menu. You can make them with chives or fresh herbs, crème fraîche or butter or soft cheese, smoked salmon or prosciutto, or vegetables. But however you have them, lots of fresh black pepper is a must—I always have my eggs with lots of fresh black pepper.

—Jody Williams, as told to Joanna Sciarrino

Makes 2 servings

4 eggs
2 tbsp butter, cut in two
+ salt and freshly ground black pepper
+ soft cheese (optional)
+ chopped herbs (optional)
+ crème fraîche (optional)
+ smoked salmon (optional)

1. Crack the eggs into a porcelain or stainless steel pitcher. Using a fork, give the eggs a quick scramble, making sure to puncture all the yolks. Add the butter.

2. Using the steamer attachment of your espresso machine, submerge the wand into the egg mixture in the pitcher. Open the valve and steam the eggs, moving the pitcher in a circular motion, until curds start to form, 60 seconds or so.

3. Spoon the eggs onto two plates and season with salt and pepper. Top with cheese, herbs, crème fraîche, smoked salmon—anything you like, really!

Anda Bhurji

Eggs in India are nearly always prepared with onions, tomatoes, and a lot of spices. *Anda bhurji,* spicy scrambled eggs, is less creamy than American-style scrambled eggs, and in our house was often served for lunch, rather than breakfast, usually with roti, naan, or *pav,* a soft bread roll. It is savory and piquant, studded with red tomatoes and green bell peppers, and smells of fresh cilantro and cumin. When I was a child, my mother would roll a spoonful into a blazing-hot paratha, a flaky, layered flatbread. I always washed it down with a cup of milky sweet tea.

—*Pooja Makhijani*

Makes 2 to 4 servings

2 tbsp vegetable oil
2 tsp ginger-garlic paste (see Note)
3 green chilies, such as serrano, slit lengthwise
1 tsp cumin seeds
1 medium onion, finely chopped
2 medium tomatoes, finely chopped
1 medium green bell pepper, finely chopped
½ tsp ground turmeric
½ tsp ground coriander
½ tsp ground cumin
4 eggs, whisked lightly
+ salt and freshly ground black pepper
¼ cup chopped cilantro leaves

1. Heat the oil in a large skillet over medium heat. Add the ginger-garlic paste and sauté until aromatic, about 30 seconds. Add the chilies and sauté until softened, about 1 minute. Add the cumin seeds and sauté until browned and sputtering, about 30 seconds. Add the onion and sauté until softened, about 2 minutes. Add the tomatoes and bell pepper and stir until tender, another 5 minutes.

2. Add the turmeric, coriander, and ground cumin. Reduce the heat to low. Add the whisked eggs, season with salt and black pepper, and stir gently until the eggs begin to curdle, 2 to 3 minutes.

3. Continue to stir until the desired texture is achieved. I prefer a uniformly crumbly bhurji. Fold in the chopped cilantro, and serve immediately.

Note: While ginger-garlic paste, a South Asian staple, can be found in most ethnic grocery stores, it is easy to make at home. Combine equal parts chopped ginger and garlic and pulse in a food processor until finely chopped. Drizzle vegetable oil, a preservative, into the mixture, and continue pulsing until the paste has a smooth, consistent texture. Store in a clean, dry airtight container in the refrigerator for up to 1 month.

Matzo Brei

I was born in Queens, New York, in 1937. I learned to make matzo brei from my mother. We never in our lives measured anything. You put in enough butter so that it's sizzly, and then you fill the pan with matzo and smush it around and cook it until it's crispy on one side, then flip it and do the same on the other side. There are some things you don't screw around with, and as far as I'm concerned, this matzo brei recipe is one of them.

My recipe is hardly a recipe: matzo, eggs, water, and butter. You buy Streit's matzo. I mean, if you have to use something else, okay, but it really should be Streit's. Matzo brei is the kind of thing you really have to try hard to screw up, but you do need to get it crispy. Frankly, nobody makes it as good as I do. I mean, there are some things I will admit that people make better than I do, but matzo brei is not one of them. The secret is making sure to get it crispy. After you soak it, you really have to get as much of the liquid out as you can; otherwise it's just mush in the middle. It's not a complicated thing, and if you fry it in enough butter it doesn't matter what you do.

When I was a kid, we used to get our eggs from the milkman. Now I try to buy my eggs at the farm, and it makes a huge difference from the ones they have in the supermarket—that's for sure. I don't always do it because it's a separate trip, but there is a tremendous difference. I don't particularly like eggs sunny-side up but when I get eggs from the farm, I like them, because the eggs are so much more flavorful.

—*Judie Baker, as told to Ashley Goldsmith*

Makes 2 servings

2 sheets unsalted Streit's matzo, broken into 1- to 2-inch pieces
2 eggs
+ salt
2 turns freshly cracked black pepper (optional)
2 to 4 tbsp butter

1. Soak the broken-up matzo in warm water (about 3 cups) until it gets kind of mushy, 3 to 5 minutes. Squeeze as much liquid out of it as you can in a colander without mashing up the natural flakes of the matzo. Put the squeezed-out matzo in a bowl and crack the eggs over the matzo. Add some salt. Add a couple turns of freshly cracked pepper if you like. Mix with your hands until the eggs are well blended. I don't season it too heavily before I cook it.

2. Heat the butter in a large nonstick or cast iron skillet over medium-high heat and fry the matzo-egg mixture until it's nice and browned and crispy on one side, about 3 minutes, then flip it over. If you're really good, you can turn it over whole and do the other side. If not, you can do it in pieces. It depends on what kind of day I'm having: Sometimes I can flip it over whole. When it is browned and crispy on the second side, after about 2 minutes, flip onto a plate and serve. You can use maple syrup or powdered sugar, but I'm not a sweet matzo-brei person. I like salt and pepper.

Bird of Paradise

Menemen

On a traditional Turkish breakfast table, there's always a feast: cucumbers, tomatoes, olives, herby feta pastries, honey, homemade jam, *kaymak* (Turkish clotted cream), and *simit* (sesame-coated bread rings). And then, center stage, there are the eggs. *Menemen* is a Turkish-style scrambled egg dish made with peppers and tomatoes. There are variations of menemen that use a white cheese like feta, garlic, onions, and *sucuk* (sausage flavored with garlic, cumin, and chili flakes), depending on which region they're from, and which chef is behind them. This is my version.

—Ozlem Warren, as told to Laura Goodman

Makes 4 servings

1 tbsp butter
1 tbsp olive oil
1 green bell pepper, finely sliced
3 scallions, finely sliced
4 medium tomatoes, diced
1 to 2 tsp chili flakes
8 eggs
4 oz feta cheese, crumbled
 (about ¾ cup)
+ salt and freshly ground black pepper
+ crusty bread, for serving

1. Heat the butter and olive oil in a skillet.

2. When the butter is melted and foaming, stir in the bell pepper and cook over low to medium heat until softened, about 5 minutes.

3. Add the scallions, tomatoes, and chili flakes and cook for 3 to 4 minutes.

4. Meanwhile, crack the eggs into a bowl and beat well. Crumble in the feta cheese and mix with a fork.

5. Pour the egg and cheese mixture into the pan and give it a good stir.

6. Scramble the eggs until they are just cooked through, retaining their juice, about 4 minutes. Season with salt and black pepper.

7. Serve warm with a little more chili flakes sprinkled on top and a chunk of crusty bread.

RECIPE PICTURE MENU

Yank Sing's Egg Tart (page 24)

Scotch Egg (page 28)

Aioli (page 30)

Egg Curry (page 31)

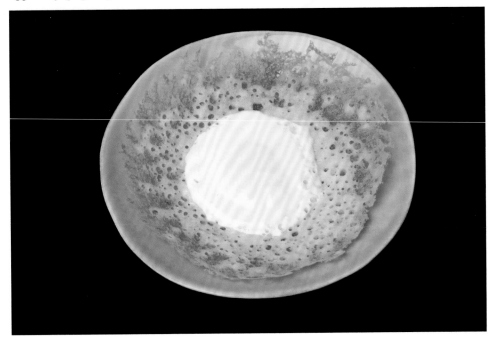

Egg Hoppers (page 32)

Shakshuka (page 34)

Huevos en Rabo de Mestiza (page 35)

Huevos Divorciados (page 36)

Spaghetti alla Carbonara (page 38)

Uitsmijter (page 39)

Eggs Kejriwal (page 54)

Egg and Beef Sandwich (page 56)

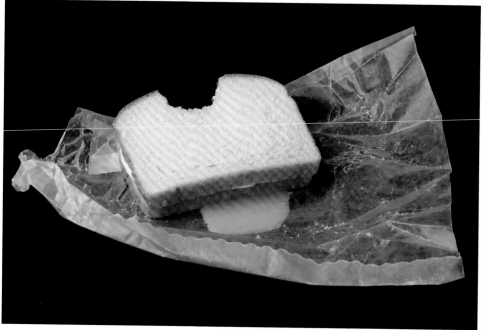

Egg Banjo (page 57)

Daniel Boulud's Omelette Farcie (page 60)

Michael Anthony's Tamagoyaki (page 62)

Tamago-no-Shinzo Yaki (page 64)

Kookoo Sabzi (page 69)

Poulard Omelet (page 70)

Hangtown Fry (page 71)

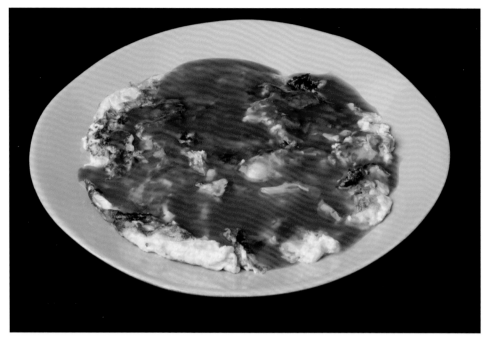

Taiwanese Oyster Omelet (page 72)

China Café's Egg Foo Young (page 74)

Tortilla Española Clásica (page 76)

Chipsi Mayai (page 78)

Denver Omelet (page 79)

Peasant's Frittata (page 80)

Chicken with Eggs Tagine (page 82)

Khai Jiao (page 83)

Courgette Omelet (page 84)

Masala Omelet (page 85)

Soft-Boiled Egg (page 90)

Hard-Boiled Egg (page 90)

Half-Boiled Eggs (page 91)

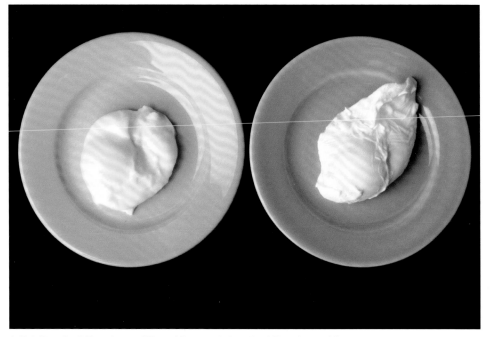

Julia's Poached Egg (page 97) and Jacques's Poached Egg (page 96)

Eggs Benedict (page 100)

Çılbır (page 102)

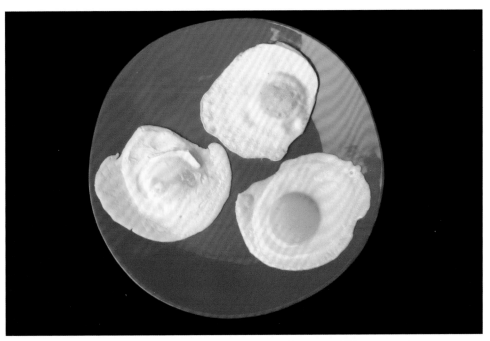

Fried Eggs (from left): Over Easy, Over Hard, Sunny-Side Up (page 103)

Huevos Motuleños (page 104)

Corned Beef Hash (page 106)

Saltie's Soft-Scrambled Eggs (page 107)

Buvette's Steamed Scrambled Eggs (page 108)

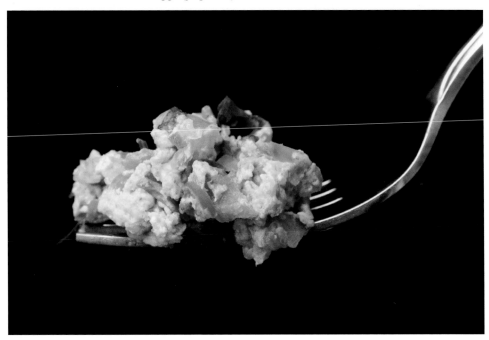

Anda Bhurji (page 109)

Matzo Brei (page 110)

Menemen (page 112)

Lourdes's Deviled Eggs with Tuna (page 165)

Anglesey Eggs (page 166)

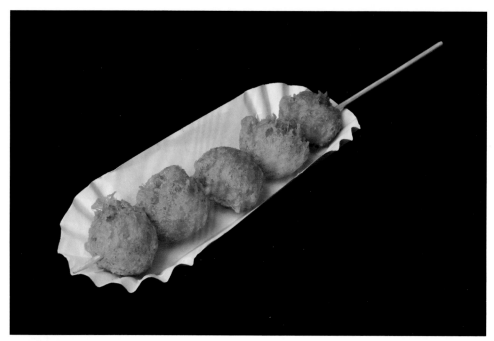

Kwek Kwek (page 168)

Egg Salad (page 170)

Salad Olivier (page 171)

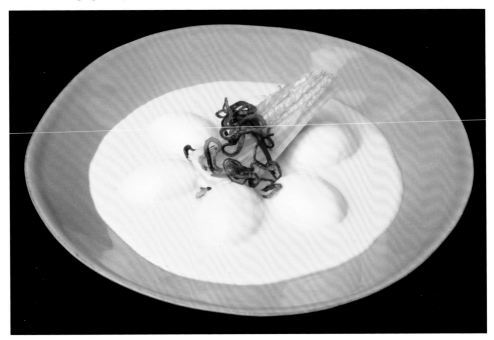

Oeufs Mayonnaise (page 172)

French Meringues (page 176)

Lemon Meringue Pie (page 178)

Crème Brûlée (page 180)

Limoncello Zabaglione (page 181)

Îles Flottantes (page 182)

Chicken Consommé (page 184)

Gin Fizz (page 185)

Yuen Yueng (page 186)

Pisco Sour (page 190)

Eggnog (page 191), Rompope (page 193), Indonesian Eggnog (STMJ) (page 194)

Vietnamese Egg Soda (page 196)

Soufflé (page 202)

Quiche Lorraine (page 203)

Eggs in Aspic (page 207)

Caesar Salad (page 208)

Steakhouse Salad (page 209)

Arpège Egg (page 210)

Arzak Egg (page 211)

Korean Steamed Eggs (page 220)

Steamed Salted Egg with Pork (page 221)

Chawanmushi (page 222)

Egg Drop Soup (page 223)

Monk Leaping into the Ocean (page 224)

Stracciatella (page 225)

Stir-Fried Egg and Tomato (page 226)

Yam Khai Dao (page 227)

Tea Egg (page 228)

Shabbat Eggs (page 229)

Onsen Tamago (page 230)

Tamago-Kake Gohan (TKG) (page 231)

Soboro Bento (page 232)

Oyakodon (page 234)

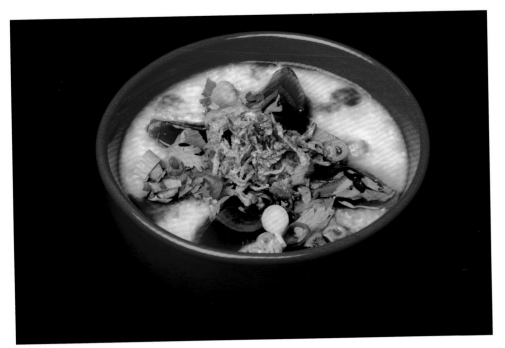

Congee with Century Eggs (page 241)

Spicy Basil and Century Egg Stir-Fry (page 242)

Salted Duck Eggs (page 244)

Bibingka (page 245)

Picklopolis Pickled Duck Egg (page 246)

Pennsylvania Dutch Pickled Beet Eggs (page 247)

Index

5.

OVER-THE-TOP EGGS

When it comes to eggs, less is more (think the perfection of a soft-boiled or soft-scrambled egg, or the simple, unadorned omelet). But more is also more. Gilding the lily—and by "lily" I mean, obviously, the egg—is par for the course. We love to make eggs—already perfect in their packages—even more decadent: We mix eggs with mayonnaise, itself an egg product, to make deviled eggs (page 165) and egg salad (page 170) and Salad Olivier (page 171). We deep-fry eggs; we bathe them in cream and butter. Think about classic pairings like eggs and truffles, eggs and caviar, and the little egg on top of your steak tartare. There's just something about eggs that lend themselves to such eggcess—they stoke our unending desire for too much of a good thing. But it's not too much! It's just much enough.

Included here, too, are the desserts we make from eggs: the custards made from just the yolks, the meringues made from just the whites—whipped to ethereal heights—and desserts that showcase the magical (okay, scientific; see page 173) properties of both. We mix eggs with booze and drink them down as nog. And speaking of nog, we celebrate with eggs—encrust them with jewels (page 162), hide them for children, eat chocolates shaped like them (or just admire the chocolates, too pretty to eat). That's pure over-the-top.

Fit for a Tsar

Marian Bull

Here is the story of how one of the world's most expensive eggs was almost scrambled.

Between 1885 and 1916, the Russian jeweler Peter Carl Fabergé crafted fifty gold Easter eggs for the Russian Imperial family. They were some of the finest works of goldsmithing the world had ever seen, intricate and opulent, the early iterations just a handful of inches high and bedecked in the shiniest representations of wealth an egg can accommodate. The first was a gift from Tsar Alexander III to his wife, Empress Maria Feodorovna, to celebrate the couple's twentieth anniversary and also Easter, the most sacred holiday in the Russian Orthodox Church. Most Russians gift painted eggs to loved ones on Easter; tsars, apparently, call up the fanciest jeweler in town. In the years that followed, he commissioned more and more eggs, each with its own little "surprise" inside: a hen specked with rubies, a crown made of diamonds, portraits of the monarchy in miniature. The eggs became a family tradition that lived on even after Alexander's death. And then the Revolution came.

In 1917, with the tsar abdicated, the Bolsheviks confiscated much of the art that filled the Romanov palaces, including a number of Imperial eggs. They sold them off to make quick cash, looking to fund their plans of industrialization. So off the eggs went, dispersed into the world, stripped of their royal family. The majority of the lot was scooped up by Armand Hammer, an American entrepreneur and art collector (who founded—get this—Arm & Hammer baking soda). But a handful of them remain lost to this day, their provenance murky, their identity unknown to their owners.

Almost a century after the eggs left home, in 2014, an anonymous man walked into London antique dealer Wartski with photos of what he thought to be one of those lost eggs. He had bought the egg for the sum of its parts, about $14,000, somewhere in the American Midwest, and had planned to sell it for scrap metal—in which case it would have been melted down, its history obliterated by alchemy. But then he found a name! A name on the little surprise watch inside, the name of Vacheron Constantin, he who had made the watch. A quick Google search shocked Anonymous Man with the realization that he may have something so small and so valuable that every square inch was worth over a million dollars: Constantin had also made the

gold watch that hid inside the Third Imperial Fabergé egg, a treasure at that time considered lost. And so he went to London bearing photos, and Wartski's Kieran McCarthy quickly flew back to the States to confirm the egg's identity.

"The story was so incredible that it really had to be true," says McCarthy, a longtime scholar and admirer of Fabergé's eggs. But a visit and verification were in order. Upon entering the house that was housing the egg, McCarthy found it sitting on the kitchen counter, a few inches away from a cupcake. "It was just such a wonderful juxtaposition," he remembers, delighted: "The cupcake is almost the picture of America, and then next to it was this Imperial treasure from Saint Petersburg. It wasn't a small one, either—it was a monster-sized chocolate cupcake." Covered in sprinkles, no less.

It was real, and it was intact: a golden egg just 2½ inches tall, decorated with diamonds and sapphires and set atop a stand with intricate golden feet that resembled the base of a very fancy chair in sparkling miniature. Shock and elation ensued. Wartski arranged a sale to an unnamed buyer for an unnamed but surely outrageous sum of money (before its discovery, the egg's worth was estimated at $33 million). After the purchase, the buyer let Wartski exhibit it in their own galleries, just before Easter 2014.

The news went worldwide in seconds. "It was like an art historical lottery win," explains McCarthy. "It really struck a chord: that this could happen to anyone. The world is a lottery, and although you can work very hard, you sometimes have to rely on pure luck. This is an example of how chance can work on anyone: You can walk along the most unlikely places and find the greatest treasures."

But how does a treasure like this become lost in the first place? How could anyone forget or overlook what it was? In 2011, Fabergé researchers figured out that the egg had been last sold, unknowingly, in 1964. But art dealers in 1964 knew about Fabergé. They knew about his eggs. How could anyone with this in their possession not know its provenance?

The thing about provenance, McCarthy told me, is that it's very delicate. As in a game of telephone, all it takes is one person not relaying whence an object came, or mixing up a fact or a name, to lose the provenance of even priceless, world-famous works of art. The art world calls these "sleepers," orphan objects that have lost their identity. The egg had last been owned by Rena Clarke, who had a lavish apartment on Park Avenue in New York. When she died, her entire estate was likely sold off, McCarthy guesses. There were ceramics, paintings, porcelain . . . so many items to sort through that the sellers in charge of the whole shebang likely didn't have enough time to spend investigating each one. And so the egg went off to its next owner unrecognized, and its own little game of telephone landed it somewhere in the Midwest.

Two Imperial eggs remain lost: They could be anywhere. The Cherub with Chariot Egg was last seen in 1934, on display at Lord & Taylor in New York City. The 1889 Nécessaire Egg, McCarthy says, is "almost certainly under somebody's bed somewhere." Maybe it's in your grandmother's attic, or on the next episode of *Antiques Roadshow.* This is the special allure of hidden treasure fairy tales: that something gleaming could be around the next corner, or under the cushion you're sitting on reading this. That what was once a king's could be in the hands of us paupers. And, hopefully, that we'll have the good sense to cherish the small treasures we find, instead of melting them down.

Lourdes's Deviled Eggs with Tuna

When you make egg salad or *oeufs mayonnaise* or deviled eggs, you're putting eggs on eggs. To take eggs and then put egg mayonnaise and foie in it, and then to have a fatty fish like tuna, it's really over the top. And yet it's hyper delicious. I actually thought the concept of it was kind of revolting, but then it was so good—it had such a delicate and elegant flavor. They're at our Christmas table every year: Every Christmas, my husband Eder's Aunt Lourdes makes these eggs *para picar,* or "to nibble," before the main courses. I appreciate that she buys a foie gras terrine and then uses it to make these doped-up surf-and-turf deviled eggs. They're pretty old school and would be very much at home at a fancy San Sebastián *pintxos* bar.

—Alex Raij

Makes 4 to 6 servings

12 **Hard-Boiled Eggs** (page 90)
½ cup mayonnaise
1 tbsp Dijon mustard
+ salt
2 tsp black truffle paste (optional)
1 can (4 oz) tuna in olive oil, drained on
    paper towels and crumbled
3 tbsp minced chives, plus more for
    garnish
1 can (2 oz) foie gras terrine, at room
    temperature (optional)

1. Peel the eggs and halve them lengthwise. (Alternatively, for a more modern presentation, peel them, then trim the ends and cut them crosswise through the center.) Remove the yolks and set aside. Rinse off the whites. Fill a bowl with water and hold the whites in it until ready to serve.

2. Place the yolks in a food processor and add the mayonnaise, mustard, and a pinch of salt. Process until smooth. Pulse in the black truffle paste (if using) until evenly combined. Transfer the mixture to a bowl.

3. Fold the tuna and chives into the yolk mixture. Use a fork to smash the foie terrine, then fold that into the egg yolk mixture as well, making sure there are no lumps. Taste and adjust with salt if needed. Spoon the yolk-foie mixture into a piping bag with a wide star tip, or into a large plastic zip-top bag (snip off the corner after chilling). Chill for 1 hour.

4. Remove the egg whites from the water and pat them dry. Pipe the filling into the egg whites and decorate them with chives, if you like. (I like to decorate them with truffle shavings, too.) You can make the filling up to a day ahead and chill it until needed, and the whites can be stored immersed in water in the refrigerator for the same amount of time. Make sure the whites are at room temperature before serving or they will be tough. The filling should be slightly chilled, so it may need a little tempering, too, if it's been chilled too long.

Anglesey Eggs

Anglesey eggs is that old-school British meal that is quintessentially British because it's at least 50 percent potato and frequently devoid of spices. In this dish, which is known as *wyau ynys môn* in its homeland of Wales, hard-boiled eggs are nestled in a leek-studded mash (i.e., mashed potatoes) and covered in a cheesy sauce blistered from the grill (i.e., broiler). Named after the northern Welsh island, it is thought that the wives of fishermen who lived on Anglesey created this dish by melting the local Caerphilly cheese into a sauce and flavoring mashed potatoes with boiled leeks, a symbolic Welsh vegetable because it was, until relatively recently, one of the only vegetables that grew in Wales.

The Welsh reverence for leeks has long been linked to Saint David, the patron saint of Wales who's been canonized as a vegetarian ascetic monk. He brought Welsh soldiers to victory against the Saxons in the mid-sixth century when he told them to wear leeks in their hats in order to distinguish themselves from their enemies. Since the twelfth century, the first of March has been a national holiday honoring Saint David, for which men and women wear leeks and feast on leek-heavy dishes such as *cawl cennin* (leek soup), leek pasties, and Anglesey eggs.

This recipe gives the holy leeks their due. Leeks get sautéed in butter, then added to a mustardy mash. The sauce is made with a classic sharp white English cheddar (which should be replaced with Caerphilly if you have access to it), spiked with smoky paprika and more mustard.

—Aralyn Beaumont

Makes 4 to 6 servings

2 medium russet (baking) potatoes, peeled and quartered
+ salt
2 tbsp butter
2 leeks, rinsed and finely chopped
3 tbsp warm milk
1 tsp Dijon mustard
½ cup grated sharp white cheddar cheese (see Note)
½ cup bread crumbs
1 tbsp finely chopped parsley
+ freshly ground black pepper
6 **Hard-Boiled Eggs** (page 90), halved
+ **Cheese Sauce** (recipe follows)

1. Make the mash: Place the quartered potatoes in a large pot, cover with 1 to 2 inches of cold water, and season with salt. Bring to a boil, then reduce to a simmer, cooking until tender, about 15 minutes.

2. While the potatoes are simmering, melt the butter in a pan over medium heat. Add the leeks and sauté until they've cooked down and released juices, about 5 minutes. Set aside.

3. When the potatoes are cooked through, drain and mash them with the warm milk and mustard. Fold in the leek-butter mixture and season to taste with salt. Set aside.

4. Heat the oven to 400°F.

5. Combine the cheese, bread crumbs, parsley, ¼ teaspoon salt, and a few turns of pepper in a small bowl.

6. Assemble the dish: Spread the mashed potatoes in an even layer in the bottom of an 8 × 8-inch glass dish. Nestle the hard-boiled egg halves over the top, softly pressing them into the mash. Evenly pour the cheese sauce over the top and cover with the bread crumb mixture.

7. Bake until the top is golden brown and the sauce is bubbling, about 20 minutes.

8. Serve hot.

Cheese Sauce

Makes about 1½ cups

2 tbsp butter
3 tbsp all-purpose flour
1¾ cups milk
1¼ cups grated sharp white cheddar
   cheese (see Note)
1 tsp Dijon mustard
¼ tsp smoked paprika
½ tsp salt
5 turns freshly ground black pepper

1. Melt the butter in a medium saucepan over medium heat. Add the flour and whisk until smooth.

2. Remove from the heat and add the milk a little bit at a time, whisking until smooth with each addition.

3. When the milk is incorporated, warm over medium-high heat to a simmer, stirring, until the sauce has thickened. Remove from the heat and add the cheese, mustard, paprika, salt, and pepper and stir until the cheese is melted and the sauce is smooth. Adjust the seasoning to taste. Keep warm and stir occasionally until ready to use.

Note: Caerphilly cheese is traditionally used in Anglesey eggs, but since it's difficult to find outside of the UK, this recipe calls for sharp white cheddar. Use Caerphilly if you can!

Kwek Kwek

Kwek kwek is Filipino street food: deep-fried quail eggs on a stick. Vendors will hawk fried foods, tofus, barbecue, maybe even chicken *balut*. Kwek kwek might be just one of maybe five different things in their arsenal. It's super simple. The eggs get their reddish orange color from the annatto. They're dipped in batter, then fried, put onto a stick, and that's it. You dip kwek kwek in all types of sauce. There's a sweet-and-sour sauce, there's Maggi sauce—it just depends on whatever the vendor's feeling for the day. Anywhere in the provinces, you can find kwek kwek. You might see it in the cities occasionally, but it's really a provincial barrio thing—in small villages, it's always available readily.

Here's our very easy and delicious recipe. We've added vodka to the batter to help keep the breading crispy.

—Chase and Chad Valencia

Makes 2 to 4 servings

12 quail eggs
+ salt
3 tbsp cornstarch
1 cup all-purpose flour
1 tbsp ground annatto
1 cup cheap vodka
2 cups vegetable oil, for deep-frying
+ sukang maanghang (Filipino spiced
    vinegar) or hot sauce, for serving

1. Hard-boil the quail eggs: Bring salted water to a boil and cook the eggs for 2½ minutes. Shock in ice water to stop the cooking. Peel the eggs (see Note).

2. Dredge the quail eggs gently in the cornstarch.

3. Make the fry batter: In a bowl, combine the flour and 1 teaspoon salt. Dissolve the annatto in the vodka, and pour the mixture into the bowl with the flour and salt. Mix well.

4. Place the dredged quail eggs into the fry batter and coat as best as you can.

5. Pour the oil into a heavy-bottomed pot. Heat the oil to 350°F. Fry the battered quail eggs until golden brown, 2 to 3 minutes, rolling them in the oil so they brown evenly. Remove with a spider and drain on paper towels.

6. Skewer the fried eggs onto wooden skewers, 3 to 6 eggs to a stick. Serve hot with *sukang maanghang* or hot sauce for dipping.

Note: Quail eggs can be a little bit trickier to peel than chicken eggs. Crack the bottom (large) end of the egg and start gently peeling from there.

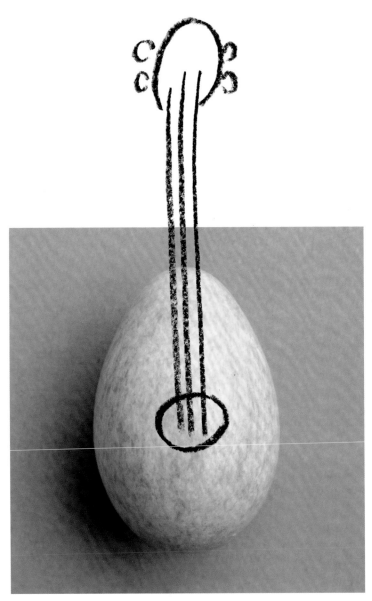

Cactus Wren

Egg Salad

I had somehow forgotten about egg salad, but with the spring herbs plentiful in the garden, eggs just coming in with the lengthening days, and some very good bread in the house, egg salad suddenly came sharply into view. I also add a small, finely diced pickled shallot to egg salad just to insert a little zing into the creamy richness of real farm (or backyard) eggs. We buy eggs from a farmer who lives on the road where my husband Patrick's studio is. You put money in their jar, and you just go in and get some. They're huge. I asked Sam, the farmer, about them, and he said they're from Wallace chickens. Henry Wallace was vice president under Franklin Roosevelt, and when he left office he started raising chickens, and he developed this breed—it's named after him—and the eggs are really big. Sam is so impeccable as a farmer: His eggs are super fresh, they're big, the whites really stand up, and the yolks are really yellow and perky; they're just a pleasure to use. I don't buy eggs anywhere else.

—*Deborah Madison*

Makes about 2 cups

1 small shallot, finely diced
1 tsp red or white wine vinegar
6 **Hard-Boiled Eggs** (page 90)
1 heaping tbsp minced tarragon leaves
1 tbsp finely snipped chives
1 tbsp minced parsley or lovage
3 tbsp mayonnaise
+ salt (preferably sea salt)
+ freshly ground black pepper
+ chive blossoms, if available

1. Toss the diced shallot with the vinegar and let stand for a few minutes. The color will change right away to a soft pink.

2. Meanwhile, peel and chop the eggs. (If they're very fresh and hard to peel, I just cut them in half crosswise and carefully scoop out the egg with a spoon. It works every time!)

3. Put the eggs in a bowl with the herbs and mayonnaise. If you use commercial mayonnaise you might not need much salt. Taste, add ¼ teaspoon, then taste again. Season with pepper.

4. If there is excess vinegar with the shallots, drain it off and add the shallots to the mix. Pile the egg salad into a serving bowl and garnish with chive blossoms, if available.

Salad Olivier

Aka "Russian salad" outside of Russia, this is an eggy, mayonnaise-y Russian holiday staple first created in Moscow by a Belgian cook named Lucien Olivier in the 1860s. (Another story circulating puts forth that it was named after the actor Laurence Olivier, to whom it was first served. Unfortunately not true!) Lucien Olivier was tight-lipped about his recipe, which is maybe why the Salad Olivier of today bears little resemblance to his, which, in true no-holds-barred eggy fashion, included caviar, jellied broth, crayfish tails, a Provençal sauce with egg yolks in it, tongue pieces arranged around the dish, and gherkins, hard-boiled egg slices, and potato skins decorating the top.

Makes 2 to 4 servings

2 medium waxy potatoes, such as
    Yukon Gold
+ salt
1 medium carrot, cut into ¼-inch dice
¼ cup fresh peas (or frozen, thawed)
3 **Hard-Boiled Eggs** (page 90)
3 tbsp diced gherkin or other pickles,
    plus 1 tbsp pickle juice
½ cup diced boiled ham or bologna
½ cup chopped scallions
¼ cup chopped dill
¼ cup mayonnaise
1 tsp Dijon mustard
+ freshly ground black pepper
+ parsley leaves, for garnish

1. Place the whole potatoes in a medium saucepan and cover with cool water. Season with salt and bring to a boil over medium-high heat. Reduce the heat and simmer until the potatoes are just tender, about 25 minutes. Drain and let the potatoes cool.

2. While the potatoes cool, clean the pan and refill with water. Bring to a boil, season with salt, and blanch the carrot until tender, about 4 minutes. Remove with a slotted spoon and add the peas, cooking until they are bright green, 30 seconds to 1 minute. Drain and let cool.

3. Dice two of the hard-boiled eggs. Use a sharp knife to slice into the third egg and remove the yolk in one piece. Thinly slice the white lengthwise into strips.

4. When the potatoes are cool, rub away the skins with a paper towel and dice them the size of the peas, about ¼ inch. Place the potatoes in a large bowl and add the carrots, peas, pickles, ham, diced eggs, scallions, and dill.

5. In a small bowl, whisk the pickle juice, mayonnaise, and mustard until smooth. Season with a pinch of salt and pepper and pour over the diced ingredients. Toss gently, taking care not to break up the potatoes and eggs. Mound the salad on a serving platter and garnish with parsley. Place the egg yolk toward the middle of the top of the salad to be the center of an egg flower. Arrange the strips of egg white to look like petals. Serve immediately.

Oeufs Mayonnaise

The French are unafraid of egg-on-egg action, and *oeufs mayo* are proof that they're onto something. At Yves Camdeborde's Comptoir du Relais in Paris, an order of "oeuf mayo" means a plate of halved hard-boiled eggs blanketed in a loose mayonnaise—lemony and bright—alongside a little segment of Little Gem, and an onion-plus-onion garnish of pickled onion and fried shallots. It's eggs in egg sauce! I love it, yet I fear it.

Makes 2 to 3 servings

¾ cup **Aioli** (page 30) or store-bought
  mayonnaise
2 tbsp olive oil
2 tbsp fresh lemon juice
+ salt
3 **Hard-Boiled Eggs** (page 90)
½ head Little Gem lettuce, quartered
  vertically
¼ red onion, sliced and quickly pickled
  in a splash of red wine vinegar and a
  pinch of salt and sugar
+ **Fried Shallots** (recipe follows)

1. Thin out the aioli by whisking in the oil and lemon juice. You want it thin enough to be pourable, but not too liquidy. Add a little bit of water if it's still too thick. Taste, and add salt and more lemon juice to taste.

2. Peel and halve the eggs lengthwise. Arrange them in a circle on a plate, pointy ends facing out. Pour the aioli mixture over the eggs, so they're completely blanketed. Put the Little Gem halves in the middle, and the pickled red onion slices on top of those. Sprinkle with fried shallots, and eat right away.

Fried Shallots
Makes 1 cup shallots and 1 cup oil

1 cup peanut or vegetable oil
2 cups thinly sliced shallots
+ salt

1. Heat the oil in a saucepan over medium heat and throw in a shallot slice. When it rises to the top and starts to sizzle, add the remaining shallot slices. Stir with a slotted spoon or spider to untangle and keep them from sticking to one another.

2. Let cook, stirring occasionally, until the shallots have browned, 13 to 15 minutes. (Reduce the heat if they start to brown too fast.)

3. Remove the pan from the heat and transfer the shallot slices to a plate lined with paper towels. Sprinkle with salt. Use right away or transfer to a jar or an airtight container. Strain the shallot oil and reserve for stir-frying or drizzling over things.

How to Understand an EGG

Arielle Johnson

Biologically

The egg is a chemically complex, sealed package of protection and food to grow a chicken embryo into a chick. Understanding what its parts are intended for by evolution sheds some light on what happens when we cook with them.

Eggs are built from the inside out, starting with the hen's germ cell, which, if fertilized by rooster sperm, will eventually become a chicken.

Food for the growing chick is added next: This is the yolk, rich in lipids—fats, emulsifiers, and cholesterol—with about 17 percent protein. The yolk also holds fat-soluble, orangey-yellow molecules like zeaxanthin and lutein from the hen's intake of leafy plants, similar to the carotenoids in carrots and other orange vegetables.

The white of the egg, or the albumen, is added in layers to buffer and protect the chick, starting with the chalazae, the twisted protein ropes attached to either end of the shell that suspend the yolk in the middle of the egg. Albumen proteins serve a variety of protective and defensive roles in the egg, in addition to cushioning the chick.

The white is wrapped in tough protein membranes, then the protein–calcium carbonate composite of the shell, then a waxy cuticle. The color of the egg—white, brown, speckled, blue, green—depends on the breed of chicken but is deposited only on the outer shell, and has no effect on flavor or functionality. The shell has thousands of tiny holes in it to let air in for the chick—these also let in carbon dioxide, which causes the egg white to gradually become more alkaline as it sits around.

Chemically

The different biological functions of the components of an egg help explain why eggs are so versatile, and so useful in cooking.

What eggs do, in food, mostly boils down to protein denaturation (foaming, setting, and scrambling) and fat-water emulsification. And these in turn all work on fat-water repulsion.

"Denaturing" a protein has to do with upsetting its formation. Every protein is a long, unbranched chain of smaller molecules called amino acids. In their natural state, protein chains are folded into a very specifically shaped ball, unique to each type of protein. The original folds are held not by permanent links, but rather by temporary interactions between the different amino acids that make up the protein chain. It's possible to essentially unravel this ball into a looser shape or a totally unfolded chain by disturbing with heat (cooking), changes in pH (acid or alkaline treatment), or even just whacking it a lot (beating or whisking).

You may recall that water and oil don't mix. The same effect is what drives protein folding and the behavior of denatured proteins. The amino acids that make up a protein chain are basically either oily, hydrophobic (water-hating) and nonpolar; or hydrophilic (water-loving) and polar. Since proteins are usually floating around in water, the hydrophilic amino acids are cool just chilling out next to the water. The hydrophobic amino acids don't mix well with water, so they get wrapped into the middle of the protein, where they can be their nonpolar selves and not have to deal with water molecules. This nonpolar-hiding-wrapping is what keeps the protein in its particular folded shape.

But disrupt these folds by heating it up, or whacking it around, or changing the chemistry of the surrounding water to become quite acidic or alkaline, and the proteins begin uncoiling and stretching out. What happens next depends on what part of the egg you're dealing with.

Whole Egg: Coagulation

Most of the basic, and some of the nonbasic, ways to cook an egg deal in coagulation. Boiled, fried, steamed, poached, scrambled, or baked eggs; eggs mixed with dairy to make a custard or flan; or even salted or century eggs all get their delightful texture this way. Heat (but sometimes chemical changes, like alkali paste) causes the egg proteins

to start unraveling and denaturing. They go from being tight little globules to loose and floppy strings, and begin connecting and binding with one another. This makes a loose net that traps water inside it, resulting in a solidified texture.

Where coagulation can go wrong: If you heat the coagulated proteins too much, their net will get tighter and tighter, squeezing out all the water, making for curdled custards and weepy scrambled eggs.

Egg White: Foams

More advanced techniques with eggs get into separating the yolk—which contains a lot of fats in addition to protein and water—from the white, which is essentially fatless: 90 percent water and 10 percent protein. Whip a whole egg and you'll get a creamy pale yellow liquid; whip egg whites and you'll get a growing cloud of foam.

Why the difference?

Like heating, whipping begins unraveling and denaturing proteins. It also incorporates air, which in nonprotein circumstances would just bubble away. But recall that the egg proteins have sections that want to get away from water. If there were fat around, these would just face toward the fat. In the absence of fat, they do the next best thing and face toward the air, with the polar amino acids on the unfolded proteins remaining pointed toward the water. This is a stable way to hang out, so the air bubbles remain incorporated into the liquid of the white, held in place by tiny, nonpolar "hands."

And this is why detergent residue on your whipping bowl, or a speck of egg yolk, spells doom for your meringues and soufflés: nonpolar amino acids would much rather get cozy with fats than with air, so the only way to get them to foam is to make sure their only stabilizing friend around is air.

Egg Yolk: Emulsification

We would be remiss not to look at the chemistry that makes luscious egg sauces, like mayonnaise and hollandaise, possible in the first place. Egg yolks are largely fat and water, which don't like to mix. To keep them together, the yolk is full of molecules that have both hydrophobic and hydrophilic parts. These are called phospholipids or lecithins, and come in the form of a fatty tail with a polar, phosphate head. We can take advantage of their capabilities by adding yolks to mixtures we want to contain both fats and water, and slowly mixing them together. Like air bubbles in egg white foams, the fats will form little droplets, and the phospholipids will gather around them, their nonpolar, fat-loving tails dipped in the droplets, their polar heads sticking out into the surrounding watery environment, and this in aggregate turning into a thick and creamy sauce.

Lecithins may not unfold as dramatically as proteins, but they are workhorses for keeping fatty things suspended in emulsions. In a mayonnaise they enable a yolk to emulsify about fifteen times its own volume in fats.

Shiso sprouts

French Meringues

In the family of meringues, French meringue would be considered the most basic. Compared to its Swiss and Italian cousins, which require heat, French meringue is whipped egg whites with a simple addition of granulated sugar.

When the meringue is baked, the sugar holds on to the water molecules, giving the protein structure of the egg whites time to coagulate into a permanent foam before all the water evaporates. This needs to happen slowly, at 200°F or lower. In the professional pastry department, I employ a dehydrator set to 180°F and leave them for 4 or more hours, depending on their size. At home, I set my oven as low as it can go, which is 200°F. I bake them for 3 hours, turn the oven off, and leave them in there for another hour or two.

Baked meringues can be shaped as simple kisses or fluted rosettes, piped and baked into individual nibbles. Bake meringue in large disks and you can layer them with mousses, whipped creams, custards, and fruits for a meringue cake. Little meringue nests can be filled with cream and fruits to make the classic French vacherin.

—*Dana Cree*

Makes about 1 quart meringue (enough for about 50 kiss-shaped meringues)

6 egg whites
2 tsp cream of tartar
½ tsp vanilla extract (optional)
1½ cups superfine sugar

1. Heat the oven to 200°F.

2. Place the egg whites and cream of tartar in the bowl of a stand mixer fitted with the whisk attachment. Add the vanilla, if using. Whip on medium speed until the egg whites are thick, have grown to about eight times their original size, and are forming soft peaks. This could take anywhere from 5 to 10 minutes.

3. Sprinkle in 2 tablespoons of the sugar. Let the meringue whip for 1 minute, then add another 2 tablespoons sugar, and again let the meringue whip for 1 minute.

Continue adding the sugar in 2-tablespoon increments, letting the meringue whip for 1 minute after each addition, until all the sugar has been added to the bowl. This should take you more than 10 minutes.

4. When you've added all of the sugar, let the meringue whip for an additional 2 minutes, then check the texture of the meringue to see if it's holding taut, glossy peaks. To do this, remove the bowl from the stand mixer, dip the whip into the meringue, and extract it. Position the whip tip-up and watch the way the meringue behaves. Does the tip of the meringue fall over and disappear into the mass it sits above? If so, you have soft peaks—keep whipping for about 4 more minutes. Does the meringue keep its shape, but the tip falls over on top of the mound? Then you've created medium peaks—you're so close!

Continue whipping for 2 more minutes. (If you were folding your meringue into a recipe, you'd likely stop here.) Is the meringue stiff and keeps a tall, proud point on top like a stalagmite? Those are stiff peaks. Congratulations, your meringue is ready to be shaped and baked! Does it break off into multiple peaks, and is kind of chunky? I'm so sorry, you've over-whipped your meringue and you'll have to start over.

5. Working quickly, shape your meringues on a Silpat-lined baking sheet and get them in the 200°F oven ASAP! Bake the meringues for 3 hours, turn the oven off, and leave them in there for another 1 or 2 hours, to ensure they are very dry. (Alternatively you can hold them in a dehydrator at 180°F for 4 hours.) Once baked, let the meringues cool completely at room temperature, then transfer them to an airtight container to help preserve their crisp texture. If you have any of those "do not eat" packets of desiccant that come in your shoes and bags of beef jerky (you can also find them for sale at most hardware stores), throw them in the container with your meringues. They will absorb any moisture in the container, preserving the meringues' crisp texture.

King Penguin

Lemon Meringue Pie

Lemon meringue pie, arguably the most beautiful of pies, is the glorious coming together of yolk and white, lemony custard coupled with sky-high Italian meringue. This pie's a cute couple: Mary-Frances Heck's perfectly tart custard is toweringly piled with all 6 cups of Dana Cree's foolproof recipe for soft, glossy Italian meringue. We ate the (Mary-Frances) *HECK* out of this pie. You will, too.

Makes one 9-inch pie

¾ cup plus 1 tbsp sugar
¼ cup cornstarch
1¼ cups water
1 egg
3 egg yolks
+ pinch of salt
1 tsp grated lemon zest
½ cup fresh lemon juice
4 tbsp butter, cubed
+ **Pie Crust** (recipe follows)
+ **Italian Meringue** (recipe follows)

1. Whisk ¾ cup of the sugar and the cornstarch together in a medium saucepan. When combined with no lumps remaining, add the water and whisk until smooth. Set over medium-high heat and bring to a simmer, stirring, until thickened. Remove from the heat.

2. Beat the whole egg and yolks with the remaining 1 tablespoon sugar and the salt. Pour one-third of the hot cornstarch mixture into the eggs while whisking. Pour the tempered eggs into the saucepan and whisk gently to combine. Switch to a heat-resistant spatula and set the mixture over medium-low heat. Cook until the mixture simmers, stirring and scraping the bottom of the pan with the spatula. Remove from the heat and stir in

the lemon zest, lemon juice, and butter until smooth. Strain the hot lemon custard into the baked pie crust and place in the refrigerator to cool.

3. Heat the oven to 400°F and arrange a single rack in the lowest slot of the oven.

4. Spoon a cup or two of Italian meringue over the cooled lemon custard, sealing the custard below the meringue. Pile on more meringue, creating peaks and valleys around the pie. Use at least 3 cups of meringue, or more for a mile-high effect. Bake the pie until the meringue is toasted to your liking, 10 to 15 minutes. (Alternatively use a blowtorch to toast the meringue.) Let cool before slicing.

Pie Crust
Makes one 9-inch pie crust

1½ cups all-purpose flour, plus more as needed
½ tsp baking powder
½ tsp salt
1 stick (4 oz) cold unsalted butter, cubed
¼ cup ice water

1. Pulse the flour, baking powder, salt, and butter in a food processor until the butter is broken down into small pebbles. Drizzle in the water and pulse just until the mixture begins to come together. Dump onto a lightly floured work surface and fold and press until the dough comes together. Shape the dough into a disk, wrap in plastic, and chill for at least 30 minutes and up to 2 days.

2. Heat the oven to 400°F.

3. Roll out the dough to an 11- or 12-inch round and fit into a 9-inch pie dish. Trim to a 1-inch overhang, crimp the edges, and dock the dough with a fork. Lay a piece of parchment over the dough and fill the pan with baking beans. Bake for 20 minutes, remove the beans and parchment paper, and continue baking until the crust is firm and tan colored, another 10 to 15 minutes. Let cool.

Italian Meringue
Makes about 6 cups

6 egg whites
1 tsp cream of tartar
6 tbsp water
1 cup sugar
1 tsp vanilla extract

1. Place the egg whites and cream of tartar in the bowl of a stand mixer fitted with the whisk attachment and begin mixing on medium speed.

2. Meanwhile, place the water and sugar in a small, heavy-bottomed pot and place over medium-high heat. Cook, stirring only enough that the sugar dissolves, until the syrup reaches a boil. When the syrup starts to boil, use a pastry brush dipped in water to wash any sugar crystals off the sides of the pot as they appear. Continue cooking until the syrup reaches 240°F.

3. Ideally, the meringue will reach soft peaks at the same moment the syrup reaches 240°F. You'll have to keep your eye on both items as they progress, increasing and decreasing the heat under the syrup if necessary to achieve this. If the egg whites reach soft peaks before the syrup has reached that temperature, turn the mixer to low speed, but do not stop it. Once you stop the motion, the proteins in the meringue continue to bond with each other, locking it in place, and will break when you begin whipping them again.

4. When the syrup has reached 240°F, reduce the mixer speed to medium-low, to prevent splatters of hot syrup flying at your face. Begin adding the syrup in a slow, steady stream. Aim for the place where the whisk and the bowl come closest to each other. Once all of the syrup has been added, turn your mixer to medium-high speed. The heat from the syrup will denature the proteins on contact and can overcook them if you don't start moving the mixture fast and grab as much air as you can.

5. The Italian meringue will reach full volume and form stiff peaks, but it's not completed until the meringue cools to below 120°F, or is warm—not hot—to the touch. Just before stiff peaks form, add the vanilla extract and whip until it's completely incorporated.

6. Bask in the glossy glow of your tall-peaked Italian meringue. Take your time—it's not going anywhere for a little while. Once you're done admiring your hard work, send it on its way to its final destination.

Crème Brûlée

You expect to see crème brûlée at a steakhouse, next to the molten chocolate cake or tiramisu. But other desserts don't actually hold a flame to crème brûlée's perfection, even though it's just yolky custard and burnt sugar. Maybe it's the simplicity, maybe it's the specks of vanilla bean flickered throughout, or the foreign accents. Most likely it's getting to theatrically break the sugar crust with your silver spoon.

—Aralyn Beaumont

Makes 4 servings

2 cups heavy cream
+ pinch of salt
1 vanilla bean
6 egg yolks
½ cup sugar
4 tsp turbinado sugar

1. Heat the oven to 300°F and heat a kettle full of water.

2. Slowly warm the cream and salt in a medium saucepan over medium heat, about 5 minutes. Remove from the heat. Split the vanilla bean lengthwise, scrape the seeds out of the pod, and add the seeds to the pot along with the vanilla bean. Cover the pot and let steep for 15 to 20 minutes.

3. Meanwhile, mix the egg yolks and sugar until you reach the ribbon stage: When you lift the whisk, it should leave a trace of a ribbon on the surface that slides back into the mixture in a couple of seconds.

4. Bring the vanilla cream back to a simmer. Pour a small amount into the egg yolk mixture to temper it and whisk, adding a little at a time until the eggs are heated. Pour the egg mixture into the cream and return to the stove over medium heat. Constantly stir in a figure-eight motion until the mixture has thickened, 3 to 5 minutes.

5. Strain the custard through a fine-mesh strainer into a pitcher or large measuring cup. Divide the custard among four 8-ounce ramekins. Place the ramekins in a large roasting pan and fill the pan with the heated water so that it reaches two-thirds of the way up the ramekins. Bake until the center has a slight jiggle but the sides are set, 30 to 40 minutes.

6. Remove from the oven and cool on a cooling rack. Refrigerate until ready to serve.

7. Once they're cooled, it's time to brûlée: Evenly coat the top of each ramekin with 1 teaspoon of turbinado sugar. Torch according to the directions on your handheld torch, or stick the ramekins under the broiler for 5 minutes.

8. Let them sit for 5 minutes before serving so the sugar can cool and harden.

Limoncello Zabaglione

Traditionally zabaglione is made with Marsala. I first had it at Felidia in New York, where Lidia Bastianich makes a very traditional Italian zabaglione—super light and fluffy, served in cups and topped with whipped cream. It's very simple.

Years later, when I started developing a menu at Mozza, I had to revisit all my memories of desserts and dishes and put my own little spin on them. I thought about the zabaglione and how I wanted to make it different and work with lighter flavors. Italy doesn't really have a lemon curd, so I thought of using the limoncello as a way to introduce a lighter element into the dessert as opposed to a boozy Marsala zabaglione.

We tend to serve it in the dead of winter, even though it's still 75 degrees here in LA. Since it is made with limoncello, we can pair it with fresh citrus fruits, such as grapefruit or blood oranges or tangerines, which are seasonal in the winter. And that's really one of my favorite ways to have it: chilled and spooned over fresh fruit. You can also layer it in a glass with cake and berries.

—Dahlia Narvaez

Makes 8 servings

8 egg yolks
½ cup sugar
¾ cup limoncello
¼ cup heavy cream
+ berries, for serving

1. Prepare a large bowl of ice water and set aside.

2. Fill a medium saucepan less than halfway with water and heat to a gentle simmer. Whisk together the egg yolks, sugar, and limoncello in a large metal bowl until well blended. Place the bowl over the saucepan and immediately start whisking at a moderate speed.

3. Beat the egg mixture with large strokes, frequently scraping the whisk around the sides and bottom of the bowl to heat and cook the zabaglione evenly—be careful not to scramble the egg yolks. Continue to steadily whisk as the zabaglione expands into a thick frothy sponge, about 5 minutes longer.

4. When the sponge is warm to the touch and thickened enough to form a ribbon when it drops back on the surface, take the bowl off the saucepan and transfer it to the bowl of ice water. Whisk the zabaglione until it's cool.

5. When the zabaglione is cool, whip the cream to medium peaks. Fold the whipped cream into the zabaglione. Chill the zabaglione until ready to serve, or refrigerate covered tightly for 1 day. Serve with berries.

Îles Flottantes

For the French, this dessert is not only a classic, but often a childhood touchstone. In a country where people are more likely to buy their desserts from a neighborhood pâtisserie than prepare them at home, *îles flottantes* (floating islands) remains a mainstay in the make-at-home repertoire, in some part because it is so easy and in some part because it's a naturally showy dessert. The islands, soft-poached meringue puffs, float in a smooth crème anglaise, which is even better when refrigerated overnight. Served in a large bowl (the dessert looks great served in a grand footed bowl) or in individual portions, the islands can be presented unadorned or given their traditional decoration—caramelized sugar strands. Making the strands is a last-minute job, but it takes only a couple of minutes and adds more than a couple of minutes' worth of oohs and aahs.

—*Dorie Greenspan*

Makes 6 servings

4 cups whole milk
6 egg yolks
¾ cup sugar
1½ tsp vanilla extract
4 egg whites, at room temperature
+ pinch of salt
+ **Caramel** (optional; recipe follows)

1. Make the crème anglaise: Bring 2 cups of the milk to a boil in a small heavy-bottomed saucepan over medium heat.

2. Meanwhile, put the yolks and ½ cup of the sugar in a heavy saucepan and whisk vigorously until thick and pale, 2 to 3 minutes.

3. Still whisking, drizzle a little of the hot milk into the yolks—this will temper, or warm, the yolks so they won't curdle. Whisking all the while, slowly pour in the remaining hot milk. Put the saucepan over medium-low heat and, stirring constantly with a wooden spoon,

cook until the crème anglaise thickens, lightens in color, and coats the spoon—if you run your finger down the spoon, the track should remain; this will take about 10 minutes. The crème anglaise should be cooked until it reaches 180°F on an instant-read thermometer.

4. Immediately remove the pan from the heat, strain the crème anglaise through a fine-mesh sieve into a bowl, and stir in the vanilla. Press a piece of plastic wrap against the surface of the crème anglaise to create an airtight seal and refrigerate until thoroughly chilled, 2 to 3 hours, or for up to 3 days. (The crème anglaise will improve with at least an overnight rest.)

5. Make the meringue islands: Spread a few clean kitchen towels on the counter near the stove and have a large slotted spoon at hand. Line a baking sheet with wax paper. Put the remaining 2 cups milk in a wide saucepan and bring it to a simmer over low heat.

6. Meanwhile, put the egg whites in the clean bowl of a stand mixer fitted with the whisk attachment (or use a large bowl and a hand mixer). Beat the whites on medium speed just until foamy, then beat in the salt. When the eggs turn opaque, increase the mixer speed to medium-high and add the remaining ¼ cup sugar about 1 tablespoon at a time. Whip until the meringue is firm but satiny and still glossy, about 5 minutes.

7. You have two choices in shaping the floating islands: You can just scoop up some meringue—specifically, an amount about twice the size of an egg—in which case you'll have the equivalent of a rocky volcanic island, or you can smooth the meringue to get a manicured island. For the smooth look, use a large oval spoon to scoop up the meringue, then use another large oval spoon to very gingerly transfer the meringue from spoon to spoon a couple of times to form a smooth oval.

8. Either way, one by one, lower the islands into the simmering milk, adding only as many islands as you can fit into the pan without crowding.

9. Poach the meringues for 1 minute, gently turn them over, and poach them for 1 minute more. Then lift the islands out of the milk and onto the towel. Repeat until you've poached 12 islands. Put the puffs (which will have inflated when poached and will deflate when cooled) on the lined baking sheet and chill them for at least 1 hour, or for up to 3 hours.

10. Either pour the crème anglaise into a large serving bowl and top with the meringue islands, or make 6 individual servings. If using the caramel, working quickly, dip the tines of a fork into the caramel and wave the fork over the floating islands to create threads that will quickly harden.

Caramel
Makes about 1 cup

½ cup sugar
⅓ cup water

1. Stir the sugar and water together in a small heavy-bottomed saucepan and cook over medium heat, stirring, until the sugar dissolves.

2. Increase the heat, bring the syrup to a boil, and cook without stirring, swirling the pan occasionally, until the caramel turns a pale gold color, 6 to 8 minutes.

3. Pull the pan from the heat and let the caramel cool just until it is thick enough to form threads when it is dropped from the tines of a fork. (If the caramel hardens, rewarm it slowly over low heat.)

Chicken Consommé

Okay, so you have too many egg whites from making all those custards, and you're feeling a little queasy from this chapter, too? What you should cook now is this simple chicken consommé, clarified with egg whites.

This is a recipe I made a couple of dozen times in culinary school. The ritual of slicing and mixing the ingredients methodically, then carefully watching the mixture simmer and the raft form, offers a form of therapy to the cook. A recipe doing exactly what it's meant to—something that you can't otherwise achieve with any piece of kitchen equipment—brings one back to the basics of the French kitchen. The bit of time invested produces something deeply nourishing for ill and well alike.

—Mary-Frances Heck

Makes 4 servings

1 leek or small onion, thinly sliced
1 celery stalk, thinly sliced
1 carrot, julienned
¼ cup 1-inch pieces parsley stems
1 tsp cracked black peppercorns
10 thyme sprigs
1 lb lean ground chicken
6 egg whites, beaten
8 cups homemade chicken stock

1. Toss the leek, celery, carrot, parsley, pepper, and thyme in a taller-than-wide stockpot. Add the chicken and egg whites and break up and stir with your fingers or a wooden spoon.

2. Pour the stock into the pot and set over medium heat. Bring to a very gentle simmer, then slide the pot one-quarter of the way off the burner (taking care that it will not tip over or spill) and "convection simmer," so the liquid bubbles up the side of the pot that's directly over the burner and up and over the raft of coagulated egg and meat that has formed. Cook in this manner until the consommé is perfectly clear and flavorful, about 45 minutes. Do not let the consommé boil or allow the raft to break up lest the stock become cloudy. Remove from the heat and let settle.

3. Gently ladle the consommé into a coffee filter–lined strainer set over a clean saucepan. Reheat to nearly boiling, then pour into heated bowls.

Gin Fizz

I absolutely subscribe to the belief that an egg makes everything better. If you have leftovers, put a poached egg on top, and they're better. Put an egg on a burger, great! Put an egg in a drink—it will make the drink better, too.

The Gin Fizz is very classically a brunch drink, and now it's the kind of thing that cocktail nerds like to order at night. But it was originally a Sunday morning kind of thing. Using an egg white makes the drink extra silky, extra foamy—gives it this extra texture that changes the drink, gives it a thicker mouthfeel, and makes it more exciting. And the other good part about egg white drinks is that you can make cool designs on the top.

—Meaghan Dorman, as told to Lauren Ro

Makes 1 cocktail

¾ oz fresh lemon juice
¾ oz simple syrup
2 oz gin
1 small egg white (about 2 tbsp)
+ ice
3 oz club soda
+ lemon peel

1. Shake the lemon juice, simple syrup, gin, and egg white together briefly in a cocktail shaker to emulsify.

2. Add ice and shake again, then strain into a Collins glass without ice. Add the club soda and the drink will foam up higher. Express lemon peel over the top, discard, and serve.

American Kestrel

Yuen Yueng

What's that? You have too many egg*shells* left over from cooking the recipes in this book? A recipe for you:

Perhaps the most famous of the milk tea drinks in Hong Kong is the *yuen yueng* (a half tea half coffee drink filtered via eggshells), whose name comes literally from the male and female names of Mandarin ducks who mate for life, and more figuratively from the complementary forces of yin and yang. When Lan Fong Yuen opened in the 1960s, the owner's wife sewed all the socks for their "silk stocking milk tea." Now they have them custom-made by a local seamstress. But that's not the real secret, says the guy manning the sixteen pots bubbling on the stove. The secret is not to boil your coffee and tea all sloppy, and then mix it all together! This process takes concentration and coordination, he says. If you really do it right, the whole process takes half an hour per pot.

—Tienlon Ho

Makes 4 servings

2½ tsp black tea leaves
4 eggshells, crushed into small shards
    (mostly uniform in size, each about
    ⅛ inch across)
1 cup coarsely ground coffee
+ sweetened condensed milk

SPECIAL EQUIPMENT
2 cotton coffee socks or 1 pair of new
    stockings

1. For the tea, mix the leaves with half of the crushed eggshells and put in a coffee sock or stocking. Bring 1 quart water to a high simmer in a pot, add the coffee sock, and steep at this steady temperature for at least 10 minutes.

2. For the coffee, mix the ground coffee with the rest of the crushed eggshells and put in a coffee sock or stocking. Pour 1 quart of 195°F water through the sock into a second pot set over a low flame. Pour that pot through the sock into a third pot set over the same flame. Repeat. You want the coffee water to pass through the sock a total of six times.

3. Fill a serving pot with the tea, then stir in sweetened condensed milk to taste (you'll want it overly sweet). Top off with an equal amount of coffee. (Lan Fong Yuen finds balance in an unbalanced 7:3 ratio of milk tea to coffee.)

4. Pour the yuen yueng into heavy mugs and serve.

Cowboys do it, too! A classic trick at church socials, camping trips, and anywhere there are no coffee filters is to drop a whole egg into coffee grounds, shell and all. The calcium in the shell neutralizes one of the seven main acids that can give coffee its acrid flavor. At the same time, the egg proteins bind to some of the bitter components, just the way egg white is used to clarify the tannins from wine, allowing them to be strained out.

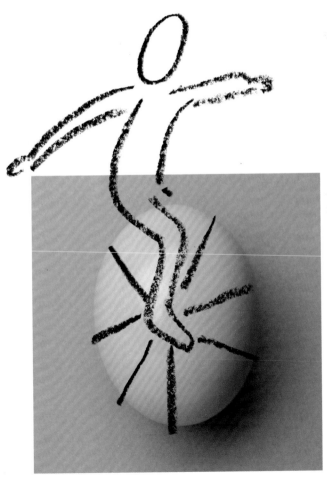

Crested Tinamou

Confetti-filled eggs from Mexico City

Life of the PARTY

Lucas Turner

The Easter egg hunt, as we know it today, is a cocktail of traditions and mythologies. Eostre was a fertility goddess, who, according to Anglo-Saxon legend, saved a broken-winged bird by transforming it into an egg-laying hare. During Easter in Germany, children are sent to find the hare's hidden egg nests. After the Christian church adopted the pagan festival of Eostre—which was a celebration of spring and fertility—as a way to celebrate Christ's resurrection, "Pace Eggs" followed. Eggs were dyed red to represent Christ's blood; the shell symbolized his three-day entombment—the breaking of which represented resurrection, and the breaking of the bonds of sin and death. In Lancashire, England, pace eggs are carefully boiled with onion skins to give their shells the appearance of mottled gold. Ukrainian pysanky eggs are intricately and brilliantly decorated with beeswax and successive dips into dye baths. In Germany and other central European countries, egg trees are made by stringing up emptied, painted eggshells with ribbons on evergreens or small leafless trees.

Today, the Easter egg hunt is executed in myriad ways: Some people plan out elaborate scavenger hunts with clues. (My own experience with them, growing up in California, was a free-for-all melee with eggs scattered around a park or backyard.) In Mexico, children bump *cascarones* (hollow chicken egg shells, painted and filled with confetti and sometimes small toys and sweets, closed again with a colored square of tissue paper) onto one another's heads. The most famed American Easter egg celebration is the White House Easter Egg Roll, a race where children push a decorated egg through the grass with a long-handled spoon, celebrated annually since the early nineteenth century. (President Rutherford B. Hayes made it an official White House event in 1878.) Different versions of the egg races abound in Scotland and England, mostly of the downhill variety.

Pisco Sour

When I went to Peru I drank so many pisco sours I thought I was tapped out forever. They make them in blenders over there because they make so many. A sour is a really good showcase for pisco—which I love as a spirit, because it's real floral, yet earthy. Support that with a little bit of citrus, and make it fluffy with the egg white, and it's a great introduction to pisco. Everyone likes it!

—*Meaghan Dorman, as told to Lauren Ro*

Makes 1 cocktail

½ oz fresh lime juice
½ oz fresh lemon juice
¾ oz simple syrup
2 oz pisco
1 small egg white (about 2 tbsp)
+ ice
+ Angostura bitters

1. Shake the citrus juices, simple syrup, pisco, and egg white briefly in a cocktail shaker to emulsify.

2. Add ice and shake again until the shaker is frosty. Strain into a coupe.

3. Add a few dashes of Angostura bitters onto the foam, then use a spoon or straw to make the bitters into a design.

Blue Grouse

Eggnog

George Washington, our country's first president and fan of innumerable boozes, loved eggnog especially. (Is it any coincidence that our first commander in chief, who hob-nobbed endlessly with powerful figures, was a fan of the world's most important food?) I can't really picture him swilling it (though I *can* picture him lovingly brushing his wig), but apparently George and Martha threw excellent parties at which they served a potent nog. They loved the stuff! This is the Washingtons' (adapted) recipe, which uses four kinds of alcohol and a dozen eggs. Of course, it serves a crowd.

Makes 24 servings

2 cups brandy
1 cup rye whiskey
1 cup Jamaican rum
½ cup dry sherry
12 eggs, separated
¾ cup sugar
4 cups milk
4 cups cream
+ nutmeg

1. Combine the brandy, whiskey, rum, and sherry in a large measuring cup.

2. Whisk the egg yolks and sugar in a large bowl until two shades paler, about 30 seconds. Add a few drops of the liquor and whisk to incorporate. Begin pouring the liquor in a thin, steady stream, whisking constantly. Add the milk, then the cream, in the same man-ner. Set the eggnog base aside.

3. Whip the egg whites to stiff peaks and then fold into the eggnog base. Pour the eggnog into a gallon container, like a jug, or four 1-quart jars. Cover and refriger-ate for at least 1 day and up to 2 weeks.

4. When ready to serve, pour into small glasses and grate nutmeg over. Serve cold.

It's ROM-PO-PAY

Naomi Tomky

That's how you pronounce *rompope*, the eggy Mexican drink that's ever present at holidays and special occasions. The ingredients—milk, sugar, spices, egg yolks, and rum—sound as much like the makings of a cookie as they do a beverage. So it's no surprise that rompope pops up in pastries and on dessert menus—as an ice cream flavor, fruit topping, and cake moistener.

It takes lots of egg yolks to get rompope to be its brilliant yellow color. Those yolks—aside from bequeathing their color—make for a creamy drink, smooth and velvety. The basic building blocks are similar to eggnog (and it is often described as Mexican eggnog), though it's made with cooked eggs—and only the yolks. Some versions are additionally thickened with nuts—usually almonds, though there are many variations (including the common and freakishly bright pink bottles colored by Mexico's pink pine nuts, as well as chocolate, pistachio, and walnut). Like American eggnog, it's often thought of as a holiday beverage, though that's spread to a general cheery reputation, meaning it's brought out for any special occasion, usually served chilled or over ice.

Versions of the drink abound in Latin America, but Puebla (birthplace of mole poblano and chiles en nogada, and a culinary center of Mexico) claims rights to the first and best version: Santa Clara brand, sold in large triangular bottles, is the original, named for the local convent whose nuns began producing the drink around 1600, after the Spanish introduced it. There, each nun had a culinary duty, including baking Santa Clara cookies and making *camote enmielado,* a crystallized sweet potato candy. Another of those jobs was to make what the Spanish had called *ponche de huevo,* or egg punch, rechristened rompope upon arrival in the New World. Sister Eduviges was the nun with the rompope gig, and it was her perfected recipe—she added an additional ingredient that she never revealed—that made the rompope wildly popular and profitable: It raised a lot of money for the convent. The story also goes that Sister Eduviges convinced the Mother Superior that the nuns be allowed to partake of their own product—and that was when the drink really took off.

Rompope

Mexico does it, too!

This rompope is a little lighter than the thirty-egg version I learned in culinary school but still decadent and aromatic from the addition of cinnamon and vanilla, and not too sweet. Drink it from a small chilled glass as a dessert or pour it on top of ice cream. Alternatively, you can serve it warm at a holiday party.

Cachaça, a distilled Brazilian sugarcane liquor, takes the place of the traditional Mexican *aguardiente,* which can be hard to find. (Cachaça adds a cleaner, more balanced flavor than the often-substituted rum.) You can also use a vanilla bean instead of extract for bigger vanilla flavor, or add a pinch of freshly grated nutmeg if you like. But definitely only use the egg yolks—adding the whites is a whole other drink.

The texture here is fairly thick; if you want it thinner, don't reduce the milk as much.

—*Lesley Téllez*

Makes 8 servings

5 cups whole milk
1 cup sugar
2 whole cloves
1 Mexican cinnamon stick (3 inches)
1 tsp vanilla extract
12 large egg yolks, beaten
¼ cup cachaça or rum, or to taste

1. Combine the milk, sugar, cloves, cinnamon stick, and vanilla in a large, heavy saucepan. Bring to a gentle boil over medium heat, stirring occasionally. Reduce the heat to medium-low and stir constantly until reduced by about one-third, 20 to 25 minutes. Let cool to room temperature.

2. Slowly whisk in the egg yolks and warm the mixture over very low heat. Stir constantly until thickened to an eggnog-like consistency, 10 to 15 minutes. Stir in the alcohol. Strain the mixture into a bowl and discard the cloves and cinnamon.

3. If serving chilled, prepare an ice bath by placing some ice cubes and a little cold water in a large bowl. Nestle the bowl containing the rompope inside. Refrigerate until cool, then transfer to an airtight container.

Indonesian Eggnog (STMJ)

Plying the underground walkways beneath Blok M, Jakarta's main bus terminal, hawkers entice morning and evening rush hour commuters with steamed or fried snacks. Their pushcarts—basically retrofitted cupboards or TV cabinets tricked out with bicycle tires on the sides and a peg-leg prop in front—go by the name of *kaki lima* ("five feet," i.e., three feet for the cart itself and two feet for the itinerant vendor behind).

Many kaki lima are gaudily painted and some blare loud Indo-pop. But the stall of Indra Kurniawan and his wife, Nena, is relatively understated: just a grapefruit-size rotating mirrored disco ball and a stream of cool Sundanese flute music to evoke the misty hills of West Java that rise above Jakarta's urban sprawl.

The Kurniawans sell a Sundanese potion designed to bolster the sick and weary and to rekindle flagging libidos on the cool winter nights in those misty hills. It's a recipe so simple and so cherished that it is denoted by just the initials of its key ingredients: milk, egg, honey, and ginger (*susu, telor, madu, jahe*). But it requires a deft touch with a wire whisk and a blowtorch, cautions the Kurniawans' fifteen-year-old son, Rakka, who runs the Blok M stall most nights.

—Melati Kaye

Makes 1 drink

3 egg yolks
1 tsp honey
2 tbsp sweetened condensed milk
1½ tsp ground cinnamon
¼ tsp ground nutmeg
¼ tsp ground cloves
¼ tsp ground black sesame seeds
    (optional)
¼ tsp ground ginseng root (optional)
+ **Ginger Tea** (recipe follows)
3 whole cloves, for garnish

1. Place the yolks in a cocktail shaker along with the honey, sweetened condensed milk, and ground spices.

2. Hold a small whisk at the center of the shaker and twirl until the concoction is fully mixed and slightly frothy.

3. Pour one-quarter of the frothy egg mixture into a heatproof serving cup. Toast the surface with a blowtorch to caramelize to a light brown color. Repeat with two more additions, toasting each time. Add about ½ cup ginger tea, or to taste. Add the final frothy addition of egg and toast again.

4. Arrange the whole cloves on top of the drink for garnish. Serve with a small glass of ginger tea the drinkers can use to dilute the potion to their preferred sweetness levels.

Ginger Tea

Makes enough for 8 servings

½ lb fresh ginger
8 cups water

1. Wash and towel dry the ginger. Roast over a charcoal flame, grill, or gas flame until lightly charred.

2. Pound the ginger with a mortar and pestle. (Alternatively, lay the ginger out on a plastic cutting board and smash with the flat side of a cleaver or a rolling pin.)

3. Put the ginger in a saucepan and fill with water (the roots should be submerged). Bring to a rolling boil, reduce the heat, and cook for 10 more minutes.

4. Strain and reserve the spicy tea in a warm spot.

White-Winged Chough

Vietnamese Egg Soda

When I visited Vietnam for the first time recently, I was surprised (and overjoyed!) to learn that people there love to drink eggs. I tried an "egg coffee"—strong, sweet coffee with a whole egg in it (the whites make an even more voluptuous foam than milk). *Soda sua hot ga* is another eggy beverage, which on the menu at my local pho shop, Pho Tan Hoa in San Francisco's Tenderloin, is listed as "Soda with egg york." Unlike the American egg cream, which contains neither egg nor cream, Vietnamese egg soda is made with eggs AND soda. And condensed milk, which nobody doesn't love.

Makes 1 drink

1 egg
1 cup club soda
2½ tbsp sweetened condensed milk
+ ice

1. Crack the egg into a large drinking glass. Puncture the yolk with a fork and beat until mixed, about 30 seconds. Add the club soda—slowly, in case it wants to bubble out—and stir vigorously until the soda is incorporated with the yolk and uniformly pale yellow, another 30 seconds or so.

2. Mix in the condensed milk (more or less to taste) and stir vigorously to dissolve and to refroth the drink.

3. Add ice cubes and drink right away!

Chocolate Eggs

Alison Kinney

Eggs are so fundamentally about origins that even egg-shaped chocolates, which generally contain no egg, can't help but point back to their antecedents. Half the pleasure—or disgust—in a Cadbury Creme Egg comes from its uncanniness: the fragile chocolate shell, the oozy innards, the fondant flavor whose intensity rivals that of a soft-cooked yolk. Then there's the Kinder Surprise: What's in that shell—food, fowl, or foul? They confuse and titillate our eyes and tongues; they evoke egginess when no real eggs are in sight.

Chocolate eggs are for philosophers, lovers, and Christians. In 1902, the French teachers' journal *Manuel général de l'instruction primaire* published a romance, "Easter Story," in which a chocolate egg transformed the love life of a melancholy schoolteacher. A century later, the (fabricated) tale of a Perugian couple's mishap with a diamond engagement ring inside a dark chocolate egg—exchanged, by the lady, for a milk chocolate egg—went viral in the Italian media. Researchers have given children chocolate eggs to test the bounds of friendship; Slavoj Žižek has used chocolate eggs to test our patience with his ideas on the central void of subjectivity; Ludwig Wittgenstein had

the good sense just to give them as gifts to friends. At the outbreak of WWI, little Simone Weil was so moved by the suffering of war that, at Easter, she donated her chocolate egg to the soldiers. And in her 1986 performance *The Constant State of Desire,* artist Karen Finley "got gourmet Easter egg candy to sell. I sell these Easter eggs to gourmet chocolate shops," in a way the Wall Street traders would never recover from.

In the chocolate shops of Paris, the Easter Chocolatier has laid the Easter eggs. It means springtime is here, gorgeous in pastel royal icing, edible gold, and velvety cocoa powder. At La Maison du Chocolat, a daisy with a mustache sprouts from a chocolate egg. Arnaud Larher has made clown- and elephant-eggs for the kiddies and glorious chocolate eggs bearing priestly breastplates made of *mendiants* for the adults. At Jean-Charles Rochoux's shop, a giraffe hatches from one massive chocolate egg, and the bust of a bewigged man—the seventeenth-century playwright Molière—looms from another. Choco-Story, the Musée Gourmand du Chocolat in Paris, is preparing a giant chocolate egg for children to destroy with tiny hammers on Easter. (How giant? "Big, but not big enough to fall over on them," a clerk tells me.)

My egg hunt had started in February in New York, when I took the subway to Jacques Torres's chocolate factory on Brooklyn's industrial waterfront. In the kitchens, pastry chefs painted chocolate molds, turning out bemused ducklings and saucy bunnies. In the lunchroom, Torres and I, wearing hairnets, hunched over his phone looking up the history of chocolate eggs.

In his native France, the traditional Easter symbols include eggs, fish, bells, and hens, but Torres noted, "In America, it's rabbits. We sell more rabbits than eggs. I actually have a bell mold, but nobody buys them!" Eggs, though, inspire him. "Eggs are a very interesting topic. I think that has something to do with the baby. The egg is a symbol of birth, renewing, beginning, spring!" Easter eggs date at least to 1290, when England's Edward I spent eighteen pence on 450 colored, gold-leafed eggs. But many cultures around the world have regarded eggs as symbols of

creation, birth, fertility—or death or witchcraft. Egg-decorating traditions have crossed the boundaries of paganism, Judaism, Islam, Christianity, and communism, reinventing folk practices around the world, especially in Eastern Europe.

What came first, the chocolate chicken or the chocolate egg? The chocolate egg may even predate the invention of solid chocolate. The sixteenth-century introduction of Aztec cacao to Europe created another hot chocolate–drinking culture. At Versailles, chocolate was whipped with sugar, almonds or orange flower water, and—wait for it—an egg yolk. According to Elisabeth de Contenson in *Chocolat et son histoire* (2010), it was the eighteenth-century chocolate-drinkers who first blew out a chicken eggshell to fill with drinking chocolate. Voilà: chocolate egg! The 1830s saw the first molds for shaping solid chocolates—including egg shapes— and the chocolatiers never looked back.

If there's something elementary about ovoid symbolism, the chocolate egg also constitutes part of a pastry chef's elementary education. Jürgen David, Senior Coordinator of Pastry Arts at New York's International Culinary Center, supervises students in tempering and molding chocolate eggs, then using the eggs for building. "If you think of the shape of a bunny or teddy bear, you can make a big egg that's the body, and smaller eggs for the feet. If the eggs are hollow, they can become ears." Even in France, there's only so much a chocolatier can do with a whelk or an Easter bell. Eggs, on the other hand, are fundamental forms whose simplicity provides opportunity for creativity, meaning, and humor.

One chocolate egg summons up not only confectionary history but also the origins in the chicken egg. All over Paris they're sold, singly from wire egg baskets or six at a time in egg cartons. I buy mine at Rochoux's: a chocolate *"oeuf dur,"* or hard-boiled egg. It's a real brown chicken eggshell, containing a hard chocolate shell filled with luscious hazelnut praline. Ronald Bilheux and Alain Escoffier, in the French Professional Pastry Series, called this an "Oeuf Surprise": "Very often purchased by our clientele to be put in the gardens on Easter—it's really a surprise egg!" How am I supposed to eat it? The staff at Rochoux's say, "Cut it with a knife, and eat it like any egg!"

Surprise eggs are commonly sold in Parisian bakeries and supermarkets, as well as chocolate shops, but they aren't common in the United States; usually it's intrepid food bloggers who make them at home. It must be said that ganache eggs are fussy to eat. Like fresh hard-boiled eggs, they're the damnedest things to peel; chips get stuck in the chocolate. Digging the ganache out with a spoon just feels anticlimactic.

All the same, they're magical. They use the eggshell itself—the inedible, discarded, beautiful-till-cracked eggshell, upon which the egg depends for its characteristic form— and turn it into a chocolate mold. Chocolate eggs were born inside real eggshells, and now they're back, as mysterious and strange as they ever were. In a way, they effect a resurrection of both chocolate and eggs, forcing us to rethink the uses of foods so common we hardly even register their marvelousness, telling us nearly forgotten food histories, restoring origins we didn't even know they had. Spring is here, beginning all over again.

6.

EGG VOGUE

The egg is timeless. But it's not immune to being the subject of our fashions—falling into style, and then falling out of it again (say, when new scientific research launches us into concern over our cholesterol levels and egg white omelets sweep the nation). Once upon a time, circa the 1960s, the soufflé was big (though mysterious, too)—thanks to Julia Child. During the years we unconscionably loved Jell-O, people put whole eggs into their molded creations (in France, they loved *oeufs en gelée,* hard-boiled eggs suspended in aspic [page 207]). Then came the 1970s, when the quiche was particularly in style—though real men didn't eat it. Salads with eggy components and/ or dressings—Caesar, green goddess, Cobb—took the runway. In the 1980s, we ate deviled eggs in our shoulder-padded power suits. The 1990s brought the sous-vide egg into the spotlight, made in a machine that could hold an egg at a steady temperature for a perfectly rendered yolk. Then there are the twentieth and twenty-first century's vaunted eggs of fine dining: Alain Passard's egg with crème fraîche and syrup; Juan Mari Arzak's poached egg; René Redzepi's hen and egg. They were innovations, to be sure, but also prime examples of eggs as occupying—and representing!—a specific moment in human time. There are the tools we use to cook and alter our eggs, changing through the years, yet the same: the in-shell scramblers, the omelet pans, the cups and coddlers and platters.

The stylish egg—trendy one decade, then disdained the next! Like bell-bottoms, we wear an egg one way, then cast it aside for another style entirely. These days we Instagram eggs with their bright orange yolks, oozing from atop toast or into ramen (follow @all_about_eggs).

Eggs in vogue not only tell us about the world we live in, they hold a mirror up to who we are: our hopes, our fears, our dreams, our ingenuity, our ineptitude. Eggs are us, and we are eggs.

Soufflé

The soufflé is a dish that proves eggs are perfect. The French soufflé dates back to the eighteenth century and is credited to the chef Antoine Beauvilliers (who was also possibly the first restaurateur in history to ever provide menus). The French verb *souffler* means "to blow," which is a constant reminder that soufflés have a reputation as a high-pressure food (*don't blow it!*). But soufflés are way easier to make than the fearmongers would have us believe. They won't fall if you make a loud noise. It's not that hard to get them to rise, if you understand the basic principles: A soufflé is frothed egg whites, plus some other stuff, that get puffed up when baked.

That said, a few guidelines are: (1) Use the right dish to hold your soufflé. The traditional soufflé dish is porcelain with straight sides, but you could use any ovenproof vessel, as long as it's the right size: Your soufflé batter should almost reach three-quarters or seven-eighths the way up. (2) Do not overbeat the egg whites! (3) Always serve your soufflé in the dish it was baked in. Don't try to transfer it to another dish.

Makes 4 servings

3 tbsp butter
2 tbsp very finely grated parmesan cheese
3 tbsp all-purpose flour
1 cup whole milk
1 tsp salt
¼ tsp freshly grated nutmeg
⅛ tsp cayenne pepper
½ tsp mustard powder
4 egg yolks, at room temperature
1 cup packed coarsely grated gruyère cheese
6 egg whites, at room temperature

1. Remove all the racks from your oven except the bottommost rack. Heat the oven to 400°F.

2. Butter a 6-cup soufflé dish (using 1 tablespoon of the butter) and sprinkle with the parmesan as you would flour a pan, tapping out the excess.

3. Melt the remaining 2 tablespoons butter in a heavy-bottomed saucepan over medium heat. Add the flour, then the milk, and heat until foamy, whisking until thickened. Remove from the heat, and add the salt, nutmeg, cayenne, and mustard. Whisk the yolks in one at a time, blending after each addition, then whisk in the gruyère until melted. Let cool to room temperature.

4. While the base is cooling, whip the egg whites until they're glossy and hold stiff peaks.

5. Fold the whipped whites into the soufflé base in three additions, incorporating until just streaky after each addition. Do not overmix. Transfer to the soufflé dish.

6. Bake for 25 minutes without peeking (though it's not the end of the world if you do). The soufflé should be puffed and golden, and should jiggle a bit. Serve right away!

Quiche Lorraine

Real men don't eat quiche, according to a 1982 book by Bruce Feirstein, which was on the *New York Times* Best Seller list for 55 weeks and sold over 1.6 million copies (just like this book, what a coincidence!). The book actually satirized gender norms. Which is to say, everyone can eat quiche, and cook it, too.

Makes 4 servings

6 oz bacon, diced
1 cup finely chopped onions
+ salt
4 eggs
1 cup half-and-half
¼ cup chopped chives
+ freshly ground black pepper
+ freshly grated nutmeg
+ baked **Pie Crust** (page 178)
1 cup grated gruyère, Swiss, or cheddar cheese

1. Heat the oven to 400°F.

2. Put the bacon in a cold, medium skillet and set over medium heat. Once the bacon sizzles, stir it occasionally and cook until crisp and well rendered, about 8 minutes. Remove the bacon from the pan with a slotted spoon.

3. Add the onions to the bacon fat. Fold them over in the fat, season lightly with salt, and sweat, folding occasionally, until they are a light, even caramel color and completely translucent, 10 to 15 minutes. Using a slotted spoon, transfer the onions to a bowl. Discard any remaining fat in the pan.

4. Whisk the eggs, half-and-half, and chives in a bowl and season generously with salt, pepper, and nutmeg. Set aside.

5. Build the quiche: Dump the bacon and onions into the cooled pie crust and spread into an even layer. Pour the egg mixture over the filling. Sprinkle with the cheese.

6. Bake until the quiche is golden brown and the custard is set, 40 to 50 minutes. Let cool to room temperature before serving.

Accoutrements

Karen Leibowitz

Ensconced in their shells, eggs are perfectly packaged and self-contained. Yet something about human nature compels us to dress our eggs up with all manner of tools and trimmings—perhaps because we feel a bit inadequate, as mammals, in the presence of an eggshell, and that spurs us to overcompensate with everything from specialized cooking tools to ostentatious tableware.

Whatever the reason, eggs activate our urge to accessorize, and every age has its own favored egg accoutrements, which reflect each era's particular cultural anxiety. Whereas egg appurtenances once testified to the class status of those who could afford to pay others to serve them from the proper dish, the twentieth century gave rise to egg-related tools meant to demonstrate culinary mastery and streamline cooking techniques. As food historian Dr. Megan Elias pointed out, when domestic help became less and less common during the period between the Depression and the Second World War, our treatment of eggs began to reflect a new focus on cooking as a form of socializing. "When the food is on display as a finished product, those things are more likely to be from the early-twentieth century, when

middle-class people were more likely to have servants," Elias said. "Things that show off your cooking are late-twentieth century, when people started to go into each other's kitchens, and cooking became more of the entertainment."

So what can we deduce from the appearance of newfangled egg objets of the twenty-first century, like bento egg shapers and in-the-shell-scramblers? Maybe that egg eaters of the twenty-first century want to have it all, to be our own servants and our own domestic goddesses at once. We want to make our eggs cute, novel, and likeable. In that sense, the archetypal contemporary egg accessory is Instagram (*cough* @all_about_eggs).

Eggcups are the original ovoid accessories, designed to mimic and bolster an eggshell while its boiled contents are spooned out. Archaeologists have found evidence of stone eggcups from Crete that date back to the eighteenth century BCE, and silver eggcups were discovered among the ruins of Pompeii. Eggcups became a standard part of many European banquets in the fifteenth century, but really gained traction in the nineteenth and early twentieth centuries, when European table manners were particularly centered on specialized place settings and dishes. Designs range from the simplest of ceramics to whimsical plastic chickens to postmodern metal prongs. And eggcups inspire enthusiasm: Collectors call themselves "pocillovists."

Deviled Egg Plates were first crafted in the late 1880s, probably inspired by oyster plates, but they really came into their own around the turn of the twentieth century, when deviling became a national fad. While Northerners in the United States liked to devil shellfish, Southerners were inclined toward deviled eggs, which were often brought to picnics, or displayed on specialized platters for indoor gatherings. "Deviled egg plates are particularly Southern," according to Liz Williams, president of the Southern Food and Beverage Museum in New Orleans. Williams said that Southern dinnerware generally includes a deviled egg plate, usually with a dozen egg-size divots arranged around a central

dipping area for extra deviled egg salad, and that it is also common for Southerners to own an additional deviled egg plate that could be used with other china sets as well. During the postwar period, the egg-size divots and bonus dipping area of deviled egg plates offered a flexible design palette for personal expression, ranging from fancy etched glass to whimsical chicken-themed ceramics, and hostesses prided themselves on their choices.

Egg Cartons in their current form—molded recycled paper, polystyrene, or clear plastic dimples topped with a flat lid—are so standardized that they seem almost timeless. In fact, the ubiquitous egg carton design was created in the 1950s, by H.G. Bennett, as an improvement upon the first egg carton invented in 1918 by Joseph Doyle and in response to postwar shopping patterns, which required eggs to be shipped from rural suppliers to urban supermarkets. These days, eggs are almost always labeled by size and sold by the dozen or half-dozen, but it was not always so. Until the dawn of the egg carton, eggs were often transported in boxes or baskets and sold by volume, weight, or individual egg.

Quiche Pans, Soufflé Dishes, and Crepe Griddles got a big boost in the early 1960s from Julia Child. Her bestselling cookbook, *Mastering the Art of French Cooking,* introduced the American public to cooking exotic foreign egg dishes, with recipes like her famous quiche Lorraine, while her award-winning TV show, *The French Chef,* revolutionized kitchen design. As Dr. Megan Elias explained, "In the fifties, all the cabinets are closed, but in the Julia Child era, people had stuff on pegboards, so you could see it. Cooking became more of the entertainment." When Julia Child hung a copper saucepan on the pegboard wall of her kitchen, it led the way to Sur La Table and the aestheticization of specialized cooking tools, for eggs and otherwise.

Single-Function Egg-Cooking Gadgets flourished in the 1980s and '90s, when convenience started to replace common sense in the kitchen. An inexperienced cook might buy into the egg piercer's dire warnings about cracked boiled eggs; the squeamish might prefer an egg separator to good old-fashioned fingers; but it's not clear what sort of person purchases a "hand powered 'in-shell' egg shaker," which makes it possible to beat an egg before it's cracked. Or perhaps these simplified egg-cooking tools are all meant for children. Margaret Fox, restaurateur and author of the egg chapter in the 1997 *Joy of Cooking,* harbors some fond memories of an egg poacher she used as a child: "You'd crack your egg into it and put it into simmering water with a lid. That would be the first way of poaching eggs without dealing with the wildness and the vinegar. When I was little and I made those, it really felt like cooking."

Egg Shapers such as egg rings have a long history in short-order restaurants, where a fried egg needs to fit neatly on a bun or an English muffin, but there's now a market for egg rings shaped like hearts, stars, guns, and genitals as well. The most traditional "egg ring," of course, is hollowed-out toast in a classic egg-in-the-basket preparation that's delighted children for generations. And though Japanese bento lunches date back to the sixteenth century, Japanese mothers today use plastic bento molds to press hard-boiled eggs into bunnies, bears, and frogs. Parents work behind the scenes to ensure that their children can have the most enviable lunch boxes, like domestic servants of yesteryear. And so we come full circle, and eggs are still the medium for our social anxieties.

Eggs in Aspic

Tatiana Levha, chef at Le Servan in Paris, serves her take on French *oeufs en gelée* at her corner bistro in the 11th arrondissement (which, if you're ever in Paris, you need to get to *tout de suite*. It's so good!). "Oeufs en gelée is something you find in very traditional butcher shops," Tatiana explains. An egg with vegetables suspended in meat broth gelatin: It was a way to use leftover meat jelly from charcuterie preparations. Along with an inexpensive egg, it made for "a way to combine everything and feed people." "It's a funny idea to put an egg in jelly," Tatiana agrees. Her version is a soft-boiled egg with an oozy yolk, a mound of salad (celery, or sometimes fava beans), trout roe, and scoops of aspic. "Between the egg yolk and the jelly and the fish roe, it's all very slimy, and it's strong. That's the idea," she explains. "It's also a bit strange because it's soft, but also cold. Some people find it too weird." I find it weird in the best way—surprising, and really good.

Makes 4 servings

2 tbsp cold water
2 tsp unflavored gelatin powder
2 cups beef or vegetable stock
¼ cup katsuobushi (dried bonito flakes)
1 tbsp soy sauce
1 tsp black vinegar
+ salt
1 cup peeled fava beans or 1 cup
    ½-inch pieces celery, cut at an angle
1 tbsp olive oil
4 eggs
¼ cup herbs or celery leaves
4 oz trout roe

1. Pour the water into a small bowl and sprinkle the gelatin over. Let stand until the gelatin is translucent.

2. Bring the stock to a simmer in a saucepan and stir in the katsuobushi. Remove from the heat and let stand for 5 minutes. Strain and season with the soy sauce, black vinegar, and a pinch of salt. The broth should be smoky and well seasoned. Stir the gelatin into the hot broth until completely dissolved. Let cool to room temperature, then refrigerate until firm, at least 6 hours.

3. Meanwhile, blanch the favas in a pot of boiling salted water until just tender, 2 to 3 minutes. Drain and transfer to a bowl. Toss with the olive oil and season lightly with salt.

4. Soft-boil the eggs: Bring water to a boil in a saucepan, then add the eggs. Cook for 4½ minutes. Remove, rinse with cold water until cool enough to handle, then carefully peel.

5. Place a peeled egg on each of 4 serving dishes, then scoop about ½ cup of the aspic around each egg. Add the herbs to the favas and toss again. Divide among the plates, arranging them prettily. Add a couple of large spoonfuls of the trout roe right next to the egg, over the aspic and favas, and serve.

Caesar Salad

My friend Tod Chubrich made this particular Caesar salad one evening in San Francisco in 2008 and I still remember everyone eating it ravenously, without forks, like it was pizza. I emailed Tod for his recipe afterward, and have been using this dressing for the last near-decade (sometimes with kale, which it is also amazing with). Recently I emailed him to ask for permission to reprint the recipe here. He wrote, "OMG Rachel! My life is now complete. I can't believe you've been using it all these years!" He elaborated with some notes, which further prove why Tod is the best: "In my book there are two schools of Caesar salad: the traditional style, for which the Zuni recipe is basically canonical and impossible to improve on, and the creamy style, which is more common and is usually mediocre at best—unless I make it! My inspiration was the glorious Caesar at my favorite lunch spot in high school, the dearly departed Café Louis in Boston, at the time a satellite of the legendary Al Forno in Providence. I think their recipe used pecorino instead of parmesan, but with a lot of tinkering I arrived at something delicious if not identical to the original."

Makes 2 to 4 servings
(1½ cups dressing)

1 egg
3 tbsp fresh lemon juice
4 salt-packed anchovies, rinsed and
    patted dry
¾ cup extra-virgin olive oil, plus more
    for the croutons
1 garlic clove, peeled
+ coarse salt
1 cup finely grated parmesan cheese,
    plus more for garnish
3 cups 1-inch cubes baguette
2 tbsp butter, melted (optional)
1 large head romaine lettuce, leaves
    separated and washed

1. Drop the egg in a blender and add the lemon juice and anchovies and blend until smooth. Drizzle the oil into the blender until you have a smooth creamy dressing. Scrape the dressing into a bowl.

2. Smash the garlic clove onto a cutting board, sprinkle with coarse salt, and scrape into a paste with the side of a chef's knife. Scrape up and add to the bowl with the dressing. Add the parmesan and stir until well blended. The dressing can be stored in the fridge for up to 2 days.

3. Heat the oven to 325°F.

4. Place the bread in a bowl and drizzle with a little oil and the melted butter (if using), tossing so the croutons become coated but not soaked. Season with salt and dump into a single layer on a baking sheet. Bake until crunchy and a bit golden, about 10 minutes.

5. Either toss the romaine with the dressing or arrange on dinner plates and drizzle with the dressing. Scatter some croutons and parmesan to finish.

Steakhouse Salad

I love House of Prime Rib in San Francisco because it's like time-machining yourself back half a century. Their prime rib comes in a silver blimp and you get a whole little shaker of martini, and the salad gets dressed and spinned over ice by a man in a chef's hat, then doled to you with great bravado. But unlike some other good-for-the-old-timey-ambience, less-for-the-food San Francisco establishments (looking at you, Tadich Grill), the food is both nostalgic and delicious. I am obsessed with their retro spinning salad, not least of all because it is EGGY.

Makes 4 servings

2 handfuls 1-inch torn pieces romaine lettuce
2 handfuls 1-inch torn pieces iceberg lettuce
1 handful watercress leaves
1 roasted or canned beet, cut into matchsticks
1 tomato, chopped
1 **Hard-Boiled Egg** (page 90), chopped
½ cup sourdough croutons
about ¼ cup **Steakhouse Dressing,** more or less to taste (recipe follows)
+ freshly ground black pepper

1. Place the salad greens in a large salad bowl. Arrange the beets and tomato over the greens and sprinkle the egg on top. Top with the croutons.

2. Pour the steakhouse dressing over the greens, and use your hands to toss well. Add more dressing if it needs it. To serve, heap high on plates and grind fresh pepper all over.

Steakhouse Dressing
Makes about 1 cup

3 tbsp apple cider vinegar
2 tsp Worcestershire sauce
1 tsp dry sherry
1½ tsp Lawry's seasoned salt
2 tbsp mayonnaise
1 tbsp sugar
½ tsp Hungarian sweet paprika
1 tbsp chopped parsley or 1 tsp dried
½ tsp mustard powder
¼ tsp cayenne pepper
1 **Hard-Boiled Egg** (page 90)
¼ cup olive oil

1. In a blender, combine everything but the olive oil. Blend on high until smooth.

2. With the motor running, slowly add the oil through the lid's hole until combined. Refrigerate until serving.

Arpège Egg

Chef Alain Passard's Arpège egg, the *chaud-froid oeuf* (hot-cold egg), is THE most famous egg in the Western restaurant world—widely imitated, never duplicated . . . though here's a recipe, anyway. At L'Arpège in Paris, the egg comes at any point Passard decides, if at all, during a meal so abundant and many-coursed that Eli, my delicate, all-things-in-moderation boyfriend, was shaken to his very core, beyond repair. This is the egg from my wildest dreams: tantalizingly warm-yolked yet cold-white-d, splashed with maple syrup and vinegary cream, served in a silver stand with a little silver spoon, and flawless.

Makes 4 eggs

¼ cup heavy cream
¾ tsp sugar
½ tsp sherry vinegar
4 eggs
4 tsp maple syrup
+ salt
1 tbsp minced chives
+ freshly ground black pepper

1. Position racks in the upper and lower thirds of the oven and heat the oven to 400°F.

2. Whip the cream to stiff peaks. Incorporate the sugar and sherry vinegar right at the end. Transfer the whipped cream to a pastry bag outfitted with a smallish (about ½-inch-diameter) tip (fluted, if you want to get fancy). This will hold in the refrigerator for a few hours.

3. Cut the tops off the eggs. You'll want to take off around a sixth of the narrower end of the shell. If you have the skills and a sharp-enough blade, more power to you, do it with a paring knife. Otherwise buy a good-quality egg topper online and use that. Gently dump the contents of the eggs out into a small bowl and even more gently use your finger to remove all the white and gooey stuff left inside the eggshell. Separate the yolks from the whites and return the yolks to their shells. (Save the whites for another use, like making meringue, page 176.)

4. Place the eggshells in ovenproof egg-cups. Add 1 teaspoon of maple syrup and a pinch of salt to each eggshell. Arrange the eggcups in a shallow baking pan. Fill with about 1 inch of very hot water and place on the upper rack of the oven. Bake for 5 to 7 minutes. The goal is to warm the yolks, to give them some body and make them a little bit more unctuous, not to cook or poach them completely.

5. Remove the eggs from the pan and fill each with whipped cream. The finished egg should have a peak of piped cream rising out of the top of the eggshell like the snowcap on a mountain. Scatter that snowcap with a pinch or two of minced chives and a twist of freshly ground black pepper. Serve at once.

Arzak Egg

The lovely and generous Nadine Redzepi, who's married to René Redzepi of the lauded Noma in Copenhagen, maintains a ridiculously beautiful Instagram of the things she cooks for her family. Every once in a while she'll post a photo of eggs as little bundles—eggs she's poached in plastic wrap, a technique that's the signature of Spanish chef Juan Mari Arzak. I emailed to ask her why she likes making Arzak eggs, and she wrote: "The main reason is the amount of seasoning and flavor that you can wrap in to the egg because it's in the cling film. When I poach eggs the traditional way I lose half of the egg white. This way there's no waste. Another of my favorite reasons for Arzak eggs is you can make a lot of them at the same time so easily. We are 6 people in our family so being able to make 8 to 10 eggs at the same time really means something. :) Our favorite thing to eat at home is roasted chicken and we always make stock with the toasted bones after. Two poached eggs in there is amazing! Sometimes I'll save the chicken fat from the roasting pan (that the roasted chicken was in) and put a spoonful of that in with the egg. Sometime herbs go in there too, it kind of depends on what I have around and what I'm going to eat the eggs with. Every time I make them it also makes me think of Juan Mari, and that puts a smile on my face."

Makes 1 to 4 eggs

+ olive oil
1 to 4 eggs
+ salt

1. Drape a large square of plastic wrap over a shallow bowl. It should extend well beyond the edges of the bowl. Brush the plastic with olive oil to keep the egg from sticking to the wrap.

2. Crack an egg into the center of the bowl. Sprinkle it with salt. Gather the ends of the plastic wrap together and twist them closed. You'll end up with a bulbous balloon with a raw egg in it, and a loose cord of plastic wrap. Tightly tie a foot-long piece of kitchen twine around the plastic-wrap cord, just above the egg, sealing it off. Trim off the wrap above the twine. Repeat for each egg.

3. Bring a large pot of water to a boil, then drop it down to a simmer. Lower the eggs into the pot. Tie the twine to a chopstick or ladle laid across the top of the pot to make sure the eggs are suspended about halfway into the water—they shouldn't touch the bottom. Simmer for 4 minutes 20 seconds.

4. To finish, remove the eggs from the heat and transfer them to a cutting board. Let the eggs sit for a minute or so, then carefully cut off the plastic wrap. Deploy at will.

BEYOND the Plate: Eggs in Medicine, Art, and Winemaking

Bridget Huber

Semen Extender

Whether issued by an anonymous donor or a prize stallion, the semen used for artificial insemination needs to be preserved until it reaches its intended target, usually by chilling or freezing. But that can hurt the little swimmers, which may be poisoned by toxic by-products that semen itself creates as it ages, or damaged by freezing and thawing. So semen extenders—often made from yolks—are added to the mix to protect and nourish the sperm until their fateful rendezvous with the egg.

Flu Vaccine

Each year, over a billion chicken eggs are used to make the flu vaccine. A tiny needle injects the live virus into a laboratory-grade fertile egg, where the virus multiplies for a few days. Then, the teeming liquid is mechanically sucked from the shell and inactivated. It's mixed with the other strains of flu virus destined for that year's shot and injected into deltoids everywhere.

Tempera Paint

From ancient Egypt to the late Renaissance, most artists painted with egg tempera, generally made by mixing yolk, pigment, and a liquid like water, vinegar, or wine. Tempera has to be applied in thin layers on smooth surfaces, but, unlike oil paint, its vivid colors don't darken over time. Botticelli's *The Birth of Venus* was painted in egg tempera, Michelangelo used it for his panel paintings, and monks used a version made with egg whites to illuminate manuscripts. When oil paint hit the scene in the 1500s it mostly displaced egg tempera, but not entirely: Marc Chagall and Andrew Wyeth were egg tempera devotees and it's still used to paint Orthodox icons.

Fining Agent

Winemakers use "fining agents" to clarify wines and temper astringency and bitterness. Egg whites are one of the most common— usually at a dose of 1 to 5 egg whites per 60 gallons of wine. The whites are said to give red wines a softer taste and their proteins bind with the tiny particles that cloud wine to make larger molecules that settle at the bottom. Using lots of whites means you're left with lots of yolks, and it's thought that canelés, the custardy, caramelized little cakes, were first made by nuns in Bordeaux with yolks they got from winemakers.

Wound Dressing

Long used in Chinese medicine, eggshell membranes have been studied as a dressing for skin grafts and severe burns and even to patch ruptured eardrums. The membranes are cheap, readily available, and, in some studies, seemed to promote healing and discourage infection or allergic reactions.

Alternative Packaging

Researchers are working to make bioplastics from egg whites that would be an alternative to petroleum-based food packaging and would be biodegradable and antimicrobial to boot.

Antidote

Scientists are working to develop infection-fighting eggs. When a chicken—or any other animal—is exposed to a virus or bacteria, it develops antibodies to it. A hen passes those antibodies to her offspring in the egg, just as a human mother does to a fetus. Scientists have harvested these antibodies—called avian immunoglobulins or IgY— from chicken eggs and successfully used them to provide temporary immunity against a number of bacteria and viruses including salmonella, *H. pylori* (which can cause ulcers and stomach cancer), norovirus (aka the stomach flu), and gingivitis (causes gum disease); and they may even provide an antidote for snake bites.

Egg Substitute Guide

Lucas Turner

EGG SUBSTITUTE	Leavener	Binder	Emulsifier	Pancakes	Cake	Brownies	Quick Bread	Soufflé	Scramble	Mayo	Meringue
Agar		✓		✓	✓	✓	✓				
Applesauce		✓	✓	✓	✓	✓	✓				
Baking soda and vinegar	✓			✓	✓	✓	✓			✓	
Bananas		✓	✓	✓	✓	✓	✓				
Blood	✓	✓	✓	✓	✓	✓	✓				✓
Buttermilk	✓		✓	✓	✓	✓	✓				
Chia seeds		✓		✓	✓	✓	✓				
Chickpea liquid (aquafaba)	✓	✓	✓	✓	✓	✓	✓	✓		✓	✓
Commercial egg replacer	✓			✓	✓	✓					
Cornstarch/potato starch/arrowroot flour		✓		✓	✓	✓	✓				
Flaxseed meal		✓		✓		✓	✓				
Gelatin		✓	✓		✓	✓	✓	✓			
Soy lecithin		✓	✓	✓	✓	✓					
Tofu		✓	✓	✓	✓	✓	✓		✓	✓	

Agar

Agar is a carbohydrate sourced from sea algae; more specifically, it is a complex mixture of polysaccharides composed of two major fractions: agarose, a neutral polymer, and agaropectin, a charged, sulfated polymer. When mixed with water, agar forms a vast gummy network similar to denatured egg protein. The tangled networks entrap moisture in baking and keep ingredients evenly dispersed.

CONS: It is useful only as a binder. Texturally, agar makes things stiffer and less creamy.

USE: 1 tbsp agar + 1 tbsp water = 1 egg

Applesauce

Moist and high in pectin fiber, apples are somewhat like bananas, and applesauce is a good egg substitute in certain baking applications.

CONS: Applesauce is generally high in sugar; even unsweetened applesauce will have much more sugar than eggs. It is not suitable as a leavener, so your cake will be denser and moister with every egg you replace.

USE: ¼ cup applesauce = 1 egg

Baking Soda and Vinegar

Sodium bicarbonate (baking soda) reacts with any acidic component to create carbon dioxide, which pushes and expands (and therefore leavens) the matter around it.

CONS: You only want to use this method in recipes with relatively few eggs to replace, to mitigate the vinegar from overwhelming the flavor profile. Baked goods also won't brown as deeply.

USE: 1 tsp baking soda + 1 tbsp vinegar = 1 egg

Bananas

A very ripe banana's starch, fiber, and high moisture content make it an effective binder in certain baking applications.

CONS: Bananas are high in sugar, are not an effective leavener, and have a strong flavor.

USE: ½ medium ripe banana = 1 egg

Blood

Blood and egg have similar protein profiles (high in albumen), making it an ideal coagulator/binder. When whipped, blood approximates egg whites very well and is an optimal substitution in things like meringues.

CONS: Blood's high iron content leads to a sharp metallic taste and strong odor that is offputting to many. Strong aromatic changes can occur in uncastrated pigs due to their production of skatole and androstenone, which women have been shown to be more sensitive to. Some recipes, especially acid-forward ones, mask these qualities better than others.

USE: 65 grams of pig's blood = 1 egg (about 58 grams), or 43 grams of blood = 1 egg white (about 33 grams)

Buttermilk

The fat and moisture content of buttermilk approximate that of eggs. It contains acid, so can be used as a leavener when combined with baking soda or powder.

CONS: Works best for subsitution in single-egg recipes because of its high moisture content and overall flavor profile, which can quickly become fairly overpowering.

USE: ½ cup buttermilk = 1 egg

Chia Seeds

When chia seeds are placed in water, they exude a mucilaginous polysaccharide that surrounds each seed, effectively creating a gel with a binding capability similar to eggs.

CONS: In a recent study, a control cake (containing eggs) favored higher overall on taste, texture, and color among the subjects, compared to cakes with up to 75 percent chia substitution. Again, to be used in moderation: Works most effectively in recipes that call for fewer eggs.

USE: 1 tbsp finely ground seeds + 3 tbsp water = 1 egg

Chickpea Liquid (Aquafaba)

The science of aquafaba is as of yet murky. A community-based webgroup has hypothesized that aquafaba may contain lipids, fatty acids, fibers, mucilage (similar to flax), and proteins (presumably albumins). When whipped, it is a strikingly accurate substitution for making meringues.

CONS: Has a strong beany flavor: best when masked with vanilla or other flavoring.

USE: 3 tablespoons drained canned chickpea liquid (each can yields ½ to ¾ cup) is the equivalent of about 1 egg white

Commercial Egg Replacer

Egg replacers are generally made up of potato starch, tapioca flour, a chemical leavener, and cellulose gum. Cellulose gum is a binder that helps stabilize proteins, improve mouthfeel, and absorb and retain water; the starches and flour also bind and give body.

CONS: Can be used only in baking. Also tends to lend a chalkier taste/texture than eggs and is not as effective at leavening (produces denser texture).

USE: For baking, 1½ tsp Ener-G Egg Replacer + 2 tbsp water = 1 egg; 1½ tsp Ener-G Egg Replacer + 1 tbsp water = 1 egg yolk

Cornstarch/Potato Starch/ Arrowroot Flour

When heated in a liquid, starch granules (long chains of plant sugars) swell, absorb water, and burst, dispersing more starch molecules and thereby thickening the liquid.

CONS: Texture and mouthfeel of starches versus eggs can be much gummier and slippier.

USE: 2 tbsp starch + 3 tbsp water = 1 egg

Flaxseed Meal

Flax is a hydrocolloid, meaning it becomes a gel when it's mixed with water. Hydrocolloids build structure, emulsify, and soften mouthfeel—many things that eggs already do in traditional baking applications. It's made up of mainly polysaccharides. Because of this, flax gel can work as a mild structure builder, low foaming agent, and emulsifier in vegan baking applications. Flax gel is able to do all three without imparting off-flavors, colors, or textures when it is used properly.

CONS: Eggs rely on proteins to do most of their work and flaxseeds use polysaccharides, so the results will not be exactly the same. Flaxseed egg replacer is not a terrific foaming agent. That means it's next to impossible to use it to make extremely airy desserts like angel food cake, choux pastry, or popovers. In fact, flaxseed egg replacer can even do more harm than good in cakes because of its tendency to hold on to excess moisture. It also is not a structure builder in that it won't form protein networks that reinforce doughs the way an egg will. It will work to stick things together instead.

USE: (1) Use the whole ground flaxseed meal dispersed in a liquid such as water, nondairy milk, or fruit juice and use it after it forms into a gel. (2) Make flax gel. Boil whole flaxseeds with water, which extracts the gel, strain the flax gel, then discard the flaxseeds.

Gelatin

Gelatin is made up of collagen molecules, which help hold together connective tissue in bone/muscles. Collagen is made up of three individual protein chains wound closely together in a helix to make a rope-like fiber. When heated in liquid, the individual protein chains come apart and dissolve into the liquid. The unwound, separate chains are what we call gelatin. As the liquid they are dispersed in cools, the collagen molecules begin to re-form their wound shape, essentially entangling all other molecules in a web, creating an emulsion.

CONS: Higher protein content, slippier mouthfeel when replacing 4 or more eggs. Cannot be used as a leavener. Not vegan!

USE: To replace 3 or 4 eggs, use 4 tbsp water + 1 tbsp gelatin. But, if replacing only 1 or 2 eggs, use 3 tbsp water + 1 tbsp gelatin.

Soy Lecithin

Lecithin is a phospholipid found in eggs; when replacing eggs with soy lecithin (or any other isolated lecithin), you are substituting like for like. Phospholipids resemble triglycerides (fat) except that a phosphate group replaces one of the fatty acids. Since phosphates are polar (water-soluble) and fatty acids are fat-soluble, phospholipids connect water and fats. Lecithin is a good emulsifier.

CONS: Most ideal for emulsions and foams in low quantities in instances where you don't want to impart egginess into the flavor profile. Can be "chemical-y" in large quantity.

USE: To make a lecithin foam, take a flavorful liquid and whisk or blend in the lecithin. It is typically used at a ratio of 0.25% to 1.0% by weight to the liquid. So, for example, for 100 grams of liquid, 0.25 to 1 gram of soy lecithin would be used. For the stabilization of emulsions, lecithin is added at a weight ratio of 0.3% to 1.0%, depending on how stabilized you want the emulsion to be.

Tofu

Tofu contains lecithin, which aids emulsification. Soy is a complete protein (provides all the necessary amino acids) and cholesterol free and thus a health-foodier replacement for many savory egg dishes.

CONS: Can lead to much heavier, denser cake texture. Most ideal for binding.

USE: ¼ cup (2 oz) silken tofu = 1 egg

7.

ASIAN EGGS

The ancestor to the chicken was possibly a bird living in the jungles of Malaysia that the Romans named *Gallus domesticus*—used for sacrifices and cockfighting long before the animal became food. The earliest records of raising egg-laying hens date back to 1400 BCE (in Egypt and China), and it's likely that the Chinese were the first to take the culinary egg seriously. I am both Malaysian *and* Chinese, and in my family, our love for eggs is deep and abiding. In the course of working on this book, I consulted my mom innumerable times. My dad excitedly took the phone at one point to tell me about the hard-boiled egg he ate from an eggcup during his first year at Leeds, in England, where he went to college. "Isn't that strange!" he exclaimed. "Did you know they do this? An egg in a little cup!" He grew up eating soft-boiled eggs from a bowl (page 90); his mother, my grandma, would steam eggs with pork in our rice cooker (page 221). Everyone's ways of eating eggs are a little strange to everybody else.

What do Asian people do with eggs? The answer, essentially, is everything that people do elsewhere, plus a few more out-of-left-fielders: They eat them even before they come out of the chicken. "Unlaid eggs," in-utero eggs from slaughtered chickens that you might see in your chicken pho, are called *kinkan* in Japan, *reng khai* in Thailand, and *eyerlekh* in Yiddish, stewed along with whole hens. *Balut* are embryos, partially formed birds, boiled and eaten in the Philippines since at least 1830, when it was a delicacy for the nobility, and in Vietnam, where it's called *hot vit lon*. "Virgin boy eggs," a delicacy from Dongyang, in eastern China, is a springtime delicacy of eggs steeped in the urine of prepubescent boys, preferably under age ten. And there are all manner of preserved eggs (page 237), like Chinese century eggs and salted eggs whose yolks are put into mooncakes eaten during the lunar festival. Quail eggs are, in Chinese medicine, more nutritious than regular chicken eggs, so sometimes you'll find them floating, hard-boiled, in herbal soups. Asians also basically already wrote this book. In 1785, *Banpou Ryouri Himitsu Bako* was published in Japan, a specialized book of egg recipes that included 103 ways to cook eggs, including a boiling recipe that somehow reverses the yolk and the white. What *else* do Asian people do with eggs, you ask?

Korean Steamed Eggs   *We steam them!*

These steamed eggs are essentially unfussy savory custard. I once watched my friend Lauren make the quickest, easiest egg dish for dinner: just a bowl of beaten eggs, scallions, jalapeño, and fish sauce, cooked entirely in the microwave. In Korea, this is apparently a thing! Called *gyeranjjim,* it's traditionally steamed or cooked in an earthenware pot and eaten as a side dish. "At restaurants sometimes they give it as 'service,'" Lauren adds. "A free treat." This microwave version is fluffy, simple, and hearty—ready in the span of a pop song.

Makes 2 servings

3 eggs
½ cup water
2 scallions, sliced
1 tbsp fish sauce
½ jalapeño chili, finely chopped
    (optional)
1 tsp sesame oil

1. Lightly beat the eggs in a microwave-safe bowl. Mix in the water, scallions, fish sauce, and jalapeño (if using).

2. Nuke on high for 3½ minutes. Poke the center with a spoon or chopstick to see if it's still liquidy. If so, nuke for 1 more minute. (Alternatively, to steam: steam the bowl over medium heat for about 15 minutes.)

3. To serve, drizzle with sesame oil.

Guira Cuckoo

220

Steamed Salted Egg
with Pork

During the production of this book, I spent a lot of time texting with moms—in some cases, other people's moms. Flora Ying is the mom of Chris, *Lucky Peach*'s editor in chief, and a fellow Chinese person. Flora published a version of this steamed egg-and-meat situation in issue 8 of our magazine, but because that was more meatloaf than egg loaf, I was left curious about the eggier version: It's one that I also ate growing up. When my Hakka grandma stayed home with us during summer vacations, she would stick an enamel dish filled with uncooked meat and egg into the rice cooker, on top of the rice, and it was magically ready when the rice was ready. This version calls for raw salted duck eggs: You can make your own, or look for them, refrigerated, in Asian supermarkets.

Makes 4 servings

½ lb ground pork
¼ tsp white pepper
1 tsp soy sauce
1 tsp cornstarch
¼ tsp minced fresh ginger
2 raw **Salted Duck Eggs** (page 244)
+ sesame oil, for serving
+ chopped cilantro and/or scallions, for
    garnish (optional)

1. Mix the ground pork, white pepper, soy sauce, cornstarch, and ginger together in a bowl.

2. Separate the salted duck egg whites from the yolks. Add the whites to the pork mixture and mix with a fork in a counterclockwise motion till thoroughly mixed.

3. Transfer the meat mix to a 7-inch round enamel pan and flatten it into an even thickness. Gently crumble the egg yolks and spread on top of the meat.

4. Set up a steamer. Steam until the pork is cooked through, 20 to 25 minutes.

5. To serve, drizzle a few drops of sesame oil over the top of the egg, and scatter with cilantro and/or scallions if using. Serve right away, while hot.

Chawanmushi

Chawanmushi, savory egg custard, is a traditional Japanese dish that's very basic—just eggs, dashi, and minimal seasoning (sometimes only salt)—but with countless variations depending on small-yet-significant tweaks: the ratio of egg to dashi, what you cook in the custard, for example. This dish is often served as a replacement for soup—it's considered in the same category as a soup—so the flavor of the dashi is just as important as the custard's delicate texture. Make sure to use rich, freshly made dashi.

My homey tofu-and-shiitake mushroom chawanmushi is something I can whip up on a busy day with ingredients that are always in my fridge. I like to use soft tofu, so the custard and the tofu will have almost the same texture when they're cooked, but you can also use medium-firm tofu, drained and patted very dry. If you like, you can upgrade the recipe by adding ingredients such as crabmeat, shrimp, gingko nuts, chicken . . . anything you like.

—*Naoko Takei Moore*

Makes 4 side-dish servings

2 eggs, at room temperature
1¼ cups dashi, at room temperature
1 tsp salt
1 tsp shiro shoyu (white soy sauce) or
    usukuchi shoyu (light-colored soy
    sauce)
6 oz soft tofu, drained and cut into large
    bite-size cubes
3 to 4 fresh shiitake mushrooms, stems
    discarded and caps sliced

1. Get a steamer ready.

2. To make the custard: Whisk together the eggs, dashi, salt, and *shiro shoyu* in a bowl until smooth.

3. Spread the tofu in a heat-resistant bowl, followed by the shiitake mushrooms. Gradually pour the egg batter through a fine-mesh strainer into the bowl.

4. Place the bowl in the steamer and cook over low heat until the custard is set (a skewer inserted in the center should come out clean), about 25 minutes.

Egg Drop Soup

We drop them!

I eat this once a week when I'm home alone for lunch, since it requires less than a moment of effort, delivers satisfaction, and leaves room for afternoon recipe tasting. It's plainer than Chinese-restaurant versions, but super delicious, and ready in no time.

—*Mary-Frances Heck*

Makes 2 to 4 servings

5 cups chicken stock
2 scallions, chopped, green and white
    parts separated
1 slice (1¼ inches) fresh ginger
1 tsp white peppercorns
+ salt
1 tbsp cornstarch mixed with 1 tbsp
    water to make a slurry
3 eggs, beaten

1. Combine the chicken stock, scallion whites, ginger, and peppercorns in a saucepan and bring to simmer over medium heat. Reduce the heat and simmer until the broth is infused with the aromatics, about 20 minutes. Strain and return the broth to the pan.

2. Bring the broth to a boil and season to taste with salt. Whisk the cornstarch mixture into the broth and return to a full boil so the broth thickens. Reduce the heat to a simmer and drizzle the egg into the pot in three or four additions. When the egg floats, remove from the heat and ladle into bowls. Sprinkle with chopped scallion greens and serve.

Monk Leaping into the Ocean

In Hong Kong, this classic energy drink is known to soothe stomachs of the young and old, and pep up partiers looking for a second wind.

—*Tienlon Ho*

Makes 1 drink

1 cup boiling water
1 egg
+ sugar

1. Fill a glass mug with the boiling water.

2. Crack a raw egg into it.

3. Serve with sugar and a spoon. The water should be hot enough to make egg flowers when stirred.

Striated Prinia

Stracciatella   *Italy does it, too!*

You probably know *stracciatella* as the Italian version of chocolate chip ice cream: It's gelato with chocolate that gets drizzled in as the ice cream churns, so the chocolate ends up in delicious, ragged shards. But stracciatella also refers to what is basically a cheesy egg drop soup, popular in central Italy. (Which came first, the soup or the ice cream, you're wondering? As it turns out, the soup!) Their shared name derives from the Italian verb *stracciare,* which means "to rip to shreds." Ripped-up shreds is exactly accurate, and this recipe has shreds of spinach too. Stracciatella (the soup) is a Roman staple around Easter, when eggs are traditionally most plentiful and most celebrated. But the soup is simple enough to make any time of the year—especially when you want something straightforwardly satisfying. It's fresh, bright, and made from ingredients you most likely have on hand already. And it's criminally easy! Say you're sick and can't muster the strength to make yourself chicken soup. You can make stracciatella.

Makes 4 appetizer servings

4 cups chicken stock
+ salt
8 oz spinach, stemmed and thinly
    sliced
2 eggs
¼ cup finely grated parmesan cheese,
    plus more for serving
+ freshly ground black pepper

1. Bring the chicken stock to a simmer in a saucepan and season with salt. Add the spinach and cook until wilted but still bright green, about 3 minutes.

2. Meanwhile, beat the eggs with the parmesan and a pinch each of salt and pepper.

3. Use a spoon to stir the soup around the pot and pour the eggs into the broth in three additions, stirring after each addition. The eggs will form wispy strands as they cook.

4. Ladle into bowls and sprinkle with a little more parmesan.

Stir-Fried Egg and Tomato

We fry them!

Stir-fried egg and tomato is a Chinese dish, I'm pretty sure, but I only know it from my youth in California and the home cooking of my Chinese-Malaysian mom, who was born and raised in Malaysia. If it's not the official Chinese version, I apologize. This is chunks of tomato scrambled with eggs that have been seasoned gently but purposefully with white pepper, Shaoxing wine, and sesame oil. It's boring sounding but actually revelatory, and seriously the easiest, best comfort food.

Makes 4 side-dish servings

5 eggs
1¼ tsp salt
½ tsp white pepper
1 tsp Shaoxing wine
½ tsp sesame oil
2 tbsp canola or vegetable oil
4 medium tomatoes (about 1 lb),
    chopped into rustic chunks
1 tsp sugar
2 scallions, sliced

1. Beat the eggs with 1 teaspoon of the salt, the white pepper, Shaoxing wine, and sesame oil—not too aggressively, and definitely not until they're frothy— just so the whites and yolks are incorporated and the mixture is uniformly yellow.

2. Heat 1 tablespoon of the oil in a large nonstick skillet or wok over medium heat. Add the egg mixture to the skillet or wok, cooking until the eggs are just barely setting and pulling together, about 10 seconds. Transfer to a bowl and wipe out the pan with a paper towel.

3. Heat the remaining 1 tablespoon oil in the same pan over medium heat. Add the tomatoes and stir until the tomatoes start to look wilted (their peels will sort of shrivel) and they release their juices, about 5 minutes. Sprinkle the sugar and remaining ¼ teaspoon salt all over, and stir for another minute.

4. Return the eggs to the pan along with the sliced scallions and cook, stirring occasionally, until the eggs are cooked through, another minute. Serve right away.

Yam Khai Dao

The best part of *yam khai dao,* Thai fried-egg salad, is the texture of the eggs: It's best when there's a perfect ratio of crisp edges to tender whites to soft and/or runny yolks. Fried in a quarter-or-so inch of oil, the egg whites blister and get crispy before the yolks completely firm up. The depth of oil bastes the egg whites, leaving the yolk exposed. That's why even though yam khai dao is typically made with chicken or duck eggs, I prefer quail eggs. With each bite of a fried quail egg, you get exactly that perfect ratio. Most Thai cooks fry their chicken or duck eggs to well done when they make this salad; with quail eggs, you can leave the yolks runny.

This is my own riff on this popular salad. You won't see fried quail egg salad anywhere on the streets of Thailand: Frying 36 quail eggs is not exactly a walk in the park. If you'd like to use chicken or duck eggs instead of quail, there's no shame in that. This salad is best enjoyed right away; it doesn't keep well. Like most Thai salads, yam khai dao is not meant to be eaten as a stand-alone dish, but as an accompaniment to rice.

—*Leela Punyaratabandhu*

Makes 6 servings

36 quail eggs or 12 large duck or
    chicken eggs
½ cup vegetable oil
2 plum tomatoes, cut lengthwise into
    ¼-inch wedges
1 cup packed roughly chopped
    Chinese celery leaves and stems
2 tbsp Thai fish sauce
3 tbsp fresh lime juice
1 tsp finely grated palm sugar or ¾ tsp
    light brown sugar
3 to 4 Thai bird's eye chilies, thinly
    sliced crosswise

1. Crack 36 quail eggs into a small bowl. Use a small sharp knife or pointed scissors to snip through the membrane, taking care to keep the yolk intact.

2. Heat the oil in a 10-inch skillet over medium heat. Line a baking sheet with double layers of paper towel and place it near the stove. When the oil is hot, gently pour one yolk and its white from the bowl at a time, dotting the pan with the 36 eggs (if using duck or chicken eggs, fry one at a time). Fry without flipping until the bottoms and edges are ruffled, crisp, puffed, and golden brown, about 2 minutes. Transfer the fried eggs to the prepared baking sheet.

3. Place the tomatoes and celery leaves in a medium bowl. Add the fish sauce, lime juice, sugar, and chilies and toss everything together. Arrange the fried eggs on a platter (quarter them if using chicken or duck eggs), and spoon the tomato mixture over them. Like any salad, this can be tossed or composed: If you choose to toss, be careful not to break the yolks. If you prefer to keep the platter composed, be sure to get equal amounts of the dressed topping and some egg in every bite.

Tea Eggs

We stew them!

To see what a country really craves, one need not look much further than its convenience stores. Bodegas, corner stores, and 7-Elevens are often stacked not only with packaged junk food but also with a few freshly prepared bites, be it pastries or hot dogs. In Taiwan, the convenience stores are always equipped with a steaming slow cooker of stewed, soy sauce–stained eggs. But they're not just soy-stained, and they're not just stewed. They're tea eggs.

The difference? Black tea is steeped in a rich, salty bath of five-spice and soy sauce, giving it an herbal undertone to otherwise classic red-braised (or *hongshao* stewed) foods. And the eggs aren't merely boiled and peeled—they're hard-boiled first, then the shells are crackled all over. The result is a crackly pattern across the eggs once you lift them from the bath and peel them. Since eggshells are porous, the flavors have steeped throughout the egg, but the color has stained the surface in marbled streaks of brown.

When making it at home, best to do a big batch, then reheat and snack on them throughout the week. The color and flavor will only get deeper and better the longer the eggs soak in their tea brine.

—Cathy Erway

Makes 12 tea eggs

12 eggs
½ cup dark soy sauce
½ cup light soy sauce
¼ cup packed black tea leaves
1 star anise
2 tsp Chinese five-spice powder

1. Place the eggs in a large pot and fill with enough water to cover. Bring to a boil over high heat and boil for 5 minutes. Drain and plunge the eggs into an ice bath until just cool enough to handle. Using the back of a spoon, tap each of the eggs all over gently to crackle the edges, being careful not to rip the shells off.

2. Return the eggs to the drained pot and add 8 cups fresh water, the soy sauces, tea leaves, and spices. Bring to a boil, then reduce to a low simmer and cook, covered, for at least 2 hours to achieve a brown stain on the eggs beneath the shells.

3. Tea eggs can be refrigerated and reheated in their liquid over the course of up to 1 week in order to acquire a darker, more flavorful tea and soy stain. Peel and enjoy as snacks.

Shabbat Eggs

Iran does it, too!

The Saturday morning breakfast in most Jewish households in Iran features these darkly stained, slow-cooked eggs. Because, in Jewish tradition, Shabbat is a day of rest, cooking is forbidden from sundown on Friday evening through sundown on Saturday. So observant Iranian Jews set these eggs over the lowest heat Friday afternoon, and allow them to cook overnight. By Saturday morning, the onion skins impart a deep brownish color to the eggs' shells, the whites take on a muted beige, and the long, slow cooking yields a creamy yolk.

These eggs are part of a breakfast spread that includes Persian flatbread like *barbari* or *sangak,* fried eggplant and zucchini—served cold as they were cooked on Friday—and *sabzi khordan,* the plate of fresh herbs like basil, tarragon, and mint ubiquitous at Persian meals and meant to be eaten along with the prepared dishes, with your fingers.

There are no fancy ingredients here, and it's a far cry from the Shah's opulent cuisine. This is haimish Jewish ghetto food that has made its way to the current day. And while the earthy tones of the eggs seem at odds with the modern taste for bright, barely cooked ingredients, for many Iranian Jews, the scent of eggs simmering on the back burner is the sweet smell of Shabbat.

—Tannaz Sassooni

Makes 6 Shabbat eggs

1 tbsp salt
8 cups water
+ skins from 1 or 2 yellow onions
6 eggs
2 tsp black tea leaves or 2 black
    tea bags

Combine the salt and water in a Dutch oven or slow cooker. Stir to dissolve the salt. Add the onion skins, eggs, and tea leaves. If cooking on the stove, place the pot over the lowest heat and simmer for at least 2 hours, up to overnight. If cooking in a slow cooker, cook at low for 2 hours, then hold on warm until ready to serve.

Onsen Tamago

We stew alongside them!

Onsen tamago translates to "hot spring egg," a name derived from its original method of cooking in Japan, where volcanoes dot the landscape like sheep. Most Japanese hot springs hover at a temperature somewhere around 154°F, decidedly north of the point at which egg yolks begin to solidify (149°F) but just south of where their whites do (158°F). To make onsen tamago traditionally, eggs would be lowered into the water in baskets or rope nets and left there for thirty to forty minutes, perhaps while you steeped yourself nearby. The resulting egg has a barely set white that is more silky than runny and a completely soft-cooked yolk. My friend-in-egg-love Kee, also known as "A Bathing Egg," tells me that in Tokyo, where he lives, people use tiny coolers to make onsen tamago. They're essentially little ice chests: insulated plastic containers into which you pour hot water, with an insert that holds the eggs upright and off the bottom. You could also sous-vide your eggs for an hour at 154°F in an immersion circulator—the perfect pseudo hot spring. Or you could follow this recipe.

Makes 4 eggs

+ ice
4 eggs, from the fridge

1. Bring 1 quart of water to a boil in a small, heavy pot, preferably an enameled cast iron Dutch oven. Add 4 oz of ice (5 standard cubes), turn off the heat, add the eggs, and cover the pot. The water should drop from 212°F to between 150° and 155°F. Let stand, covered, for 45 minutes. The water should not drop below 140°F; if it does, turn the burner to low and heat until the water reaches 154°F.

2. Drain the eggs and serve, or refrigerate for up to 2 days.

Double-Crested Cormorant

Tamago-Kake Gohan (TKG)

We put them over rice!

Tamago-kake gohan in Japanese means "raw egg over rice." Along with grilled fish and miso soup, it's one of the staples of a traditional Japanese-style breakfast, but it can be enjoyed at other times of the day, too. Most Japanese people, including myself, have a soft spot for tamago-kake gohan, and we even refer to it as "TKG," with affection.

The most basic TKG is rice, egg, and soy sauce. But there are two main methods: Some people stir together the egg and soy sauce first, then pour it over the rice, while others drop the unbeaten egg over the rice and drizzle some soy sauce over it before breaking the egg yolk and letting it ooze over the rice. I own a special egg whisk stick designed specifically for perfect TKG! The tip of this stick is a small blade that can blend the yolk and white thoroughly so you won't experience some gooey white-only part when you pour the egg over.

TKG continues to evolve. At grocery stores, you can find special sauces made only for TKG. In Japan, there are restaurants that specialize in TKG. Whether it's a simple egg with katsuobushi (dried bonito flakes) or a decadent TKG topped with shaved black truffles, always make sure the rice is freshly made and steaming hot, for the best-tasting TKG. Here I've included ideas for simple toppings and more unique ones.

—*Naoko Takei Moore*

Makes 1 serving

1 very fresh egg (make sure it's from a
    reliable source)
1 serving freshly cooked Japanese
    short-grain rice in a bowl
+ soy sauce
+ toppings (optional)

OPTIONAL SIMPLE TOPPINGS
+ minced chives or scallion
+ katsuobushi (dried bonito flakes)
+ shredded nori or ao-nori (dried green
    seaweed powder)
+ toasted sesame seeds
+ wasabi
+ sesame oil

OPTIONAL UNIQUE TOPPINGS
+ mentaiko (spicy cod roe)
+ la-yu (hot chili oil)
+ kimchi and mayonnaise
+ bottarga
+ parmesan cheese and butter
+ shaved truffle and butter
+ avocado and wasabi

1. Crack the egg into a small bowl. Make a small dent in the center of the rice, and pour the egg over the rice. Drizzle with some soy sauce. (Alternatively, crack the egg into a small bowl and drizzle with some soy sauce. Pour the mixture over the rice.)

2. Add toppings, if using. Enjoy by mixing (or not mixing!) the egg and rice.

Soboro Bento

When I was in junior high school in Tokyo, I had a regimented school life: dull uniforms, cramming for exams, and compulsorily going to school on Saturdays, even when kids in other parts of the world had no school. But the saving grace was our mother's bento box, which we brought to school on Saturdays because there was no free-lunch program available on the weekend. It was the only chance to show off something colorful and special. Some kids brought store-bought sandwiches and *onigiri,* because their mothers were working and didn't have time to make bento, which was kind of sad. Most mothers, however, were stay-at-home types, eager to please their children with the prettiest bentos.

The most popular bento at school was the tri-color *soboro* bento, a bed of rice blanketed with rows of soboro eggs (yellow), seasoned ground chicken (brown), and something green. "Soboro" is a topping for rice or vegetables—coarse crumbles made by mincing eggs, fish, meat, or tofu. My mom wouldn't use beef because it was too expensive. For greens, you used sliced snow peas, green beans, or spinach. There was some red pickled ginger to accent the flavors, and also, if you got lucky, an apple wedge sliced to looked like a rabbit with long ears sitting in the corner of the box. Back when I was a child, that was the extent of *kawaii* figures. No Hello Kitty. No Mickey Mouse. Even so, it was your mother's expressionist piece.

My best friend Peichun Wang's mother made the best-looking soboro bento. The rows were so clean and the soboro was cooked to perfection. The yellow egg shone like the sun. The brown chicken soboro looked juicy. I would watch her eat the whole thing, working from the ground chicken and finishing with the egg, dexterously using her pair of chopsticks, not leaving a grain of rice or soboro in the bento box.

Soboro bento is easy to make. Scrambled eggs are already something you're familiar with. Just scramble the eggs a little further until they turn into coarse soboro crumbles. I bunch together long kitchen chopsticks with a rubber band and use the dull end to scramble the eggs. The secret of a good egg soboro is that once the eggs are cooked, remove them from the heat and continue stirring. This is how you get the fine crumbles.

For a classic soboro bento, arrange the yellow, brown, and green into whatever pattern you like: diagonal, cross, tic-tac-toe, Mondrian.

—*Sonoko Sakai*

Makes 3 bentos

2 handfuls green beans, trimmed
3 cups cooked Japanese short-grain
  rice

+ **Chicken Soboro** (recipe follows)
+ **Egg Soboro** (recipe follows)
+ sesame oil
+ toasted sesame seeds

1. In a small saucepan of boiling water, cook the green beans to al dente, a couple of minutes. Drain and let cool. Julienne the green beans and set aside.

2. To serve, divide and pack the rice into bento boxes, and top with rows of chicken soboro, egg soboro, and green beans. Garnish with a drizzle of sesame oil and the sesame seeds.

Chicken Soboro
Makes 3 servings

1 (3-inch) piece kombu
1 cup water
1 tbsp vegetable oil
¾ lb ground chicken (use thigh meat with some fat)
¼ cup sake
2 tbsp mirin
1½ tbsp sugar
3 tbsp soy sauce
1 tsp grated fresh ginger
1½ tsp cornstarch mixed with 2 tbsp water to make a slurry

1. First, make a quick dashi: Soak the kombu in the 1 cup water for 30 minutes to overnight. Remove the kombu. The dashi can be made a day in advance and refrigerated.

2. Heat the oil in a skillet over medium heat. Add the ground chicken and cook until the meat is crumbly and loose, using a bundle of chopsticks or a whisk to break the meat apart to create fine even crumbles, about 3 minutes.

3. Season the chicken mixture with the dashi, sake, mirin, sugar, and soy sauce. Bring to a boil, then reduce to a simmer and cook until 80 percent of the liquid is absorbed, 7 to 8 minutes. Stir occasionally. Add the grated ginger. Taste and adjust the seasonings if necessary. If the soboro chicken appears dry, add a few more tablespoons of dashi or water. Then stir in the cornstarch slurry. When you get a shiny coat, in about 1½ minutes, remove from the heat.

Egg Soboro
Makes 3 servings

3 eggs
1 tsp sugar
+ pinch of salt
1 tbsp vegetable oil

1. Combine the eggs with the sugar and salt in a bowl and mix well.

2. Heat the oil in a skillet over medium heat. Once hot, pour the eggs into the pan. Reduce the heat to low and scramble the eggs with a bundle of chopsticks or a whisk until the eggs become crumbly, about 3 minutes. Be very careful not to overcook or burn the eggs. Remove from the heat and continue stirring for a couple more minutes to create fine even crumbles.

Oyakodon

The Japanese use relationships to name rice bowls—I like that. Take *oyakodon,* my favorite rice bowl. It means "parent and child in a bowl." You have chunks of *amakara* (sweet and salty) chicken, and runny eggs simmered in dashi, served over rice. If you make the rice bowl with duck and chicken eggs, that would make them *itokodon,* "cousin bowl," but if you use beef and eggs, you are no longer family, so what you get is *tanindon,* "stranger bowl."

Oyakodon is equally delicious at breakfast, lunch, and dinner. The thing to be careful of is not to overcook the eggs. They must remain *torotoro,* trembling and barely set, to allow the custardy egg sauce to seep into the hot bed of rice.

Tamahide, a 250-year-old restaurant in Nihonbashi, Tokyo, claims it is the inventor of oyakodon. Tamahide began as an eatery specializing in shamo, a game fowl brought into Japan from Thailand during the Edo period (1603–1867). The bird was bred and pampered for cockfighting, and the losers were usually killed—taken out of the fighting pit and sent to the shamo restaurants to be made into savory delicacies that were a favorite of Tokugawa shoguns. Generations later, one of the chefs at Tamahide is said to have made the first oyakodon, using chicken and eggs simmered in broth and served with rice. It was delicious but the owners felt oyakodon was not classy enough to put on their regular menu, so they sold it as street food. The rest is history.

My mother made a communal-style oyakodon in a large cast iron skillet, so it looked like a large pizza. Mother had a habit of cooking for fifteen, even though we had seven in our family. Slices of oyakodon were served on dinner plates, American style, with mounds of rice on the side. I could eat two plates full in one sitting.

A traditional oyakodon pan makes a single serving. It comes with a unique handle that sticks straight up and allows you to slide the oyakodon right onto a bowl of rice, without losing any of its delicious amakara sauce. A few years ago, I finally bought my dream pan in Kyoto. I keep reminding myself that it's there waiting for me to season it. But I love my large cast iron skillet and the pizza-size oyakodon that I can make with it. *Oyako*—mother and daughter—are so much alike.

—*Sonoko Sakai*

Makes 4 servings

2 cups short-grain white or brown rice
1½ cups water
1 cup katsuobushi (dried bonito flakes)
2 tbsp sugar
¼ cup soy sauce
2 tbsp sake
¼ cup mirin

1 onion, halved lengthwise and cut crosswise into ¼-inch slices
1 lb boneless and skinless chicken thighs, cut into 1-inch cubes
8 eggs, lightly beaten
4 mitsuba sprigs, leaves removed from stems (optional)
1 sheet nori, crumbled (optional)

1. Cook the rice according to the package directions. While the rice is cooking, make the oyakodon topping.

2. Bring the water to a boil in a small saucepan. Add the bonito flakes and simmer the dashi for 2 minutes. Strain the broth through a strainer. Measure out 1 cup of the dashi.

3. Transfer the dashi to a well-seasoned 10-inch cast iron or nonstick skillet and add the sugar, soy sauce, sake, and mirin. Bring to a boil over medium-high heat, stirring to dissolve the sugar. Add the onion and chicken and cook, stirring occasionally, until the onion is soft and the chicken is no longer pink, 3 to 4 minutes.

4. Reduce the heat to medium-low, then pour two-thirds of the beaten eggs into the skillet and continue cooking until the eggs just start to set around the edges, about 2 minutes. Add the remaining eggs, cover, and let cook for 1 minute, until they look mostly set all the way through. Turn off the heat and let the oyakodon sit for another minute.

5. Slice the oyakodon and serve over the rice, a generous cup of cooked rice per serving. Garnish with mitsuba leaves and crumbled nori, if you like.

Chestnut-Collared Swift

8.
IMMORTAL EGGS

And so we come—almost!—to the end. Eggs existed before you and me, and eggs will outlive us all. This thought is either comforting or terrifying, depending on the sort of day you're having—and how acute your sense of mortality. In so many cultures, eggs were the very first things to exist. Ancient Greek Orphic tradition describes a cosmic egg that hatched the first hermaphroditic deity, from which all other gods came. In Egyptian mythology, the god Ra was hatched from an egg laid by a celestial bird. The universe began as an egg in the Chinese myth of Pangu, a god who was born from an egg in which he developed and slept for 18,000 years; when it split, the egg created the universe. The lighter elements drifted up to make the sky, and heavier, less pure elements settled to create the earth. A Finnish story has it that a yolk from an egg laid by a duck made the sun, and the white made the moon. And as eggs were at the beginning, eggs will be at the exciting end. After we're all gone from this planet—that is, if we haven't destroyed it completely—eggs will outlast and outlive us all.

A fresh egg is a very good thing (page 46), because eggs begin to break down as soon as the egg leaves the hen: The last one in is a rotten egg, as we all know. (Eggs come to such smelly ends because hydrogen sulfide and other gases are produced by the bacterial breakdown of egg proteins.) But it turns out that fresher isn't always better, and there is something very wonderful about old eggs, too, when properly preserved—pickled, fermented, alkaline-cured, dried, crystallized. They're food for the apocalypse—nearly immortal—ready for travel to the ends of the earth, and beyond.

RIP us. Long live the egg!

The Century Egg

Tienlon Ho

There was a time when making *pi dan* was a specialty, as much as hand-pulling noodles, hammering into shape a well-balanced wok, or fermenting rich soy sauce. When my dad was a kid in southern China, there was a guy in the village whose trade was making pi dan and caring for the ducks that laid the eggs to make them. And, of course, he had learned how to do these things from his father before him.

Pi dan means roughly "leather-skinned egg" in Chinese, a name that describes how they were once most commonly made: Clay was applied to the shell of raw eggs (usually duck), which dried into a leathery coating. After a month or so, it transformed their insides into a gel of dark amber surrounding a creamy yolk of many shades of green.

In the West, pi dan are commonly known as thousand-year eggs, millennium eggs, or century eggs, which are all misnomers. Transformed, pi dan can last a few months without refrigeration—though, like most everything in the world, they do eventually shrivel up into smelly, brown goop.

The magic ingredient for making pi dan is not the clay but rice husks, or more precisely, rice husks burned into ash. Blended with water, they become a strongly alkaline concoction known as lime. Humans have found all sorts of ways to use alkalis in cooking—from the nixtamalization of corn into digestible masa to creating the golden crust on pretzels, curing olives, and giving ramen that pleasant bite. With enough time and enough concentration, alkalis also cure eggs.

The alkali was for millennia a product of the seasonal cycle of rice farming and the ducks that waddled around freely, tilling and weeding the rice paddies. Everything was in synchronicity. The first rice crop went in the ground just after the Chinese New Year and was harvested in early summer, just when the ducks were at their egg-laying peak. The piles of coarse rice husks and plant stalks left over from the harvest were burned into the ash that would be used to turn all those eggs into something pungent, delicious, and readily saved. In other parts of Asia where rice was not as abundant, alkaline substitutes like the yellow clay churned up by the rivers, termite mounds, and the dust spit out by volcanoes were used to make pi dan instead.

Each pi dan maker would mix his own proprietary blend of salt, tea, and ash (rice husks and pine, for instance) into the clay, then cover the duck eggs with it. The coating would slow evaporation through the porous shell while the alkalis and trace elements penetrated it, making the egg inhospitable to bacteria while breaking down proteins into smaller, tastier compounds, such as the glutamates responsible for imparting a meaty, umami flavor. The eggs would go into an earthenware vessel, or simply a dry hole in the ground, for around forty days in the summer, or fifty days in the winter (depending on the local climate), to undergo metamorphosis.

This technique resulted in a lot of flops. Sometimes the eggs would ripen only partly, while others would decompose. The mark of a quality pi dan is the appearance of *song hua,* frosty pine branch shapes on their glassy, amber surface, but these only form if proteins have denatured sufficiently and at just the right rate.

In Taiwan, chemists in the 1950s perfected a mass production method using a liquid brine, immersing the eggs in a solution of salt, lye, and lime for a couple weeks, followed by a few weeks of dry-aging in wax or plastic. Village pi dan makers were soon replaced by factories. In the beginning, some added lead oxide to the mix to keep the texture soft while ensuring song hua, but eventually they learned less worrisome zinc or magnesium salts did the trick. While pi dan makers have always tested for doneness by tapping each egg, feeling for just the right rebound and jiggle, a Taiwan university recently unveiled technology that tests eggs ten times faster in an acoustic chamber. There are always new ways to improve the process, it seems.

*

In Hong Kong, the narrow street of Wing Wo in the neighborhood of Sheung Wan is packed with herbalists, but even a couple years ago it was still known to locals as Pidan Street, where vendors sold their eggs stacked high on carts. In recent years, they were encouraged to pack up and move to a concrete wholesale market by the wharf, out of sight.

One of the last of the egg vendors still on the street is Shun Xing Xing, which serves customers promptly from 10:30 to 3:30 Monday through Saturday through a small window cut out of a corrugated steel door. Shun Xing Xing is rumored to supply some of the best restaurants with its pi dan, and when I arrived, a spry, elderly man was already loading up a handcart with cartons to deliver to various groceries and restaurants unnamed.

The woman at the window was Mrs. Kwok, whose father had opened the shop selling all kinds of eggs—pi dan, salted eggs, salted yolks, and more—sixty years before. Growing up in the business, she told me, she had watched her father's pi dan specialist make the eggs by burning rice husks and fragrant branches. He was a Chinese man from the mainland whom her father had hired just to make them, she said.

But now, she admitted, she did not make the pi dan at her shop anymore. She bought them all from the mainland. Despite what everyone says, she said, everyone imports their eggs. It is too time intensive, too unpredictable a process to run a business on, she said. In fact, she was closing up shop permanently, as soon as possible. "I'm ready to cook dinner for my two sons every night and relax," she said.

Later, I went to see the wholesale market to find where all the other egg sellers had gone. It was a huge industrial concrete warehouse of stalls set up like storefronts and living rooms. In the egg section, there were thousands of boxes of small quail to large goose eggs, stamped for export to everywhere in the world. Little kids watched TV next to their parents as they sifted through all their cracked eggs.

On the top floor, I met a woman who explained that all the best pi dan in Hong Kong—in Asia really—were coming from central China and Taiwan. But she could not, or would not, say definitively how they were made. She pulled out samples from producers who still used rice husks and clay, but she thought some might have been brined first and then aged in the coating for appearance's sake. When I wanted to buy some, she took one out of my hand and wouldn't give it back. It was no good, apparently, but she wouldn't explain why.

*

In Hong Kong, pi dan have long been a staple even though the process by which they are made remains mysterious. They are served at breakfast and *yum cha* with congee (rice porridge), and late at night in noodle shops as an appetizer with a side of pickles or simply soy sauce and ginger. At Yung Kee, a Michelin-starred restaurant that began as a *dai pai dong,* a cart serving roast goose by the pier, the pi dan with their *tang xin,* a yolk more molten than creamy, are one of the main draws.

They serve their eggs quartered and accompanied by a mound of thinly sliced pickled ginger. Sometimes diners add a glass of Bordeaux. Others request sugar for dipping.

Carrel Kam, the grandson of Yung Kee's founder, said they still made their eggs by the barrel at their own factory using a liquid brining method. They had been using largely the same technique since the 1970s, trying to perfect the ratios, temperature, and time that would yield the most eggs with soft jelly whites, a creamy yolk, and no trace of a "horse urine smell." When an egg goes too far, it's the worst, he said. "You can really feel it in the throat."

Yung Kee had set up a climate-controlled room held at a steady 80 percent humidity, and found the right ratios for adjusting the salt, lye, or lime, depending on the weather report. They had figured out that they generally got the best results somewhere between forty and fifty days of brining time. But even with all that in place, the experts at the factory, the precision measurements, and the climate control, they still ended up with plenty of bad eggs.

Another hitch was the eggs themselves, which came from Hubei, a lake province in central China. Every year in the late spring, the ducks gorged on little river shrimp and fish, and their egg yolks turned bright red and oily. Even that changed the chemistry.

"That's just the way it goes with weather and nature and handmade things," Kam said. "Everyone is still trying to find the best way."

Iceland Does It, Too!

In northeast Iceland around Lake Mývatn, duck eggs are stored in boxes of dry ash, which both desiccates and preserves them; they are then boiled before eating. The alkaline ash is collected from the smokehouses (which use sheep dung as fuel) but the tradition may have sprung from finding ways to use the alkaline ash periodically tossed out by the still active nearby volcano.

Congee with Century Eggs

Congee (*jook*) topped with quartered century eggs is the kind of thing I want when I'm sick—it makes me miss my mom's cooking. I emailed her for congee guidance. She likes to soak her rice overnight with salt and oil because "some people think that the jook will be smoother and easier to boil the next day," she emailed. I call for dried scallops here, but dried oysters are a good swap-in, too. The point is a gingery, peppery congee that's a backdrop to those funky, savory eggs.

Makes 6 servings

1 cup jasmine rice
8 cups water
+ salt
½ tsp vegetable oil
1 piece (1½ inches) fresh ginger, peeled and smashed
4 dried scallops
½ lb ground pork
1 tsp sesame oil, plus more for serving
2 tsp soy sauce, plus more for serving
½ tsp white pepper, plus more for serving
1 tsp Shaoxing wine
½ tsp oyster sauce
2 century eggs, quartered
+ thinly sliced scallions
+ roughly chopped cilantro
+ **Fried Shallots**, store-bought or homemade (page 172)

1. In a pot, soak the rice for 4 hours or overnight in the water with a generous pinch of salt and the vegetable oil.

2. The next day, add the ginger and scallops and bring the pot to a boil. Reduce to a simmer and cook until the rice grains have broken down and the porridge has thickened, about 30 minutes. Stir periodically to keep it from sticking to the bottom.

3. Meanwhile, mix the pork with the sesame oil, soy sauce, white pepper, Shaoxing wine, and oyster sauce and let it marinate while the porridge cooks.

4. When the porridge has thickened, add a splash of water to the pork mass and break it up with your fingers. Add the marinated meat to the pot, and cook for another 10 minutes, until the pork bits are cooked through.

5. Taste and adjust the seasoning. If you like your porridge thinner, add more water.

6. To serve, ladle portions into bowls. Drizzle extra soy sauce and sesame oil over the top, and more white pepper if you like it peppery (I do). Finish with the century egg pieces, scallions, cilantro, and fried shallots.

Spicy Basil and Century Egg Stir-Fry

In Thailand, century eggs, affectionately called *khai yiao ma* (literally "horse piss egg"), were once a staple at Teochew-style rice porridge shops and would be served as one of the many accompaniments to rice as well as quite on their own—just peeled, halved or quartered, and plated. But over the decades, century eggs have made their way into several traditional Thai dishes, creating either entirely new dishes or new spins on old classics. This dish, *khai yiao ma phat ka-phrao,* a newish favorite of many Bangkokians, falls into the latter category.

—*Leela Punyaratabandhu*

Makes 3 to 4 servings

6 garlic cloves
3 to 4 Thai bird's eye chilies or 2 serrano
    chilies (or to taste)
1 tbsp fish sauce
1 tbsp oyster sauce
1 tbsp dark soy sauce
1½ tbsp grated palm sugar or
    1 tbsp packed light brown sugar
+ vegetable oil, for frying
3 cups tightly packed holy basil leaves
6 century eggs, peeled and quartered
    lengthwise
½ lb ground pork
1 serrano or jalapeño chili, cut into
    slivers
+ jasmine rice, for serving

1. Grind the garlic and bird's eye chilies in a mortar or mini food processor until you get a coarse paste with each bit being the size of a match head. Set aside.

2. Combine the fish sauce, oyster sauce, dark soy sauce, and sugar in a small bowl. Set aside.

3. Line a baking sheet with two layers of paper towel and place it near the stove.

4. Pour enough vegetable oil into a wok to form a ¾-inch-deep pool. Heat the oil over medium-high heat.

5. When the oil is hot, throw 2 cups of the holy basil leaves into it and quickly step back, because it will splatter. In just a few seconds, the splattering will subside. Approach the wok and stir the basil around with a fine-mesh skimmer. When the leaves become crisp and translucent, in less than a minute, scoop them out onto one side of the prepared baking sheet. Don't turn off the stove just yet. While the oil is still hot, add the egg quarters and deep-fry, stirring gently but constantly, until they're golden brown, about a minute. Transfer them to the vacant side of the prepared baking sheet.

6. Pour the oil out of the wok, leaving only 2 tablespoons, and put the wok back on the stove. Immediately add the garlic-chili paste and stir-fry quickly until fragrant, about a minute (do not brown the garlic). Add the pork and stir-fry until no longer pink, separating it into tiny chunks as you go. Add the prepared sea-soning sauce, scraping every bit out of the bowl. Continue to stir-fry until everything is well mixed. Add the remaining 1 cup basil leaves and the slivered chili to the wok and stir-fry until they wilt a little. Add the deep-fried eggs and stir just until heated through.

7. Plate the stir-fry and top it with the crispy basil leaves. Serve immediately with warm jasmine rice.

African Golden Oriole

Salted Duck Eggs

The Essential Techniques for the Peasantry, written for the Chinese home cook 1,500 years ago, includes this instruction for preparing salted eggs: "Soak a duck egg in brine for one month." Today, *xian dan* on Asian grocery store shelves are still made this way in a brine of typically one part salt to four parts water.

Another way of making salted eggs in the shell is encasing it in a paste of salt and clay, which hardens, creating a skin that protects like plastic but breathes like skin. Treated this way, eggs last unrefrigerated for many months. Wet or dry, the salt slows bacterial growth and draws out moisture through the shell. The salt molecules disrupt the bonds in the proteins of the egg yolk and with time separate them from the fats, eventually turning the yolks richly oily and dense, and thickening the egg whites.

This recipe is not traditional but gets the eggs where we want them: It's a piece of cake except for the four-week wait.

—*Tienlon Ho*

Makes 1 dozen salted eggs

¾ cup Shaoxing wine
¾ cup fine sea salt
12 duck eggs

1. Pour the Shaoxing wine into a small bowl and pour the salt into another. Roll the eggs, one by one, into the wine and then into the salt, so a layer of salt coats the egg.

2. Put the salt-covered eggs into a zip-top freezer bag. Press out the air and place the eggs in a plastic container, and cover. Date your eggs and let sit in a cool, dark place for 4 weeks.

3. Rinse the eggs and either use or store them. You can hard-boil the eggs to eat with congee or use in Bibingka (opposite), or use fresh in Steamed Salted Egg with Pork (page 221). Refrigerated, they will keep for a month.

Bibingka

Bibingka—it's dope: It's a Filipino street dessert and it's usually rice flour, mad egg, and butter wrapped in a banana leaf (sometimes with cheese, like white cheese or sharp cheddar). And there's salted duck egg in it, too—pieces of duck egg on top or inside, so you get bites of the salty duck egg to cut through all the richness, and counterbalance the sweetness of the butter. It's really good.

In the Philippines, in the provinces, there are small little neighborhoods, barrios. By six a.m. you're hearing roosters and people whistling and yelling. Hawking already starts by six thirty, and you wake up to that. Outside, people are running or walking, going to their next thing—they're in jerseys and sandals because it's a little poorer in the provinces. It's a little microeconomy where they're taking care of one another. We were driving in our car one day, and my mom was like, "Oh, you know who makes the best bibingka? My so-and-so, she makes it best . . ." And she rolled down the window and she said, "Oh, that's her! Maria, come over here!" We were driving all slow in traffic and Maria walked up to us and she just slanted it toward us—boom!—and we ate it hot. It was wrapped up in a banana leaf—buttery and hot as hell.

Growing up, we tasted a lot of different takes on bibingka: Some were breadier, some were more airy. Some families use Bisquick pancake mix—probably an American influence. We settled on this recipe, which is in between.

—Chase and Chad Valencia

Makes 8 servings

1 cup rice flour
2½ tsp baking powder
⅛ tsp salt
3 tbsp butter, at room temperature
1 cup sugar
3 eggs, beaten
1¼ cups coconut milk
1 piece banana leaf
1 **Salted Duck Egg** (opposite),
    hard-boiled, peeled, and sliced
½ cup grated coconut

1. Heat the oven to 375°F.

2. Combine the rice flour, baking powder, and salt in a bowl. Set aside.

3. Cream the butter in a large bowl, and gradually add the sugar while whisking. Add the beaten eggs, incorporating them into the butter-and-sugar mixture well. Gradually add the flour mixture and then add the coconut milk.

4. Line a pie plate or cake pan with the banana leaf. Pour the well-mixed batter into the lined pan. Bake for 15 minutes. Remove and add the sliced salted duck egg on top and continue to bake until a toothpick comes out clean, 15 to 20 minutes.

5. Garnish with the grated coconut and serve warm.

Picklopolis Pickled Duck Eggs

I've always loved duck eggs for their density. The yolks are extremely heavy and dark—perfect for baking, and especially for making pasta. I started using them a lot when one of our fellow vendors at Portland Farmers' Market had a surplus and asked me if I could do anything amazing with them. I had always made pickled eggs and thought duck eggs would be perfect for pickling. I like to undercook them so that the yolks are still runny. At the market, we sell them on sticks. They are wonderful on their own—the first bite is hot and salty, and the yolk is custardy and mild—but even better on a salad niçoise or lightly decorated and served like a deviled egg. I also do a green jalapeño one, but the red is the best.

—David Barber

Makes 6 pickled eggs

½ lb red cherry peppers or red Fresno
    chilies
6 garlic cloves
1 tsp salt
1 cup distilled white vinegar
6 duck eggs

1. Wash and stem the peppers. Combine them in a blender or food processor with the garlic and salt and process until finely chopped. Add the vinegar and continue processing until smooth.

2. Place the duck eggs in a large saucepan and cover with cool water. Set over medium-high heat and bring to a boil. Cover, remove from the heat, and let stand for 8 minutes, until soft-boiled. Drain and shock the eggs in cold water. Peel the eggs.

3. Arrange the eggs in a 2-quart jar and add the pepper purée. Seal, gently turn upside down a couple of times to distribute everything, and refrigerate for 1 week. The eggs are ready when the yolk becomes firm and pliable and the egg tastes seasoned throughout.

Pennsylvania Dutch
Pickled Beet Eggs

While there are a great many foodstuffs from Pennsylvania's breadbasket that could undoubtedly endure the apocalypse, the question really is: Which of them will sate the hunger of the discerning survivor? My bet is on pickled beet eggs. They are pickled, of course, and ubiquitous. Menacingly rosy jars of them haunt the back bars or counters next to the cash register of many of the greater Lancaster area's finer and not-so-fine establishments. Most are graced by a gray halo of dust that says, "I've been here since the seventies, and I'll be here after you're gone." No doubt that's the attitude you'll want to take into the looming zombie/robot/alien wars, and with their mix of fortifying protein and piquant beetiness, these eggs will help keep your fighting spirits high!

—*Mark Ibold*

Makes 12 pickled eggs

12 **Hard-Boiled Eggs** (page 90),
    peeled
+ tarragon (optional)
1 garlic clove (optional)
1 jar (12 oz) pickled red beets
    (in their liquid)
1 cup apple cider vinegar
1 cup water
3 tbsp sugar
1 tbsp salt

1. Put the hard-boiled eggs into a 2-quart glass jar. If you want the End Times to be fancy, you could tuck some tarragon and a clove of garlic in there, too.

2. Heat the beets and the liquid from the jar, vinegar, water, sugar, and salt in a saucepan until just boiling. Dump over the eggs. Put into the fridge (or the coldest area of the cave you are hiding out in) for a few days and they should be ready to eat. The longer the eggs stay in the liquid, the more colorful they will be when cut in half.

Eggs at the END of the World

Kate Greene

Here's a twist on an old hypothetical. Imagine, instead of a deserted island, you're on Mars. You can cook and bake, so long as all the ingredients are shelf stable. Given these constraints, what's your comfort food?

I thought mine might be peanut butter on toast. Or chocolate milk. Something I was used to eating or drinking back home. I did not expect my comfort food to be a Julia Child–style French omelet with parsley and cheese. But French omelet it was, thanks to one of the most delicious inventions of the twenty-first century: egg crystals.

Okay, I wasn't technically on Mars. But in 2013 I was a participant in a four-month isolation mission sponsored by NASA. Along with five others, I lived in a dome halfway up the Hawaiian volcano of Mauna Loa as though we were astronauts on Mars. This meant eating only shelf-stable foods, wearing spacesuits whenever we went outside, and communicating with everyone back on Earth via delayed email servers. (It will take as long as twenty-four minutes to send information between Earth and Mars, depending on orbital positions.)

On Mauna Loa Mars, I was grateful for simple pleasures: a spacesuited walk on an overcast day (the suits tended to get stuffy when it was too sunny out), a breakthrough in my sleep experiment, and a good omelet on a quiet Sunday morning.

We are living in the golden era of powdered eggs. Powdered eggs, until now, have been the stuff of campers' nightmares—with their off-tasting additives and lack of resemblance to actual eggs. But the egg crystals we ate during the mission reconstituted perfectly, and cooked into scrambles and omelets that were indistinguishable from the ones I would make with fresh eggs back home in California.

How did our Martian outpost come to be stocked with such delicious shelf-stable eggs? I asked Dr. Jean Hunter, associate professor of biological and environmental engineering at Cornell, and the principal investigator of our NASA study. She told me that in 2007, while choosing the food for a food study in a different simulated Mars mission just outside of Hanksville, Utah, she taste-tested traditional egg powders side by side with egg crystals. The egg crystals, a brand called OvaEasy, won her over. Hunter decided our four months of food rations would also include a generous supply of these eggs.

OvaEasy is the product of a company called Nutriom, a family-run business based in Lacey, Washington. Nutriom got its start in cheese—concentrating whey—in the 1980s and '90s. In 1995, a business opportunity prompted the company to develop a "fully functional egg powder," Leo Etcheto, son of the founder and the head of operations, tells me.

"We spent five years," he explains, "jet-pulse drying, microwave drying . . . all kinds of stuff." Finally, Nutriom discovered a company in Tacoma, Washington, that made vegetable belt dryers—basically conveyer belts that ferry vegetables into a kind of elongated pizza oven where they're dried. It turned out to be great for dehydrating eggs. They bought one and modified it, Etcheto says. By 2000, Nutriom was using a full, industrial-size dryer and running its own custom-made egg-drying processes to create what the company now calls "egg crystals."

*

Nutriom did not invent dehydrated eggs, of course. By 1865, Charles La Mont received a US patent for "Improvement in Preserving Eggs" by using warm air to desiccate a thin layer of egg batter on metal plates. In 1880, preserved eggs became a hot

OvaEasy Egg Crystals

topic in the *New York Times* after a fresh egg shortage struck the region. In 1881, preserved eggs traveled to the Arctic on Adolphus Greely's North Pole expedition, and in the late 1890s, they were critical to prospectors in the Klondike Gold Rush. By the turn of the century, preserving eggs by drying was something anyone with access to *Mrs. Rorer's New Cook Book, A Manual of Housekeeping* (1902) could feel emboldened to do.

"Separate the whites and the yolks, spread a few at a time on a clean stoneware or china platter and slowly evaporate or dry in a very cool oven. This powder . . . may then be used the same as fresh eggs," Mrs. Rorer wrote.

Today, thanks to a prominent online community of doomsday preppers, there is no shortage of YouTube videos that demonstrate the making of powdered whole eggs at home. You'll need: eggs, a dehydrator with multiple trays, a knife to scrape the resultant egg chips off the trays, and a blender or food processor to mill the egg chips. You can dehydrate the powder again for good measure. Store in jars. When all hell breaks loose and grocery stores and chickens are hard to come by, you'll still be able to make your family a frittata.

It's not as easy, however, to find videos of powdered egg reconstitution or videos of the joyful cooking and eating of them.

*

Today's powdered eggs are largely not homemade. The majority of powdered eggs come from large-scale industrial processes, which usually start with an egg-breaking machine, a stainless steel contraption into which eggs are conveyed. The liquid then gets pasteurized—tricky business because you have to heat the egg enough to kill bacteria, but not enough "to make an omelet in the system," says François Quenard, the director of egg processing at Actini. Actini is a French thermal technology company that makes pasteurizing and egg-drying equipment. Their equipment pasteurizes liquid egg as it flows through a tube at temperatures a little higher than 140°F.

Some of this liquid egg is then shipped to restaurants or other food-service facilities; the rest stays around for drying inside a spray-dryer, the most common way eggs become powder.

In spray-drying, liquid egg is pumped at high pressure through a nozzle that jets nebulized egg into an enormous, room-size chamber. At the same time hot air, nearly 400°F, blasts in. The hot air evaporates water from the egg, and solid particles rain down for collection. Then the powder goes through the dryer again, which makes finer particles so the egg dissolves more easily in water when it is reconstituted—"like Nescafé," Quenard says.

Why doesn't the hot air in a spray-dryer cook the egg? While it's true that egg proteins change shape when heated and when agitated (which is what allows them to become solid when fried or whipped into a meringue), the heating inside the spray-dryer is such a quick blast that it doesn't warp the egg proteins as cooking at such a high temperature normally would.

Freeze-drying is the method preferred by the military for feeding soldiers in combat, and by NASA. Eggs are prepared normally—a batch of scrambled with scallions and cheese, say—but then frozen in a chamber at very low pressure. The freezing turns the water within the cooked egg to ice, and the low pressure sublimates the ice into a gas, leaving preserved chunks of dry egg. Just add hot water, drain, and they're (almost) back to their original state.

*

Nutriom's process of making egg crystals, in contrast, sounds as artisanal as an industrialized egg process can be. First, it's slow. "We process in one week what a modern spray-dryer does in ten hours," Leo Etcheto says. Second, the drying is done at low heat, never reaching above 110°F.

The egg liquid is spread in an extremely thin layer on a drying belt. Hot water below evaporates the liquid while warm air on top absorbs the water, Etcheto explains. What comes off the belt are egg "crystals": They go directly into the package you buy, he says. There are no additives.

"Because of the low temperatures and because we never freeze the egg, you don't have any of those issues [that other preserved eggs have], and then we don't change the color," Etcheto says. "It binds. It's fluffy."

*

Nutriom's belt-dried egg crystals were good enough for my crew on Mars. And maybe, eventually, they'll make their way to real Mars, too—though probably not for a while. Vickie Kloeris, the manager of the International Space Station's food system, says that eggs in space are all freeze-dried—dating back at least to the Apollo program.

Astronauts add hot water to pouches that contain eggs (scrambled eggs with cheese, or quiche are two current options), heat in the galley oven if necessary, and then eat. Of course there's no real cooking in space. Even salting your food is different—a squirt of saline solution as opposed to a messy salt-shaker. And though the eggs can be a little "crumbly," and astronauts have to be careful when they eat them because crumbs can clog filters on the space station, Kloeris confirms that eggs have always been popular in space.

My beloved powdered eggs don't make much sense in space right now: in a zero-g environment, you can't cook or bake. But Mars has some gravity, about a third of Earth's. In a 2014 experiment led by a group of Cornell and Makel Engineering researchers, Drs. Apollo Arquiza, Bryan Caldwell, Susana Carranza, and Jean Hunter tried to find out just what it would be like to cook with Mars gravity. To do so, the team took a ride on NASA's airplane, nicknamed the Vomit Comet, which simulates a range of low gravity scenarios by looping along a parabolic path. The researchers brought with them a frying pan and some canola oil (dyed red to see where it splattered), tofu, and hash browns. They discovered that cooking foods on Mars in an open pan would likely be a messy business with oil flying farther than on Earth and settling down in slow motion.

For this and other reasons, it's unlikely anyone will scramble an egg or fold an omelet on Mars anytime soon. The first NASA astronauts to the Red Planet, estimated to arrive in the 2030s, will be expedition crews that will eat meals similar to those on the space station, says Dr. Grace Douglas, food scientist at NASA. "The idea initially would be to use the prepackaged foods," she says. Although, she adds, colonization of Mars might allow for some cooking, but if it ever happens it could be many years away.

Still, for me, Mars will always mean omelets. During our four-month mission, we ate almost all meals together. This meant cooking and cleaning for six, on a rotating basis. We were also very busy, hewing to a fairly demanding work schedule. But on Sunday mornings we could eat what we wanted, alone or with others. I remember well sitting down to my French omelet, Finn Crisp crackers with jam, and tea—Earl Grey (hot), relishing the opportunity for quiet and calm. Behind me, just beyond our habitat's walls, miles upon miles of red rock extended, uninterrupted.

Ostrich

CONTRIBUTORS

Nina Bai is a science writer based in San Francisco.

Judie Baker is Ashley Goldsmith's grandmother. She grew up in Great Neck, New York, before moving to Jericho, where she made matzo brei for her five children and nine grandchildren.

David Barber has been cooking professionally for more than forty years. In 2005 he founded Picklopolis Pickles, the Kingdom of the Brine, and has never looked back.

Aralyn Beaumont is the research editor of *Lucky Peach*. She lives in San Francisco and loves to ride horses almost as much as she loves to eat eggs.

Sascha Bos is a freelance writer whose work has appeared in *Render, LA Weekly,* and *East Bay Express*. She has edited titles including *Little Flower Baking*, *Das Cookbook*, and *Drink: Los Angeles* and spent a year researching nineteenth-century cookbooks and feminism for her UC Berkeley honors thesis.

Marian Bull is a writer living in Brooklyn. Her preferred egg-cooking technique is Caroline Fidanza's scramble.

Rinco and **Susie Cheung** are the owners of China Café, which opened in Los Angeles's Grand Central Market in 1959.

Liz Crain is the author of *Food Lover's Guide to Portland; Toro Bravo: Stories. Recipes. No Bull.; Grow Your Own: Understanding, Cultivating, and Enjoying Cannabis;* and the forthcoming *Hello, My Name Is Tasty: Global Diner Favorites from Portland's Tasty Restaurants*. She is also a fiction writer, a longtime writer on Pacific Northwest food and drink, and the co-organizer of the annual Portland Fermentation Festival.

A Seattle native, **Dana Cree** landed in Chicago in 2012 to helm the pastry department of Blackbird and Avec restaurants, where she earned two James Beard nominations for Outstanding Pastry Chef. She is now executive pastry chef of the Publican, Publican Quality Meats, Publican Tavern, and Publican Anker.

Frank DeCarlo is the chef and owner of Peasant restaurant and Bacaro wine bar in New York City.

Raúl Ramírez Degollado is the son of Titita Ramírez Degollado, owner of El Bajío restaurants in Mexico City.

Meaghan Dorman is the head bartender at Raines Law Room in New York City.

Cathy Erway is the author of *The Art of Eating In* and *The Food of Taiwan*. She writes the blog *Not Eating Out in New York* and hosts the podcast *Eat Your Words* on Heritage Radio Network. She lives in Brooklyn with her dog, Doug.

Caroline Fidanza is one of the founders, chefs, and owners of Saltie, an eatery in Williamsburg, Brooklyn, and an author of the *Saltie* cookbook.

Peter Freed is an egg lover currently living in Menlo Park, California. He has eaten eggs all over the world! He and his wife recently became the parents of two girl children.

Adam Gollner is the author of *The Fruit Hunters* and *The Book of Immortality*. He lives in Montreal.

Laura Goodman is a writer living in London, and a regular contributor to the *Sunday Times* and *Lucky Peach*. She blogs at sheisbutters.com.

Kate Greene was trained as a laser physicist in Kansas; worked as a science and technology journalist in London, Washington, DC, and San Francisco; and in 2013 was an inaugural crew member for NASA's long-duration simulated Mars mission called HI-SEAS. Four months on Mars changed her; she now writes mostly essays and poems.

Dorie Greenspan is the author of *Around My French Table,* a *New York Times* bestseller that was named Cookbook of the Year by the IACP; *Baking Chez Moi;* and *Baking: From My Home to Yours,* a James Beard Award winner. She lives in Westbrook, Connecticut, New York, and Paris.

Mary-Frances Heck is a freelance food editor and contributor to *Lucky Peach*. Her recipes and writing have appeared in *Bon Appétit, Saveur, Redbook, Rodale's Organic Life, Fitness, Rachael Ray Every Day, SELF, SHAPE, All You,* and numerous cookbooks. Her areas of interest include biodynamic agriculture, childhood food security, and getting dinner on the table. Heck's first cookbook will be published by Clarkson Potter in the fall of 2017.

Anissa Helou is a chef, food writer, journalist, broadcaster, consultant, and blogger focusing on the cuisines and culinary heritage of the Middle East, Mediterranean, and North Africa. Find her at anissas.com.

Tienlon Ho writes about food, the environment, and where these intersect. She is based in San Francisco. Her favorite eggs don't have shells but come from animals with shells.

Bridget Huber is a writer and radio producer based in Oakland, California.

Mark Ibold is *Lucky Peach's* Southeastern Pennsylvania correspondent and the former bassist of the band Pavement.

Arielle Johnson is a flavor scientist and the head of research at the food think tank MAD. She is also the resident scientist at restaurant Noma in Copenhagen, where she works with the R&D team to translate scientific and scholarly knowledge into new techniques and tools. Johnson received her PhD from UC Davis, where she was a National Science Foundation research fellow.

Anna Ling Kaye's fiction has most recently been short-listed for the 2015 Journey Prize. Her journalism and nonfiction can be found in the *International Herald Tribune,* the *New York Times,* and *The Tyee,* and her creative work in *subTerrain* and *Prairie Fire* magazines. She reads and writes in Vancouver.

Melati Kaye is a reporter based in central Java and northern California.

Alison Kinney is the author of *Hood.* She has written for *Lucky Peach, Harper's, The Paris Review Daily, Lapham's Quarterly, Hyperallergic, New Republic, Gastronomica, The Atlantic,* the *New York Times,* and other publications.

Genevieve Ko is a food writer, recipe developer, and culinary consultant based in New York City. She is the author of *Better Baking,* a cookbook of delicious, wholesome desserts.

Padma Lakshmi is the Emmy-nominated host and producer of *Top Chef* and the author of award-winning cookbooks and a *New York Times* bestselling memoir. Her latest book is *The Encyclopedia of Spices and Herbs: An Essential Guide to the Flavors of the World.*

Karen Leibowitz is a writer and a restaurant person whose most recent project is the Perennial, an environmentally sustainable restaurant and bar in San Francisco of which she is the cofounder with her husband, Anthony Myint. She is also a partner in Mission Chinese Food and Commonwealth and the coauthor of *Atelier Crenn: Metamorphosis of Taste* and *Mission Street Food: Recipes and Ideas from an Improbable Restaurant.*

Rachel Levin is a San Francisco–based writer who has been published in *The New Yorker,* the *New York Times, San Francisco* magazine, and *Lucky Peach.* She is a contributing editor at OZY and likes her yolks runny. Find her at byrachellevin.com.

Michael Light is a writer and an editor from Dayton, Ohio.

Deborah Madison is a chef, writer, and cooking teacher. She is the founding chef of Greens Restaurant in San Francisco. She is the author of many books, including *Vegetarian Cooking for Everyone* and *Vegetable Literacy.*

Pooja Makhijani writes children's books, essays, and articles, and also develops educational media and curricula. She divides her time between Singapore and the United States.

Harold McGee writes about the science of food and cooking. He is the author of *On Food and Cooking: The Science and Lore of the Kitchen* and *Keys to Good Cooking,* and he posts at curiouscook.com.

Originally from Tokyo, Japan, **Naoko Takei Moore** is a *donabe* (Japanese clay pot) and Japanese home-cooking expert, based in Los Angeles. She operates Toiro Kitchen, a shop of artisanal donabe and Japanese kitchen tools, and also hosts cooking classes in her kitchen in Los Angeles. Visit Naoko's website toirokitchen.com and her blog at naokomoore.com.

Dahlia Narvaez is the executive pastry chef of Osteria Mozza and Pizzeria Mozza. Dahlia developed the menus and pastry departments for all of Mozza's Los Angeles restaurants and oversees the department in Newport Beach, San Diego, and Singapore. Dahlia has been thrice nominated for the James Beard Foundation's Outstanding Pastry Chef Award.

Jacques Pépin is the author of twenty-one cookbooks, including the bestselling *The Apprentice* and the award-winning *Jacques Pépin Celebrates* and *Julia and Jacques Cooking at Home* (with Julia Child). He has appeared regularly on PBS programs for more than a decade, hosting over three hundred cooking shows.

Leela Punyaratabandhu is the author of *Bangkok* and *Simple Thai Food.* She writes about Thai food and culture for various publications as well as on her award-winning blog, *SheSimmers.* Leela divides her time between Chicago and Bangkok.

Alex Raij is the chef and owner of Txikito, El Quinto Pino, and La Vara restaurants in New York.

Lauren Ro is a writer and an editor living in New York, covering food, film, and all things related to the home.

Sonoko Sakai is a mobile cooking teacher, food writer, and soba yogi based in Los Angeles and Tehachapi. Her new cookbook, *Rice Craft,* is all about making *onigiri.*

Tannaz Sassooni is a food writer and blogger living in Los Angeles and specializing in Iranian Jewish foods.

Michael Snyder is a freelance food and culture journalist with more than four years' experience reporting from the subcontinent. His work has appeared in the *New York Times,* the *Washington Post, Saveur, The Art of Eating,* and *Lucky Peach.*

Karen Taylor is the chef and owner of El Molino Central in Sonoma, California.

Lesley Téllez is a freelance journalist and the author of *Eat Mexico: Recipes from Mexico City's Streets, Markets & Fondas.* She runs Eat Mexico Culinary Tours, which operates food tours in Mexico City and Puebla.

Aaron Thier is the author of two novels, *Mr. Eternity* and *The Ghost Apple,* and is a columnist for *Lucky Peach.*

Naomi Tomky uses her enthusiasm as an eater, a photographer, and a writer to propel herself around the world. From trailing a street-food hawker in Singapore to navigating the ancient roads of the Mayan jungle, she explores the world for publications like *Lucky Peach* and *Saveur,* and *The Atlantic*'s CityLab.

Lucas Turner is a cook, musician, and mattress salesman currently residing in the Bay Area.

Second-generation Filipino American brothers **Chase** and **Chad Valencia** are behind the modern LA Filipino restaurant LASA. LASA currently resides at the culinary incubator Unit 120 in Chinatown. Their food combines Filipino cuisine with So Cal market-driven cooking.

Nathan Waller is the director of food and beverage at Yank Sing, the San Francisco dim sum restaurant founded by Alice Chan in 1958.

Ozlem Warren was born in Turkey and lived there for thirty years. She now lives in London, where she teaches Turkish cookery classes.

Jody Williams is the chef and owner of Buvette, a French-inspired restaurant she opened in New York City in 2010.

EGGKNOWLEDGMENTS

You can't spell "BOOK" without "BOO," and this book would not exist were it not for its many girlfriends and earth mothers. First and foremost, the Egg Team: Aralyn Beaumont, Joanna Sciarrino, Mary-Frances Heck, Tamara Shopsin, and Jason Fulford. Without you I'd be weeping, naked, and slimy beneath a pile of broken eggshells. Thank you, Aralyn, for your eagle eye and wisdom beyond your too-few years; MF for your tireless coddling (pun intended), and for deglazing our brains with rosé when we needed it most; Joanna for your acumen, smarts, and fury; Tamara and Jason for being indefatigable collaborators and brilliant artists. How did I get so lucky? Your genius design not only shaped this book but steered this eggy ship. Thank you to our Clarkson Potter team, including Rica Allannic, Marysarah Quinn, Christine Tanigawa, Kelli Tokos, Derek Gullino, Kevin Sweeting, and Natasha Martin. Thanks to copy editor Kate Slate.

Second (but still foremost!): thank you to all of this book's contributors, including the authors of pieces that didn't quite make it in the end due to my personal ineptitude. Thank you to every friend who recipe tested. This book is yours.

Thank you to the Western Foundation of Vertebrate Zoology in Los Angeles, and to Linnea Hall and René Corado for your time and generosity. This book would not have been the same without your stunning collection of eggs. Thanks to Brian Chung in Hong Kong for showing Tienlon Ho around. Thanks to Kristen Miglore for the clutch tagine.

Thank you to the *Lucky Peach* interns who jumped to help me answer my every egg question (and more): Sascha Bos, Ashley Goldsmith, Michael Light, Taylor Lee, Lily Starbuck, Lucas Turner, and Nicole Wong.

Thank you to everyone at *Lucky Peach*: David Chang for being our tiger mom, Ryan Healey for the #eggs support, Brette Warshaw for ladies cabbage, Rupa Bhattarchaya for mad matambre skillz, Emily Johnson for running our ridiculous errands, the New York office for letting us cook 100+ egg recipes in your brand-new kitchen—and then helping to eat many, many of those eggs (shout-out to Bobby Lomez for laffs; Peter Romero for sharing whiskey with us late into the nights; Devin Washburn, we stole some Bombas socks from you since you were in Brazil; and Kate Neuhaus, who's gonna make this book a bestseller). Thanks, too, to Priya Krishna, Adam Krefman, and Walter Green—my sweet, original peaches, and peaches forever.

Thank you to Peter Meehan and Chris "Christmas" Ying for taking a chance on a young foodie (JK! I'm old) and giving me a job at a fledgling food magazine back in 2011. Thanks, Peter, for buying me Chucks when it rains (metaphorically and literally), and Chris, for always saying "kazoo" when I sneeze.

Thanks to my mom, Lynn, whose egg became me, and my dad, Edward, whose . . . anyway! Thanks to my parents for instilling in me my eggbiding love for this great food, and to my brothers, Clement and Ben, egg lovers themselves.

Thanks to Eli Horowitz, who egged me gently yet firmly on through this alternatingly eggscruciating and eggciting project (and every other), and scrambles the eggs of my heart, day in and day out.

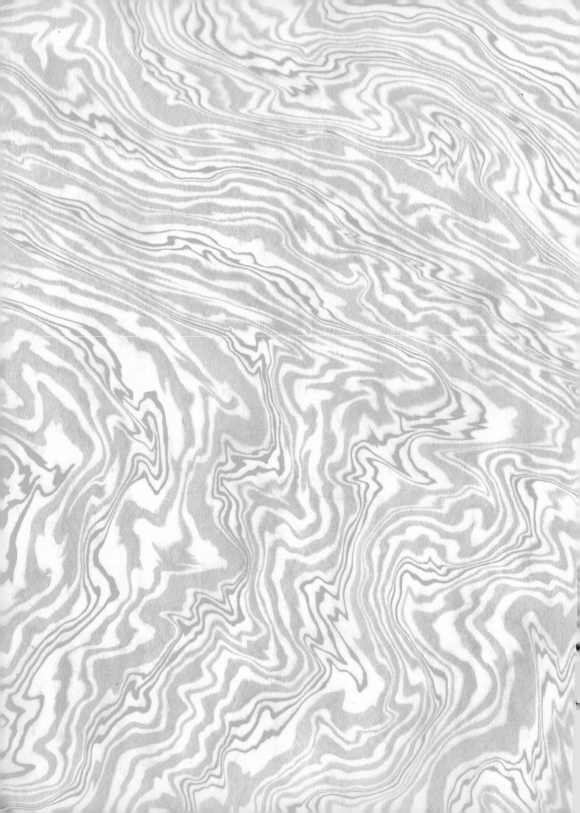